Our Final Say, Not Hearsay

Our Final Say, Not Hearsay
- Allied Accounts From 100 Years
of Military Conflict

Produced and Edited by
Grahame Warby

Mansion Field

Mansion Field
An imprint of Zeticula Ltd
Unit 13,
196 Rose Street,
Edinburgh,
EH2 4AT,
Scotland

http://www.mansionfield.co.uk
First published in 2018
This collection © 2018 Graham Warby and contributors
Cover based on an image by Friederike Hiepko

ISBN 9781905021161

Dedication

This book is dedicated to all of the contributors of the accounts featured herein, whether in the words of those depicted, or by those who have provided the accounts of the same.

It is also dedicated to those contributors who featured in the first book of this kind, *"Our Say, Not Hearsay – Wartime Accounts from an Anglo-French Community in Paris"*, without whom this book would never likely have been produced.

This book, and its predecessor, has as one of its undercurrent themes, the value of life. As such, the Editor would particularly like to dedicate this work to:

Simona Acaru and Ovidiu Mihai Vintila, upon the birth of their newborn son, David, and

Claudia Freire and Alec Harvey, upon the birth of their newborn daughter, Clara.

Acknowledgements

The Editor would like to thank:

Janet Warby for her tireless efforts in collecting all of the materials for this book; she has been the true hero in this exercise.

Her Majesty's Ambassador to France, Lord Edward Llewellyn of Steep, for his kind support of this book and related book launch.

David Bean, Chairman of the Royal British Legion (Paris Branch) for his continued support of this work.

Susan Woodward, Head Mistress of the Lycee International for her support with the provision of the poetry by the various children who wrote the same herein.

The children who wrote the various poems in this work.

Colonel Chris Borneman, Military Attaché to France.

Contents

Part 3 – More Recent Times of Conflict 153

List of Illustrations

All images and illustrations in this work have been provided by the contributors of the stories herein; the copyright and permissions remains the property of the owners.

Foreword

As the current President of the Paris Branch of The Royal British Legion I am delighted to have been invited to write the foreword for this book. It is refreshing to see how the oldest Branch in the Legion can come up with some of the newest and brightest ideas in support of those who have taken the military path, and this book is a shining example of such great initiatives.

This is the second volume of collected reminiscences, biographies and autobiographies, historical accounts and more, related to one subject - that of unequivocal commitment and loyal service, both in times of war and peace. These are the very human stories, of which sometimes only fragments remain, that serve as an important reminder of our history as well as the human sacrifices made during conflict and the costs paid by families and friends.

This book, whilst sold to raise all-important funds for the Legion, is aimed at helping us understand the human element. The Legion is well known for its presence at ceremonies where its Standards are proudly carried by members, keeping the flame alive, but equally (if not more) important is the extensive welfare work undertaken by the Legion. This work helps many ex-service personnel and their families who, having served their country, now require our support for a variety of reasons. It is to them as well as to our forebears that this book is dedicated.

Colonel Chris Borneman,
Military Attaché
Paris 2018

Introduction

Around the late Summer of 2013, I experienced some form of epiphany. A vision of sorts came to my mind. I decided that I wanted to produce a book about the experiences of a community I knew in Paris, both English and French, who all had between them a wealth of stories pertaining to their experiences largely during World War II. That book had accounts from people who had been refugees, military, spies, victims of the concentration camps and much more. As a scholar of history, it was my opinion that such stories which until then had not been largely told (at least to a truly wide audience), really ought to be in the interests of posterity at least, if nothing else. I should say, it took some time before people were totally convinced about my idea, but ultimately all the right people came on board to this idea and supported it.

As such, some fifteen months later, the collaborators of that work and myself produced and published, *"Our Say, Not Hearsay – Wartime Accounts from an Anglo-French Community in Paris"*. The book was first launched at the British Embassy in Paris in late October 2014, selling a fair amount of copies (and still does so), with all proceeds going to the Royal British Legion. I have to admit, I was very proud of its relative success.

Interestingly perhaps, I never quite thought I'd later be in a position to be undertaking a follow-up tome to that original idea. I was certain, perhaps at least, that any and all stories provided in the original work were the culmination of an exhausted search for such stories and therefore any other similar stories would be few. In fact, when approached on the subject to undertake a second similar work, I was surprised to learn that there was indeed still a good selection of original or secondary source stories needing similar production, and touched by the notion that support for a second work was also there.

I am now very proud to produce and edit this second work, titled *"Our Final Say, Not Hearsay: Allied Accounts From 100 Years of Military Conflict"* – largely similar in title to its predecessor for obvious reasons. Whilst however this work carries on in the same vein as the first book, this book has one or two interesting differences and focuses. The main one of these is that unlike the first book, we have explored stories provided from secondary sources pertaining to World War I (let's face it, originally sourced stories from World War I would be somewhat more difficult to find now given that we are talking about a period around 100 years ago).

Furthermore this account features stories not only from an Anglo/French community, but also from some of our other allies in the United States, all veterans of one conflict or another themselves. One knows one is doing well when one goes transatlantic!

Finally, this book includes some poetic insights by a handful of children in the Parisian community who were encouraged by the Royal British Legion Paris Branch to compose their own range of poems upon the subject of remembrance and conflict generally. I have to admit I was unsure at first if inclusion of such poems was appropriate or feasible; but in fact I believe, having read these quite wonderful poems that in fact I need not have had any anxiety hereto. I have been positively surprised by the level of insight from these children, and well done to them all.

The first of these two books, having been published and launched in 2014, emerged therefore on the 100th anniversary of the year of outbreak of the First World War. This was purely by chance and because of the way the stars at the time were aligned. Similarly, this follow-up work coincides with the 100th anniversary of the cessation of the First World War – indeed, it will have been launched at the British Embassy in Paris some 5 days before the 100th anniversary of the famous eleventh day of the eleventh month of the eleventh hour, which brought an end to that conflict. I like the poignancy of this fact, so I thought I'd mention it.

In closing, I should like to make the following point. Both the collaborators of this work (and it's predecessor) and myself have proffered these stories because they are both interesting and of historic worth; but they are also, in my opinion fundamental to posterity. Whilst as human beings we seem to have this in-built propensity to wage war against each other throughout history, part of the reason I think we produce books like these is in the vain hope that we may learn from our history. This book, and the previous one, has many themes; but one of them to my mind is the futility omnipresent in war and similar conflict. I shall end this note with the words of Mark Knopfler of the musical group *Dire Straits*, which I think are very poignant to this undercurrent theme:

"We're fools to make war on our brothers in arms".

Grahame Warby, August 2018

Part 1 – World War I

Remembrance

by Molly

On a crisp November morning
The clock had struck eleven;
The old men gathered to remember
Their fallen friends and comrades.
There were old and young,
No one was moving.

A child was with his mother,
A flower in his hand.
He looked up at his mother
And saw a tear slowly slide down.
A lady nearby asked the child
Who his flower was for;
He replied: "For my Daddy" who
Had given his all.

The lady asked what had happened,
And the mother said proud and tall,
That he had served in the desert
With his comrades who had
Protected the people of that land.
He was one of the unlucky ones
Who had fallen for the cause.

The flowers were laid by the old ones
The boy came forth and saluted before
He laid his flower for his daddy;
A young man straight and tall.

On a crisp November morning,
The band began to play.
The leaves began to fall and flutter
As if to say:
"Thank you for your courage
And We Will Remember
You All.

Brothers At War

Janet Warby

This is the story of two brothers, who having emigrated at different times from the U.K. to Canada before World War I, both joined up to help the land of their birth.
These two men were Janet Warby's great-great-uncles.

Arthur William Morris – 1873-1915

Arthur William Morris was born on 25th October 1873 in Bristol, England. His father was in the building trade and was sent to work in Bristol from London hence Arthur being born there. Arthur was the eldest of nine children.

Arthur's youngest brother, Alfred, decided to emigrate with his wife Edith and young son to Canada for a better life. He wrote to his brother that there were plenty of jobs and that he could have a good life in Oshawa, Ontario where Alfred and Edith lived. Arthur emigrated to Canada in June 1911 from Southampton on the ship *Albania* arriving in Quebec. Once settled, he started work as a carpenter.

At the outbreak of war, Canada joined the other dominions of Great Britain and asked their men to sign up to fight the Germans. Arthur, although 42 by this time and not required to sign up, did so on 21st June 1915 at Port Hope. His Attestation Papers state his date and place of birth, that he was married to Emilia, (a fact that was not known to his family in the UK as we were always told he did not marry) and lived in Oshawa, Ontario, his trade was that of a carpenter and that he had served in a military force before, namely The Naval Brigade. His height was recorded as 5ft 9in and he was of fair complexion with grey eyes and dark hair. He stated that he was Church of England. He was sent to the 59th Battalion, number 54286, with the rank of Private, he was later transferred to 39th Battalion (Reserve) Canadian Expeditionary Force (C.E.F.). Together with his battalion, he left Canada on 15th August 1915 sailing on the ship *Scandinavia* heading eventually for Shornecliffe, Folkestone, Kent. It is not sure if Arthur ever saw action but his name appears on a Memorial Plaque of those who saw action at both St. Julien and Frezenberg in 1915 so we assume he was in action at these battles. His unit would likely have been sent to fill up the places of men killed in action. It was thought that his unit was part of The Princess Patricia's Canadian Light Infantry formed in early January 1915. We do not have much information of his time in the battlefield.

Grave of Arthur W. Morris.

Graveyard where Arthur W. Morris is buried.

Arthur is likely to have been sent on leave to Shornecliffe after these conflicts. During his time on leave in October 1915 he complained of pain in the frontal region of his head. On the afternoon of 16th October he was standing on the platform of Shornecliffe Station when he felt himself becoming dizzy with a mist arising before his eyes. He stumbled, fell backwards and only regained consciousness after about five minutes. He was taken to hospital where he had various tests. The findings were that his physical condition was only fair upon walking, his left leg dragged, there was partial paralysis of facial muscles on the left side, and there was no sign of his tongue being listless at that time of the report but it can be assumed he had suffered a stroke. He complained of headaches on the right side and his memory was poor, and cerebrations show his pupils and other faculties were immobile.

After further investigation by the doctors they found that Arthur had contracted syphilis some 20 years before whilst serving in the Naval Brigade (good old Navy!) This had been dormant until stress, probably from battle engagements, and was the likely cause of the stroke.

Arthur was declared unfit for duty under Para 392 XVI Kings Regs. He was sent back to Canada by ship but died on 25th December 1915. His body was transferred back to his family in Oshawa and his body was buried in the Union Cemetery there. The Commonwealth War Graves Photographic Society kindly took photos, opposite, of his grave and sent them to me.

The details I have for Arthur are sketchy but considering his medical history and age we are not surprised. I have also provided photographic images, on following pages, regarding his Attestation Papers, medical documents and Discharge paperwork.

A54286

B Coy 12

ATTESTATION PAPER

No.

Folio.

CANADIAN OVER-SEAS EXPEDITIONARY FORCE

QUESTIONS TO BE PUT BEFORE ATTESTATION.

(ANSWERS)

1. What is your name?.................................... *Arthur W. Morris*
2. In what Town, Township, or Parish, and in what Country were you born? *Bristol England*
3. What is the name of your next-of-kin?........ *Mrs Emila Morris*
4. What is the address of your next-of-kin?.... *Oshawa Ont*
5. What is the date of your birth?.................... *Oct 25th 1873*
6. What is your trade or calling?...................... *Carpenter*
7. Are you married?... *yes*
8. Are you willing to be vaccinated or re-vaccinated? *yes*
9. Do you now belong to the Active Militia?.... *no*
10. Have you ever served in any Military Force?. *yes naval Brigade*
    If so, state particulars of former Service.
11. Do you understand the nature and terms of your engagement? *yes*
12. Are you willing to be attested to serve in the CANADIAN OVER-SEAS EXPEDITIONARY FORCE? *yes*

Arthur W Morris ....(Signature of Man.)

Chas Nolan ....(Signature of Witness.)

DECLARATION TO BE MADE BY MAN ON ATTESTATION.

I, *Arthur W Morris* , do solemnly declare that the above answers made by me to the above questions are true, and that I am willing to fulfil the engagements by me now made, and I hereby engage and agree to serve in the **Canadian Over-Seas Expeditionary Force**, and to be attached to any arm of the service therein, for the term of one year, or during the war now existing between Great Britain and Germany should that war last longer than one year, and for six months after the termination of that war provided His Majesty should so long require my services, or until legally discharged.

Arthur W Morris (Signature of Recruit.)

Date *June 14* 1915 *Chas Nolan* (Signature of Witness.)

OATH TO BE TAKEN BY MAN ON ATTESTATION.

I, *Arthur W Morris* , do make Oath, that I will be faithful and bear true Allegiance to His Majesty **King George the Fifth**, His Heirs and Successors, and that I will as in duty bound honestly and faithfully defend His Majesty, His Heirs and Successors, in Person, Crown and Dignity, against all enemies, and will observe and obey all orders of His Majesty, His Heirs and Successors, and of all the Generals and Officers set over me. So help me God.

Arth W Morris (Signature of Recruit.)

Date *July 2* 1915 *B M Morris* (Signature of Witness.)

CERTIFICATE OF MAGISTRATE.

The Recruit above-named was cautioned by me that if he made any false answer to any of the above questions he would be liable to be punished as provided in the Army Act.

The above questions were then read to the Recruit in my presence.

I have taken care that he understands each question, and that his answer to each question has been duly entered as replied to, and the said Recruit has made and signed the declaration and taken the oath before me, at *3 P M* this *2nd* day of *July* 191 *5*

G Hunter (Signature of Justice.)

I certify that the above is a true copy of the Attestation of the above-named Recruit.

H Dawson Li-Col (Approving Officer.)

M. F. W. 23.
200 M.—3-15.
H.Q. 1772-39-841.

Attestation Paper for Arthur William Morris

DESCRIPTION OF *Arthur Wm Morris* ON ENLISTMENT.

Apparent Age *43* years *........* months. <small>(To be determined according to the instructions given in the Regulations for Army Medical Services.)</small>	Distinctive marks, and marks indicating congenital peculiarities or previous disease. <small>(Should the Medical Officer be of opinion that the recruit has served before, he will, unless the man acknowledges to any previous service, attach a slip to that effect, for the information of the Approving Officer.)</small>

Height...... *5 ft 9* ins.

Chest measurement {
Girth when fully expanded...... *37½* ins.
Range of expansion...... *2* ins.
}

Complexion...... *Fair*

Eyes...... *Grey*

Hair...... *Dark*

Religious Denominations {
Church of England...... *X*
Presbyterian......
Wesleyan......
Baptist or Congregationalist......
Other Protestants......
<small>(Denomination to be stated.)</small>
Roman Catholic......
Jewish......
}

CERTIFICATE OF MEDICAL EXAMINATION.

I have examined the above-named Recruit and find that he does not present any of the causes of rejection specified in the Regulations for Army Medical Services.

He can see at the required distance with either eye; his heart and lungs are healthy; he has the free use of his joints and limbs, and he declares that he is not subject to fits of any description.

I consider him* *fit* for the Canadian Over-Seas Expeditionary Force.

Date *June 14* 191*5*

Place *Port Hope Ont*   *F. G. Brockensire M B*
                                                              Medical Officer.

*Insert here "fit" or "unfit."

<small>NOTE.—Should the Medical Officer consider the Recruit unfit, he will fill in the foregoing Certificate only in the case of those who have been attested, and will briefly state below the cause of unfitness:—</small>

CERTIFICATE OF OFFICER COMMANDING UNIT

Arthur W Morris having been finally approved and inspected by me this day, and his Name, Age, Date of Attestation, and every prescribed particular having been recorded, I certify that I am satisfied with the correctness of this Attestation.

Date *July 2nd* 191*5*   *H. Dawson Lt-Col* (Signature of Officer.)

7

Opinion of the Medical Board.

NOTES.—(i.) Clear and decisive answers to the following questions are to be carefully filled in by the Board, as, in the event of the man being invalided, it is essential that the Commissioners of Chelsea Hospital should be in possession of the most reliable information to **enable them to decide upon the man's claim to pension.**

(ii.) Expressions such as "may," "might," "probably," &c., should be avoided.

(iii.) The rates of pension vary directly according to whether the disability is attributed to (a) active service, (b) climate, or (c) ordinary military service. It is therefore essential when assigning the cause of the disability to differentiate between them (see Articles 1162 and 1165, Pay Warrant, 1913).

(iv.) In answering question 20 the Board should be careful to discriminate between disease resulting from military conditions and disease to which the soldier would have been equally liable in civil life.

(v.) A disability is to be regarded as due to climate when it is caused by military service abroad in climates where there is a special liability to contract the disease.

20. (a) State whether the disability is the result of (i.) active service, (ii.) climate, or (iii) ordinary military service.

No

Yes.

   (b) If due to one of these causes, to what specific conditions do the Board attribute it?

Strain, following specific infection.

Disposal by Militia Authorities in Canada.

21. Has the disability been aggravated by

(Signed) G.H.Bowlby, Capt for
Lt.Col.A.D.M.S.

   (a) Intemperance ?   No

   (b) Misconduct ?   No

22. Is the disability permanent ?   Yes

Approved!

23. If not permanent, what is its probable minimum duration ?
To be stated in months.

Not applicable.   T.T.Kirkby.

24. To what extent is his capacity for earning a full livelihood in the general labour market lessened at present ?

Total

In defining the extent of his inability to earn a livelihood, estimate it at ¼, ½, ¾, or total incapacity.

25. If an operation was advised and declined, was the refusal unreasonable ?

Not applicable.

26. Do the Board recommend

   (a) Discharge as permanently unfit, or

   (b) Change to England ?
   Invalided to Canada - Yes.

   Signatures :—

_____G.S.McKeown, Lt.Col._____ President.

Chas.Hunter, Capt.C.A.M.C.   }

Station Shorncliffe   } Members.

Date 22nd Nov.1915.

Approved.

Station Shorncliffe

_____W.G.Dalpe. Capt._____
Administrative Medical Officer.

Date 23rd Nov.1915

Opinion of the Medical Board for Arthur William Morris

(On leaving Corps or Station where invalided.)

Transfer { Date_____ Station_____ }

or

Embark-ation { Date_____ Port_____ }

Name of { Conveyance_____ Vessel_____ Officer in medical charge }_____

Brief remarks on case during transit, and state on transfer for final disposal.

Re-transferred { Date_____ Hospital or } _____ Station }

Officer in medical charge.

(At Station or Hospital where finally disposed of.)

Station and Hospital } _____

Arrived from_____ Date_____

If admitted	If under treatment		Disease	How finally disposed of	Date of Discharge, &c.
Date	From	To			

Detailed statement as to condition on discharge and whether discharged as an invalid, to corps, to station, or to depôt. In cases of discharge from the service it should be stated whether the answers to questions 22, 23 and 24 are concurred in.

Date of final Medical Board, or decision }

Administrative Medical Officer.

Army Form B. 179.

MEDICAL REPORT ON AN INVALID.

Station

Corps

Regimental No.

Rank

Name

Disability

Date:

Hospital or Station transferred to for final disposal }

Date of final disposal }

How finally disposed of }

The original Report is invariably to accompany the discharge documents of Invalids.

(231) (88579). Wt. 1856 475M 5-15 W B & L

Forms B. 179. 34

9

Medical Report on an Invalid.

Station **Moore Barracks**

Date **19th Nov.1915**

1. Unit **(59th) 39th Res.**
2. Regimental No. **454286**
3. Rank **Pte.**
4. Name **Morris, A.W.**

5. Age last birthday **44**
6. Enlisted { on **June 21st 15.** { at **Port Hope.**
7. Former Trade or Occupation { **Carpenter.**

8. Disability.

Cerebral Thrombosis.
Syphilis tertiary.

Statement of Case.

Note.—The answers to the following questions are to be filled in by the Officer in medical charge of the case. In answering them he will carefully discriminate between the man's unsupported statements and evidence recorded in his military and medical documents. He will also carefully distinguish cases entirely due to venereal disease.

9. Date of origin of disability. **Oct.16th 1915.**

10. Place of origin of disability. **Shorncliffe Station.**

11. Give concisely the essential facts of the history of the disability, noting entries on the Medical History Sheet bearing on the case.

Syphilis 20 years ago in Navy

on Oct.14th & 15th 1915 he complained of pain in the frontal region on the afternoon of the 16th Oct. he was standing on the platform of Shorncliffe station when he felt himself becoming dizzy and a mist arising before his eyes. He stumbled backwards and fell and recovered consciousness five minutes afterwards.

12. (a) Give your opinion as to the causation of the disability.

(b) If you consider it to have been caused by active service, climate, or ordinary military service, explain the specific conditions to which you attribute it (See notes on page 3).

Syphilis.

Conditions prior to enlistment not due to Active Service.

Medical Report for Arthur William Morris

13. What is his present condition ?

Weight should be given in all cases when it is likely to afford evidence of the progress of the disability.

Physical condition only fair.

In walking the left leg drags. There has been partial paralysis of jacial muscles on left side and devxation of tongue but these symptoms are not prominent at present. He has slight aphasia. He complains of headaches on right side. His memory is poor and his cerebrations slow. He still takes indistinctly patellar reflexes. Exaggerated vision poor in right eye. Wasserman x x x. Phombergs sign not present. Pupils almost immobile.

14. If the disability is an injury, was it caused

    (a) In action ?

    (b) On field service ?   Not applicable.

    (c) On duty ?

    (d) Off duty ?

15. Was a Court of Inquiry held on the injury ?

    If so—(a) When ?   Not applicanle.

        (b) Where ?

        (c) Opinion ?

16. Was an operation performed ? If so, what ?   Not applicable.

17. If not, was an operation advised and declined ?   Not applicable.

18. *In case of loss or decay of teeth.* Is the loss of teeth the result of wounds, injury or disease, directly* attributable to active service ?   Not applicable.

19. Do you recommend

    (a) Discharge as permanently unfit, or   Yes.
    (b) Change to England ?

<u>   R.H.McGibbon,   Capt. C.A.M.C.   </u>
Officer in medical charge of case.

    I have satisfied myself of the general accuracy of this report, and concur therewith, *except†*

Station <u>Shorncliffe</u>   <u>W.A.Swift, Lt.Col.   </u>
                    Officer in charge of Hospital.
Date <u>20th Nov.1915.</u>

* Loss of teeth on, or immediately after, active service, should be attributed thereto, unless there is evidence that it is due to some other cause.
† Delete this word if no exceptions are to be made.

Army Form B. 268.

This space to be left blank
for the Chelsea Number.

Proceedings on Discharge.

DISCHARGE DEPOT
DEC 26 1915
C.E.F. EO

(When forwarded for confirmation the documents named on page 4 should be enclosed.)

No. **454286**   Army Rank **Private**

Name **Arthur W. Morris**
(The name must agree strictly with that on enlistment, unless changed subsequently by authority.)

Corps **39ª Battalion C.E.F.**

Battalion, Battery, Company, Depôt, &c.
(If attached to the Regular Establishment of the Special Reserve or Permanent Staff of the Territorial Force, &c., or to General Staff of the Army, it should be so stated.)

Date of discharge **25·12·15**

Place of discharge **Canada**

1.   *Description at the time of discharge.*

Age **44** years **1** months   Descriptive marks.
Height **5** feet **9** inches
Chest ⎰ girth when fully expanded **37½** ins.   **None**
measure- ⎱ range of expansion **2½** ins.
ment
Complexion **Fair**
Eyes **Grey**
Hair **Dark**
Trade **Carpenter**
Intended place of
residence
(To be given as fully
as practicable)
(The measurements and description should be carefully taken on the day the man leaves his unit, but in the case of men sent home from abroad for discharge, the age and intended place of residence should be left blank to be filled in by the Officer who confirms the discharge at home.)

2. The above-named man is discharged in consequence of **Para 392 XVI Kingships**
Having been found Medically unfit
for further service) DECEASED
(The cause of discharge must be worded as prescribed in the King's Regulations and be identical with that on the discharge certificate. If discharged by superior authority, the No. and date of the letter to be quoted.)

3. Military character :— **Good.**

4. Character awarded in accordance with King's Regulations :—

Good.

(left margin, rotated) To be filled in on the soldier quitting the Colours.

Certified that the above is an accurate copy of the character given by me on Army Form B. 2067* and that Army Form D. 489 was awarded in this case.
J.B. O.C.
Initials of Commanding Officer.

(right margin, rotated) Printed 3-1-16 *J.M.*

Army Form B. 2088 has been issued to*

Wt. W. 13141/283 430,000 3/15 M.&C. Ld.   Forms
B. 268
30   *Strike out if not applicable.   [OVER.

12   *Proceedings on Discharge for Arthur William Morris*

5. He is in possession of the following number of G.C. badges (if the man is a N C.O. and enlisted prior to 1st July, 1881, the number he would have been entitled to had he not been promoted should be stated).

   Is it probable that he will be entitled to another good conduct badge before the confirmation of these proceedings ?

   Classification for service, or proficiency pay   ...   . Class_____

6. Campaigns, Medals and Decorations

   Certificate of education ....

7. His accounts are correctly balanced, and I have impartially inquired into all matters brought before me in accordance with Regulations.

   (Place) *West Sandling*

   (Date) *Nov 27ᵃ 1915*

   F. D. Boggs Major for Lt Col.

   Commanding *39ᵃ* Battn. *C. E. F.* Regiment.

   absent on duty.

8. *Certificate to be signed by the soldier on discharge.*

   I hereby acknowledge that I have received all my pay and allowances (including clothing allowance), and all just demands up to the present date, subject to the reservations of the claims noted on the 3rd page.

   (Place) _____   *(Signature of Soldier.)*

   (Date) _____   *(Signature of Witness.)*

   (When a soldier is absent through illness or any other cause, and it is not desirable to forward these proceedings to him for signature, a manuscript copy should be sent for the man to sign, and when returned should be attached here.)

9.   *Additional certificate in the case of a soldier who takes his discharge at his own request.*

   I hereby declare that I do of my own free will request to be discharged from His Majesty's Service.

   _____*(Signature of Soldier.)*

10.   *Statement of service.*

   Service towards engagement to _____ (the date to which the record of service is completed)   years   days.

   Further service   „   „ _____ (the date of confirmation of discharge)   ...   ..._____ „ _____ „

   Total ...   „ _____ „

11.   *Confirmation of discharge.*

   The discharge of the above-named man is hereby confirmed for _____ (date)

   (Place)_____

   Signature _____

   (Date)_____

   Commanding officers (or the Paymaster, if at Netley) will issue to every discharged soldier whose claim to pension, either on account of service or disability, is to be brought under the consideration of the Chelsea Board, a memorandum for his guidance on Army Form D. 401, and will at the same time transmit to the Secretary, Royal Hospital, Chelsea, a descriptive return of the man on Army Form D. 400.

13

Army Form B. 103.

Casualty Form—Active Service.

Regiment or Corps. 39ᵗʰ Battalion C.E.F.

Regimental No. 454286 Rank Pte. Name A. W. Morris

Enlisted (a) 14–6–15 Terms of Service (a) War. Service reckons from (a) 14–6–15

Date of promotion } —— Date of appointment } —— Numerical position on }
to present rank } to lance rank } roll of N.C.Os.. }

Extended —— Re-engaged —— Qualification (b) ——

Report		Record of promotions, reductions, transfers, casualties, etc., during active service, as reported on Army Form B. 213, Army Form A. 36, or in other official documents. The authority to be quoted in each case.	Place	Date	Remarks taken from Army Form B. 213, Army Form A. 36, or other official documents.
Date	From whom received				
15·12·15	39 Bn	S.o.S to Canada	Op ecvo 27–8–15 Woodmaling	10·12·15	Nk 1½ 247.
		F.O. Loggston Lt.-Col. Commanding 39th Battalion, C.E.F. absent on duty.			
	Dis Deput	S.o.S Deceased Quebec.		25·12·15	Anth Neiyalees.

(a) In the case of a man who has re-engaged for, or enlisted into Section D. Army Reserve, particulars of such re-engagement or enlistment will be entered.
(b) e.g., Signaller, Shoeing Smith, etc., etc., also special qualifications in technical Corps duties.

I.P.T.O

Casualty Form for Arthur William Morris

14

Alfred Thomas Morris – 1884-1917

Alfred Thomas Morris was born in Cardiff, Wales, as were the rest of his siblings other than the eldest brother Arthur, due to his father moving from Bristol to work on the Cardiff Docks in the late 1800s. He was born 5th February 1884, the youngest son of William and Emily Morris.

Alfred married his wife Edith sometime in 1905 and had one son, Arthur, when they decided to emigrate to Canada for a better life. They left Liverpool in May 1907 on the *Empress of Britain*, as shown on the Passenger List for that year. They settled in Oshawa, Ontario where Alfred was thought to have worked for General Motors although his trade was that of a bricklayer. It would appear that all of the brothers in the family worked in the construction industry.

Once Canada entered World War I, Alfred joined the 116th Battalion C.E.F. His Regimental number was 746064, the rank of Private. He enlisted on 19th January 1916, whether this was because his elder brother Arthur had died, returning on board ship on Christmas Day 1915, is not clear, but it is a possible motivation. It may just have been down to how many men had gone before and been Killed in Action (KIA).

He embarked from Halifax on 23rd July 1916 sailing on the *SS Olympic* and arrived in Liverpool on 31st July 1916. Training was then undertaken. He was transferred for overseas service to 2nd Battalion on 10th October 1916. He arrived at C.B.D in France on 11th October 1916, which he then left for 2nd Battalion in the field.

His battalion took part in the Battle for Vimy Ridge and were initially near Neuville St. Vaast. After breaking through the German front line they got to Thélus and because its front broadened as it broke through the German lines, the battalion was assisted by 13 Brigade from the British 5th Division. The object was to take Hill 145 (which is where the Vimy Memorial now stands) and where the German defences were particularly strong.

The hard lessons learned by the Allies in the previous years prompted the continual evolution of Canadian tactics and planning. Once the Canadian Corps moved to the Vimy area and had begun intensive training for the attack, Canadian soldiers would be briefed and even private-ranked soldiers would be told the objectives. Maps would be widely distributed and rehearsals over scale models of the terrain would be conducted. The Infantry Section, which Alfred was part of, was created after the Somme, and infantry platoons were changed from being simply an administrative entity to a truly tactical unit. Each platoon was given a specific task in the battle plan rather than vague instructions.

Contrary to popular belief, Vimy Ridge converted into a fortress by the Germans, with the Canadians tasked with taking it back. It is now known

that the Germans were less well prepared than the popular histories of the war may have portrayed.

Because Vimy is close to Arras the town took a hammering with 'big stuff'. One recording of the bombardment said "When they were coming over (shells) it sounded as though all the trains in the world were rushing through the air at the same time". Not only did the troops have to put up with cannon shellfire coming their way, they also had German planes strafing them.

The Canadians eventually took most of Vimy on 9th April 1917. It took another three days for them to take Hill 145. The next task for the 2nd Battalion was to capture the town of Arleux-en-Gohelle and at the same time to go onto the next town of Fresnoy-en-Gohelle.

Arleux proved troublesome to the British because of the loop at the village which lay at the end of a low spur reaching into the Hindenburg Line at Quéant (some twelve miles south-east of Arras). General Douglas Haig launched a preliminary offensive aimed at eliminating the Arleux Loop and linking together two salients which had been formed on the 23rd by advances north and south of the Scarpe. The British 2nd Division (First Army) assaulted opposite Oppy and on its left the 1st Canadian Division stormed the Arleux Loop. Alfred's unit was nearby in case extra support was needed.

The Canadian assult on the Arleux Loop was the only tangible success of the whole operation, according to one Historian. Arleux was a Battle Honour granted to Canadian units participating in the battle to take the town in April 1917, during the battles on the Western Front.

The village of Fresnoy-en-Gohelle was the next objective of the Canadian Corps after their victory at Arleux in April. Fresnoy was the retreating point for the German forces from the village of Arleux-en-Gohelle, and an important part of the Oppy-Méricourt Line, one of Haig's objectives for what was known to the British as the Third Battle of the Scarpe, or the Battle of Bullecourt.

Like Arleux, Fresnoy was heavily fortified, and the area for manoeuvring was very small. It had been decided that all operations along the line would take place at night, which worked to the advantage of the Canadians since they had a very small advance area. The plan of attack at Fresnoy was similar to Arleux, with practice runs beforehand.

Fresnoy was taken within several hours, but the Canadian brigades were now up against the typical problem facing armies on the Western Front – holding their position. The Canadians managed to take Fresnoy for the British to lose it three days later!

It was during the attack to take Fresnoy that Alfred was seriously wounded in the abdomen by an enemy rifle bullet. We were told the

FORM OF WILL.

I, __Alfred Thomas Morris_____ (Name in full)

Regimental Number __746064_____ serving in ____116th O.S.Battalion C.E.F.

of the Canadian Expeditionary Force, do hereby revoke all former Wills by me
made and declare this to be my last Will.

I bequeath all my real estate unto

Mr s Edith Rachael Morris Whiting Ave. Cedardale, Ont. Canada	Name and Address of person or persons to whom it is to go.

absolutely, and my personal estate I bequeath to

Mrs. Edith Rachael Morris Whiting Ave. Cedardale, Ont. Canada	Name and Address of person or persons to receive personal estate* (See note).

IMPORTANT
NOTE this ___8th___ day of ___July_____ A.D. 191 6
This must be Signed
and Dated by
THE SOLDIER
HIMSELF. *Alfred Thomas Morris* Signature of Soldier.

*N.B.—Personal estate includes pay, effects, money in bank, insurance policy, in fact everything
except real estate.

Signed and acknowledged by the Testator as and for his last Will in the presence
of us both present at the same time, who in his presence, at his request, and in
the presence of each other have hereunto subscribed our names as Witnesses.

Signature of First Witness _Hilbert Clemens_____

Address of Witness _A Coy 14th Bn C.O.t___

THE TWO
WITNESSES Occupation of Witness _Soldier Serge.___

MUST
SIGN HERE Signature of Second Witness _George Froud_

Address of Witness _D. Coy 116 O/S Bⁿ CEF_

Occupation of Witness _Soldier Corpl_

:. F. W. 82
:66M-5-16.
1772-39-963.

18

story as children that the stretcher-bearers went out to pick him up and take him back to the dressing station when a mortar shell came over and blew the three men up. Alfred died on 3rd May 1917. He has no known grave but his name is on the Vimy Memorial, which I have located during visits to Vimy.

Like Arthur in the previous story, Alfred's wife Edith received a War Service Gratuity which she would have needed, as by this time she had three children to look after. Alfred was also awarded the Victory Medal and the British War Medal and decorations plus plaques, scroll and Memorial Cross which were sent to his widow Edith. His mother, Emily, applied for a Memorial Cross but sadly she died before she could received it.

In all William and Emily Morris lost four of their sons to the war. One was seriously wounded but survived. My great grandfather was Sidney James Morris, who served in the Royal Garrison Artillery. He was also awarded the Victory Medal and British War Medal. After the war William Morris was told that his family would be awarded the British Empire Medal for Services to the War Effort by his sons. William's reply was "Thank you, but this will not bring my sons back to me". He never collected the medal – such was his disgust at a War that was supposed to end all wars.

On page 16 is a photo of William and Emily with five of their sons. Alfred is the one wearing the cap and next to him is our great grandfather. The gap after Emily is where Arthur would have stood had he have survived. No one knows what happened to the other son.

I have included a map of the British front line (page 22), paperwork including the Form of Will (page 18), Attestation Paper (pages 20-21), Casualty Form on Active Service (page 23), War Service Gratuity document for relatives of deceased (page 24), and and image of the memorial at Vimy Ridge, also on page 24.

TRIPLICATE

ATTESTATION PAPER.
116TH OVERSEAS BATTALION C.E.F.
CANADIAN OVER-SEAS EXPEDITIONARY FORCE.

No. 746064

Folio.

QUESTIONS TO BE PUT BEFORE ATTESTATION.
(ANSWERS)

1. What is your surname? ... *Morris*
1a. What are your Christian names? ... *Alfred Thomas*
1b. What is your present address? ... *Cedar Dale East Whitby*
2. In what Town, Township or Parish, and in what Country were you born? ... *Cardiff Wales*
3. What is the name of your next-of-kin? ... *Edith Morris*
4. What is the address of your next-of-kin? ... *Cedar Dale East Whitby Ont*
4a. What is the relationship of your next-of-kin? ... *wife*
5. What is the date of your birth? ... *Feb 5th 1884*
6. What is your Trade or Calling? ... *Bricklayer*
7. Are you married? ... *Yes*
8. Are you willing to be vaccinated or re-vaccinated and inoculated? ... *Yes*
9. Do you now belong to the Active Militia? ... *Yes*
10. Have you ever served in any Military Force? ... *No*
    If so, state particulars of former Service.
11. Do you understand the nature and terms of your engagement? ... *Yes*
12. Are you willing to be attested to serve in the CANADIAN OVER-SEAS EXPEDITIONARY FORCE? ... *Yes*

DECLARATION TO BE MADE BY MAN ON ATTESTATION.

I, *Alfred Thomas Morris*, do solemnly declare that the above are answers made by me to the above questions and that they are true, and that I am willing to fulfil the engagements by me now made, and I hereby engage and agree to serve in the Canadian Over-Seas Expeditionary Force, and to be attached to any arm of the service therein, for the term of one year, or during the war now existing between Great Britain and Germany should that war last longer than one year, and for six months after the termination of that war provided His Majesty should so long require my services, or until legally discharged.

Date *Jan 19th* 1916   *Alfred Thomas Morris* (Signature of Recruit)

Thos Fayes Lt (Signature of Witness)

OATH TO BE TAKEN BY MAN ON ATTESTATION.

I, *Alfred Thomas Morris*, do make Oath, that I will be faithful and bear true Allegiance to His Majesty King George the Fifth, His Heirs and Successors, and that I will as in duty bound honestly and faithfully defend His Majesty, His Heirs and Successors, in Person, Crown and Dignity, against all enemies, and will observe and obey all orders of His Majesty, His Heirs and Successors, and of all the Generals and Officers set over me. So help me God.

Date *Jan 19th* 1916   *Alfred Thomas Morris* (Signature of Recruit)

Thos Fayes Lt (Signature of Witness)

CERTIFICATE OF MAGISTRATE.

The Recruit above-named was cautioned by me that if he made any false answer to any of the above questions he would be liable to be punished as provided in the Army Act.

The above questions were then read to the Recruit in my presence.

I have taken care that he understands each question, and that his answer to each question has been duly entered as replied to, and the said Recruit has made and signed the declaration and taken the oath

before me, at *Town of Oshawa* this *19* day of *Jan* 1916

C. N. Carsdale (Signature of Justice)

M. F. W. 23.
200 M.—11-15.
H. Q. 1772-39-841.

   Attestation Paper for Alfred Thomas Morris

Description of *Alfred Thomas Morris* on Enlistment.

Apparent Age. **3 2** years. *11* months.
(To be determined according to the instructions given in the Regulations for Army Medical Services.)

Distinctive marks, and marks indicating congenital peculiarities or previous disease.
(Should the Medical Officer be of opinion that the recruit has served before, he will, unless the man acknowledges to any previous service, attach a slip to that effect, for the information of the Approving Officer).

Height .... **5** ft. **7** ins.

Chest measurement.
Girth when fully expanded .... **33½** ins.
Range of expansion .... **2½** ins.

Complexion .... *Dark*

Eyes .... *Brown*

Hair .... *Brown*

Religious denominations
Church of England ....
Presbyterian ....
Methodist .... *✓*
Baptist or Congregationalist ....
Roman Catholic ....
Jewish ....
Other denominations ....
(Denomination to be stated.)

CERTIFICATE OF MEDICAL EXAMINATION.

I have examined the above-named Recruit and find that he does not present any of the causes of rejection specified in the Regulations for Army Medical Services.

He can see at the required distance with either eye; his heart and lungs are healthy; he has the free use of his joints and limbs, and he declares that he is not subject to fits of any description.

I consider him* *fit* .... for the Canadian Over-Seas Expeditionary Force.

Date. *Jan. 19th* 191 *6* .... *James Moore*

Place. *Oshawa* .... *Capt*
Medical Officer.

*Insert here "fit" or "unfit."

NOTE.—Should the Medical Officer consider the Recruit unfit, he will fill in the foregoing Certificate only in the case of those who have been attested, and will briefly state below the cause of unfitness:—

....
....
....
....
....

CERTIFICATE OF OFFICER COMMANDING UNIT.

.... *Alfred Thos. Morris* .... having been finally approved and inspected by me this day, and his Name, Age, Date of Attestation, and every prescribed particular having been recorded, I certify that I am satisfied with the correctness of this Attestation.

.... *A. Thorpe* L.I. Co(Signature of Officer)
O. C. 116TH OVERSEAS BATTALION C.E.F.

Date. **MAY 15 1916** 191 .

21

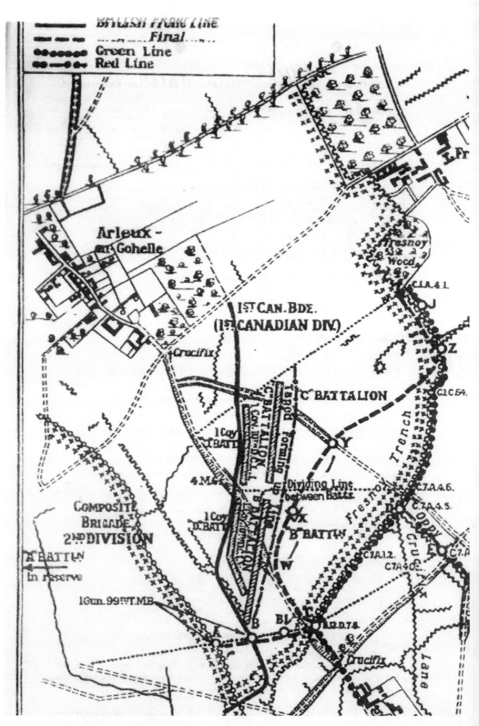

Map of the British front line

Casualty Form—Active Service.

M. F. W. 54.
15thM. 10-15.
H.Q. 1772-30-006.

Unit, Regiment or Corps ___116th Battalion,C.E.F.___

Regimental No. ___746064___ Rank ___Pte.___ Name ___Morris,Alfred Thomas___

Enlisted (a) ___19/1/16___ Terms of Service (a) ___War + 6 Month___ Service reckons from (a) ___19/1/16___

Date of promotion to present rank. }		Date of appointment to lance rank }		Numerical position on roll of N.C.Os. }

Extended_____ Re-engaged_____ Qualification (b)_____

	Date	Report From whom received	Record of promotions, reductions, transfers, casualties, etc., during active service, as reported on Army Form B. 213, Army Form A. 36, or in other official documents. The authority to be quoted in each case.	Place	Date	Remarks taken from Army Form B. 213, Army Form A. 36, or other official documents
CERTIFIED CORRECT. 21 OCT.1916	N. RECORDS, LONDON.		Embarked, Canada,	Halifax.	23/7/16.	
			Arrived. England.	Liverpool	31/7/16.	
			Transferred for Overseas service to 2nd Battalion Oct.10th 1916.			O.C.
	11.10.16	C.B.D.	ARRIVED C.B.D.	FRANCE	11.10.16	N.R. 11.10.16 PART 2 08 26.10.16
	30.10.16	C.B.D.	LEFT C.B.D. FOR	2ND BN	30.10.16	N.R.D. 30.10.16
	5.11.16	O C 2 BN	ARRIVED 2ND BN.	FIELD	1.11.16	B 213 C.S 383 2/13.11.16
	5.5.17	do	Killed in Action	do.	3.5.17	Letter P.S.II Ord 43 4/9.5/17

Lieut.
for Major A.A.G.

(a) In the case of a man who has re-engaged for, or enlisted into Section D. Army Reserve, particulars of such re-engagement or enlistment will be entered.
(b) e.g. Signaller, Shoeing Smith, etc., etc., also special qualifications in technical Corps duties.
[P.T.O

Date	Report From whom received	Record of promotions, reductions, transfers, casualties, etc., during active service, as reported on Army Form B. 213, Army Form A. 36, or in other official documents. The authority to be quoted in each case.	Place	Date	Remarks taken from Army Form B. 213, Army Form A. 36, or other official documents.

Casualty Form for Alfred Thomas Morris

War Service Gratuity for Alfred Thomas Morris

From the Vimy Ridge Memorial

The Senses of a Soldier

by Nathaniel

The smell was ghastly.
The rotten bodies,
All the blood of soldiers,
Mixed with the mud of the trenches.

A gun would feel cold,
Some wouldn't dare pull the trigger,
Our feet would never feel dry,
And everything would be slippery.

Bully beef tasted salty,
The bread was dry,
The biscuits were soggy,
The blood taste was dreadful.

All I could hear was
The cries of people in agony,
The firing of guns,
The explosions,
And the generals screaming.

All I could see was,
Innocent men fighting for their countries.
The dead all around me,
And my friends dead or frightened.

Arthur William Phillips, 1897-1973, World War One Record

Janet Warby

Arthur Phillips was in the British army from 1915 to 1919 serving exactly one month short of four years. Half of his service was spent on active service in Flanders, Western France, Salonica and Macedonia. The other half of his service was taken up with training, hospitalisation and convalescence.

He served with Royal Field Artillery units attached at different times to 33rd Division, 47th (London Division) and finally the 27th Division.

Whilst living with his parents at 29 Farlton Road, Wandsworth, Arthur Phillips enlisted in April 1915, aged 17 at East Dulwich and became part of the 'Camberwell' Royal Field Artillery 162 Brigade, 'B' Battery. He commenced serving as Gunner No. L/13181.

After training in England, along with the rest of his Brigade, he was sent to France in December 1915 and became part of the 33rd Infantry Division Artillery, itself one of Lord Kitchener's new armies.

Here is a summary of a War Diary* during his time in the Field.

January to April 1916
Further preparation in the first months of 1916 before the Brigade saw action supporting the 33rd Division just north of Lens, east of Bethune in the Annequin and Vermelles area. This was known as the La Bassee front.

May to June 1916
Artillery support for the 33rd Division continued on the Givenchy and Auchy fronts.

July 1916
The Brigade moved to near Albert at Becordel Becourt in reserve for the Somme offensive.
Each of the four Batteries of 162nd Brigade now comprise 3–18 pounders and 1– .5ins howitzers.

---

*   RFA 1st World War Diaries. PRO Nat Archives
       33rd Division 162nd Brigade WO 95/2413
       47th Division 235th (5th London Brigade) WO 95/2717
       33rd Divisional Artillery 1914-1918 by J. Macartney-Filgate (Major)
       A.W. Phillips Army Service and Medical Records. WO 363-P809

Arthur William Phillips

July 16th to 31st July 1916

Batteries in action near Mametz and Caterpillar Wood in Caterpillar Valley north of Montabaun.

High Wood, Delville Wood and Switch trench bombarded.

162nd Brigade support 51st Infantry Division when 33rd Infantry are relieved. Six inch enemy shell lands on 'B' Battery and five men are killed.

August 1st 1916

162nd Brigade relieved and return to Becordel Becourt for rest.

August 11th - 31st August 1916

162nd Brigade 'B' Battery return to front. Attached to 14th Infantry Division and attack Wood Lane and Orchard trenches.

C.O. of 'B' Battery, Major R.J.M. Johnston killed in heavy enemy bombardment whilst ordering his gun crews to shelter in trenches.

September 1916

162nd Brigade continue to bombard High Wood and Delville Wood Brigade relocates to Wanquetin on the Arras front.

October 4th 1916

Brigade batteries move south of Foncquevillers and attack trenches in the Gommecourt and Hebuterne area at Rossignol Wood. 76 men gassed by enemy attack.

October 19th - 25th October 1916

'B' Battery move south of Hebuterne and forms part of 13th Corp. Artillery now attached to 31st Infantry Division.

The artillery attack on the fronts extending west of Puisieux and south of Serre.

October 26th 1916

Brigade batteries support raids by 93rd Infantry Brigade of the 31st Division.

October 29th 1916

Eighteen pounder batteries heavily shelled. Disused gun pit doing duty as signallers dug-out received a direct hit from a four inch HV shell resulting in nine casualties; five killed and four wounded. One of the wounded was Gunner Arthur Phillips sustaining gunshot wounds to the chest and shrapnel wounds to the head and body.

Following admittance to No. 20 ccs and time spent in No 16 General Hospital in France, he was repatriated in December to England.

January – June 1917
Further training and signallers course whilst in England prior to posting to Belgium.

July 5th 1917
Joined 235th Brigade, 'C' Battery (5th London Brigade RFA). This formed the Artillery of 47th (London) Infantry Division.

July – August 1917
'C' Battery engaged in the Third Battle of Ypres whilst now in support of 41st Infantry Division as part of the 'Bluff' group.
In action south of Ypres in the following areas – Birchoote, Hollebecke, St. Julien, Klein Zillerbecke, Boescheppe, Hooge, Ouderdom, St. Eloi and Lock 7.

September 1917
Around Ypres now in support of 19th Infantry Division around Poperinghe, Oosthock, Lock 7 still part of 'Bluff' group.

October – November 1917
Brigade moves back south to the Somme region via Strazeele, Meteren, Frevincappelle, Ochele, Aubigny, Gaurelle, Gauchin-legal, Villers au Boix, Aix Noulette, continuing on to Mingoval, Wanqetin, Boyelles Ervillers, Bapaume, Happincourt, Le Transloy, Rocquiny and finally south of Cambrai via Ypres, Neuville Bourjonval, Gouzeaucourt and Villers-Plouich arriving at Flesquieres on the 24th.

November – December 1917
Brigade Artillery in attacks on Gonnelieu and Gauche Woods, Havrincourt Wood, Flesqieres and Havrincourt.

January 1918
2nd – attacks on Trescault assisting 17th Divisional Artillery
6th – 'C' Battery now comes under 19th Divisional Artillery
8th – 'C' Battery reverts back under 47th Divisional Command
10th – Nine Wood bombarded with gas
15th – 'C' Battery at map location K28.C.05.10 Premy Salient and defence of Bilhelm Chapel Switch.
20th – Under enemy shelling at Ribecourt

23rd – Arthur Phillips suffered from gas attack and was repatriated to England

February – July 1918
Following convalescence, further training and became 1st class signaller

---

Signal Section 5 "C" (Reserve) Brigade, R.F.A.

Certificate. No. 518/18

No. 13181. Gr. Phillips A.W. was examined at the *Classification* held by Capt. J. H. Ketchur *Classification Officer, Eastern Command, on the* 18th May 1918, and qualified First *Class Signaller.*

	S	R		
Buzzer	100	99.5	Semaphore	
Lamp	100	100	Map Reading	92 /.
Disc	100	100	Instrument	83 /.
Morse Flag	100	100	T.M.S.	80 /.

LESSNESS PARK,
ABBEY WOOD, KENT.

.... Captain, R.F.A.
Brigade Signalling Officer.

First Class Signaller Certificate for Arthur Phillips

August 1918
Posted to Salonica to join the 27th Divisional Artillery

August – December 1918
Took part in Battle of Dojran and Stumica Valley in Macedonia. Contracted malaria and after being confined to 29th General Hospital was repatriated to England. He was finally discharged from the army in March 1919.

CERTIFICATE of* { Discharge Transfer to Reserve Disembodiment Demobilisation } on Demobilization.

Army Form Z. 21.

Regtl. No. *13,181* ..... Rank ..... *Signaller*

Names in full ..... *Phillips Arthur*
(Surname first)

Unit and Regiment or Corps from which
*Discharged
Transferred to Reserve
Enlisted on the ..... *3rd April* 191.*5*

For ..... *R. H. & R. F. A*
(Here state Regiment or Corps to which first appointed)

..... R.H. & R.F.A.

Also served in .....

Only Regiments or Corps in which the Soldier served since August 4th, 1914 are to be stated. If inapplicable, this space is to be ruled through in ink and initialled.

†Medals and Decorations awarded during present engagement
*Has
Has not } served Overseas on Active Service.

Place of Rejoining in case of emergency } *Charlton Park* ..... Medical Category *B. II*

Specialist Military qualifications } *Signaller* ..... Year of birth *1895*

He is* { Discharged Transferred to Army Reserve Disembodied Demobilized } on ..... 191..

in consequence of Demobilization.

..... Signature and Rank.

Officer i/c ..... Records. ..... (Place).

* Strike out whichever is inapplicable.   † The word "Nil" to be inserted when necessary.

(20996). Wt. W 8211—P.P. 2329. 3,000m. 1/19. D & S. (E 1256.);

Demobilisation Certificate for Arthur Phillips

Arthur William Phillips, 1897-1973

GUNNER L/13181 - ROYAL HORSE AND FIELD ARTILLERY, 1915 - 1919

33rd Division Field Artillery
162nd Brigade 'B' Battery
also supported :
1st, 5th, 7th, 14th, 24th, 31st and 51st Divisions

Battle of the Somme
July/November 1916

33rd DIVISION ARTILLERY
162nd BRIGADE
'B' BATTERY
***
SOMME
JULY/NOV 1916
....
27th DIVISION ARTILLERY
***
SALONICA
AUG/DEC 1918

47th Division Field Artillery
235th Brigade (5th London) 'C' Battery
also supported :
41st Division
19th Divisional

3rd Battle of Ypres
July/November 1917

47th DIVISION ARTILLERY
235th BRIGADE
(5th LONDON)
'C' BATTERY
***
3rd YPRES (PASSCHENDAELE)
JULY/NOV 1917
***
CAMBRAI
NOV 1917/JAN 1918

47th Division Field Artillery

also supported
17th Division
19th Division

Battle of Cambrai
November.January 1917/18

27th Division Field Artillery

Salonica
August/December 1918

Victory

by Lottie

Silence hung heavy in the air
When the guns stopped booming
And the bombs stopped dropping
But with so many dead
Was it really a victory?

In the field of crosses
With poppies blowing at their side
Men rested after triumph
But with so many dead
Was it really a victory?

The day peace was signed
Crowds cried out with joy
"Victory, victory!"
But with so many dead
Was it really a victory?

Families wept
When they heard the news
And were they right to think that
With so many dead
Was it really a victory?

Captain Cecil Patrick Thomas Foster

Caroline Clopet

Master Mariner, Captain Cecil Patrick Thomas Foster passed away on August 8th 1930 aged 43 years. His wife Minnie Foster died on April 14th 1982 aged 98, and the couple are buried at Merthyr Dyfan Cemetery, Barry, South Wales. The grave was recently restored by people of the town and is now also regarded as a memorial to all that have sailed. The grave is now also recorded as a Treasure of the County of the Vale of Glamorgan.

Cecil Foster is remembered worldwide for the *SS. Trevessa* foundering in 1923 and the resulting safety of the lifeboats enabling the minimal loss of life for over three weeks. The majority of the London newspapers commented at the time on the foundering of the *Trevessa* as one of the most thrilling sea stories ever told. They described Captain Foster's exploit as amazing. The *Daily Telegraph* said: "*We may think with pride that our British sailors can match in daring, resolution, and loyalty those who won for their flag the realm of the circling sea*".

Captain Foster's Earlier Exploits

During World War I, while a Chief Mate, his ship was torpedoed and the liner that rescued him was also sunk. Foster, with 36 others, drifted in an open boat for 10 days before being rescued. Some went mad. When the boat eventually reached the coast of Spain, only 16 were alive. His experiences on those occasions had affected him so much that he had often discussed with his steward of the *Trevessa* the question of how a lifeboat should be provisioned in the event of having to leave the ship on the high seas.

In June 1923 the Hain Line steamer *Trevessa* loaded with zinc concentrates and *en route* from Fremantle to Durban sank very quickly in the Indian Ocean during a violent storm. Owing to the foresight on the part of the captain the steward knew exactly what provisions to put into the lifeboats. The chief items were water, condensed milk, and cigarettes. Although an SOS message had been sent out, *Trevessa's* position, 1,000 miles out in the Indian Ocean and miles from the nearest landfall to the west, made him prepare for the worst. He divided his crew between two lifeboats and had each of them provided with all the condensed milk, ship's biscuits and water they could carry.

When the *Trevessa* plunged to the seabed soon afterwards, her crew – 20 of them in the Captain's boat and 24 in a boat commanded by the first

Captain Cecil Foster

officer James Stewart Smith – faced a doubtful future, yet they remained confident in their chances of saving themselves if they were not picked up. Two ships of the company's fleet were in that ocean when the distress signal was picked up and they were diverted to search for any survivors. All that was found was a broken oar that had snapped off when one of the boats was being launched. The conclusion was that they had all perished. The 44 crew members had actually managed to get into two lifeboats, some with very little clothing on, and the Captain, Cecil Foster, had decided to endeavour to make for Mauritius some 2,000 miles away.

With no compass and only enough water for 7 pints per man, 550 biscuits and two cases of condensed milk, they were immediately put on strict rations. In the weeks which followed the men in the two boats – fed twice a day on measured rations of condensed milk, biscuits and water – sailed towards the islands of Mauritius and Rodriguez, keeping together for much of the time, but separating eventually. An abundance of cigarettes, packed in round tins which were later used to catch rainwater, helped their morale, yet it was the condensed milk which helped them to swallow the dry biscuits and kept up their stamina.

Water had to be issued most sparingly, while generally the men's mouths were so dry that any biscuits issued for food were seldom touched. As the boats soon became separated, and with the soaring heat of the tropics, some of the men succumbed to drinking salt water which caused them to become delirious and death followed quickly. With the absence of any wind, the men had to row, which aggravated not only their swollen hands and feet but also their bodies, which were suffering from extensive salt water boils. It was only by perfect discipline and obedience to the Captain's orders that they stuck together and on the 23rd day one boat landed on the island of Rodriguez and three days later the second boat landed on Bel-Ombre, Mauritius; a total of 34 men survived.

The story of these events was provided to the public by Cecil Foster, captain of the ship, in a book entitled *Seventeen Hundred Miles in Open Boats*. This plain unvarnished tale comes essentially from the logs kept by the commanders of the two open boats that carried the crew of the *Trevessa* to safety – one to Rodriguez Island, the other to Mauritius. In the account, Captain Foster remarked on the benefit they all received from the cigarettes as smoking appeared to have comforted and soothed the sufferers; indeed, Captain Foster, writing of this stated; "*When indulged in it revived everyone's spirits and added the touch of cheerfulness necessary to enable us to carry on and keep smiling*". The daily ration of water allotted to every man was one-third of a cigarette tin, which was issued at 2 o'clock in the afternoon, when the worst of the heat of the day was over. At 8am each man had a ration of milk and one

The Ovaltine advertisement featuring Captain Foster

biscuit, and another small ration of milk in the evening. While those who drank sea-water died of thirst, much relief was derived from bathing the head and body in sea-water, soaking their clothes in the sea, and, after partially wringing them out, putting them on again; the men who did this suffered less from thirst than those who relied only upon their ration of drinking water.

Capt. Foster's wife and the vessel's owners received cable messages on 30th June, 1923, stating that the captain and 16 of his crew had arrived at Mauritius Island, after having landed first at Rodriguez.

When Captain Foster's boat reached Rodriguez after 22 days adrift all but two of the boat's 20 occupants had survived the ordeal. The first officer's boat reached Mauritius after 25 days at sea, having lost eight of its 24 occupants through drinking seawater, falling overboard or from general deprivation.

When the news was first flashed over the world that an open boat containing survivors from the *SS. Trevessa* had landed at Rodriguez Island, a sense of pride as well as relief was felt in general by all. A monument to the crew of *Trevessa* was erected on Bel-Ombre and on the anniversary of their landing on Mauritius – *Trevessa Day* – was celebrated, which has now become *The Seafarers Day* so that the islanders can ponder the fact that they are indebted to seafarers of many nations.

The reunited survivors were greeted as if they were men returning from the dead. When the captain and his chief officer and their surviving crew arrived at Gravesend in a Union Castle Line mail steamer in August 1923 they received a heroes' welcome. The flags were flying and ships' sirens saluted them.

The captain was received by the King at Buckingham Palace and his obituary was recorded as far around the globe as New Zealand. His actions then, continues to save lives at sea to this very day.

World War One Poem

by Madeleine

I couldn't sleep last night
So I read your letter
For the tenth time at least
And it felt as if
I was in Flanders by your side.

I could feel the cold,
I could feel the pouring rain
I could hear the guns through the blazing skies,
I could hear your heart beating
Like the boom of a German bomb.

You were holding your gun,
But I wish you were holding me.
The winter wind was whizzling
Making me shiver
Like a poppy in a field.

So I put the letter
Right against my heart.
Hoping that protecting it
Would be like protecting you.

Ivanhoe Avon

Caroline Clopet

This is the story of Ivanhoe Avon, who was Caroline Clopet's grandmother's brother, who was a young Welsh soldier, one of just 36 of the Cardiff Pals to return to his home town after WWI following five weeks of fierce fighting in the Somme, before being sent on an 11 day journey to Salonika where he stayed four long years. Ivanhoe's story is one of incredible courage and determination on the battlefields of World War I. He signed on to the war effort in August 1914, as a 17-year old young man without telling his family, and was one of only 36 out of 800 men from the Cardiff Pals to return from the First World War to his seaside town of Penarth in South Wales in 1919.

At the outbreak of the Great War, Cardiff was one of 50 other cities across the United Kingdom to create a Pals battalion – the 11th Battalion, Welsh Regiment. Being mainly composed of professional men, the Regiment was also known as the 'collar and tie battalion'. The Pals Battalions were new units created by Lord Kitchener to encourage men from towns and cities to train and fight together, and, often, die together. For most of the young men in and around Cardiff, Penarth and Barry, bonding into a cohesive military unit was more like a Boy Scout camp, and the young men/teenage boys encouraged each other to join up and train together.

Before setting off for the War, the Pals left for training on the South Coast on the 14th September 1914. Ivanhoe's Father, Ernest gave him a Union Jack flag to carry with him every day, together with a camera, diary, notepad, and some money. When Ivanhoe said goodbye to his parents, Ernest and Elizabeth, brother Alex and sister Molly, he had no idea of what was awaiting him on the Front.

Ivanhoe spent five weeks at the battle of the Somme. While in the trenches, he witnessed an unimaginable amount of horror and tragedy which he diligently recorded almost every day in his diary. He was gassed, probably more than once, and was trapped behind enemy lines while rescuing a fellow serviceman who was badly injured. He came under direct fire on numerous occasions, and in one episode was saved from a direct hit by two pennies which deflected the bullet. While in the Trenches, Ivanhoe worked as a Rifleman, a Signalman and a Red Cross Medic. He kept his Union Jack flag on him almost everyday. Meanwhile at home in the Welsh town of Penarth, his father went every morning to the local church to pray for his son's safety.

Ivanhoe Avon

In 1915, the 11th Battalion of the Cardiff Pals were told to leave France and head for Salonika in Macedonia, Northern Greece, to reinforce the Allies' efforts against the German and Bulgarian troops. Not only was the fighting ferocious, but living and weather conditions were terrible: freezing cold and scorching hot, at varying times. Diseases were rife and malaria was rampant. Ivanhoe and the Cardiff Pals fought in Salonika for around three years. They suffered terrible losses, particularly in one attack on the Grande Couronne on the Doiran Front on the 18th September 1918, when almost 100 men from the Battalion died in the assault.

Ivanhoe recorded much about life during the Great War, including the meals he was given, his letters from home, bouts of dysentery, etc. But some of his diary entries breathed fresh air into the horror of war around him. In October 1914 he wrote "Caught the 1.13 to Brighton. Football match. England 21 points, Wales 0."

In Salonika he recorded how, in October 1916, he was positioned only fifteen yards away from the trenches of the Germans. He stated: '*I am fed up; it is so cold that I cannot hold my rifle*'. In November of that same year, he wrote about attending an art class after going through an activity-packed day, and how on Christmas day the monotony of the trenches was eased by a "fine feed of ham" and "I am so happy to have received two parcels from home".

There was a time when news reached his family in Penarth that their loved one was missing and was presumed dead, but Ivanhoe Avon was a survivor, and returned home to Penarth from the war in 1919.

Throughout the years that followed, Ivanhoe hardly spoke about his experiences in the trenches, recounting only briefly to his family the "carnage" he witnessed while on the front lines. It was only after his death at 90 years old in 1987, that his son Bill, and daughter-in-law Marion, discovered what Ivanhoe had been through as a young soldier in World War I.

His life and survival in the Great War serves as a witness for so many brave men that never had the chance to come home to their families.

With thanks to the Avon Family.

Silent Night

by Harry

I could hear that all the artillery guns
had stopped firing, even before night comes.
Everyone was starting to get into bed,
Until someone said "What's that strange noise ahead"?

Another soldier raised his hand,
"I think it's coming from NO MANS Land"
It was the great German Christmas carol,
So everyone decided to sing along afterall.

The next morning, It was Christmas day,
I remembered what had happened that particular day.
A German soldier was walking through the mud,
With his grey uniform covered with blood.

Everyone thought it was a trap, but he was unarmed.
He walked towards us with a white flag, he didn't want to do any
harm.
I came out of my trench and walked towards the soldier,
As if all those battles I've fought hadn't existed that year.

So everyone joined in for a football match,
And our goalkeeper did a really good catch!
But soon, we had to go back to the fight,
But before that, we enjoyed our Silent Night.

Lyons-La-Forêt, a Village Full of Secrets

Alexander Brzeski

Lyons-La-Forêt is a name not known by many; however this quiet, small Norman village tucked away in the heart of the forest of Lyons, 30 kms east of Rouen, has a deep and rich history with connections to Britain dating back as early as the 11th century. William the Conqueror, Duke of Normandy, King of England, had a castle built here.

In fact, if you were to look at aerial photos of the village, the formation of some of the houses show where the inner and outer keeps of the castle once stood. On the 1st December 1135 William's son, Henri Plantagenet, died within the castle walls of Lyons after eating a portion of locally caught Lamprey eels (once a delicacy in France and in the U.K), which were later found to be unfit for human consumption.

William the Conqueror and Henri 1st were not the only members of British royalty to grace the streets of Lyons. Others who favoured the surrounding forest for hunting included Richard II, also known as 'Richard the Lionheart'.

As time wore on, the links between Britain and this small Norman village faded like grains of sand being blown away in the wind until the claws of death gripped Europe. The death of Franz Ferdinand triggered the start of war in 1914. The tallons of the German empire tore into the guts of Europe ripping it from limb to limb – Europe was at war!

Whilst the cogs of the war machine turned across the world, materials such as wood for the building of trench fortifications and the fabrication of charcoal for heat as well as the production of the high explosive ammonal became more in demand. Lyons-La-Forêt, as the name suggests stands in the middle of France's largest and Europe's second largest Beech forest, a forest which now spans an area of 10,700 hectares. Images taken by local amateur photographer Joseph Venambre dating as early as 1915, indicate that the British were hard at work on the surrounding forest, treating the timber to be sent to the front. In 1917 the Lushai Labour Corps (from Northern India) and the South African Labour corps were in the area working almost side by side with German POWs. It is believed by local historians that there were at least two labour camps in the area plus at least one POW camp run by the British and Canadians. The camp is thought to have been in the grounds of the Cistercian Abbaye de Mortemer in Lisors. Evidence indicates that a second may have been based at the chateau de Vascoeuil, about 10 kms north west of Lyons.

British soldiers on the square (1921)

The exact number of German POWs is still unknown as records no long exist in this area and nothing has been found to date in the archives at Kew in the UK. Departmental records indicate that at least 500 prisoners lived and worked in the area. Photographs taken by second Lieutenant David McKlellan, an official war photographer for the British press, show prison labourers working in the forest, transporting vast logs to the saw mills around the area. American born YMCA canteen assistant Marian Baldwin describes in her book '*Canteening Overseas*' (first published in 1920) seeing German prisoners tilling the fields for local farmers. According to Emmanuel Boivin, the present chief for the ONF (Office Nationale des Forets) if you were to take a walk in certain areas of the forest today some of the douglas fir trees that now stand tall were planted by the labour corps.

Whilst the forest was filled with the sound of hard labour during the bitter years of the Great War, the village of Lyons became a popular tourist destination by one of France's famous composers Maurice Ravel. He spent two summers in Lyons writing sections of music to help his friend Modest Mussorgsky who was at the time creating the masterpiece *Pictures at an exhibition.*

The house of Maurice Ravel.

In contrast to guns blazing across northern France during the Great War, romance blossomed between a young Scottish military officer James

Richard Saige Sutherland and Huguette Lambert, a young local girl whose parents owned the Abbaye de Mortemer. Their romance came to an end after his offer of marriage was turned down, apparently by mademoiselle Lambert's family due to religious differences, he being Presbyterian and she being Catholic. Although their marriage was not to be, their friendship remained very strong until the death of Mr Sutherland in 1950.

James Sutherland of the Lovat Scouts Regiment circa WW1

When visiting this area the term '*I wish the trees could talk*' may spring to mind. If they could, I am sure the secrets they hold would fascinate all. One regular visitor's reports to this area inspired Ian Fleming to create that most famous of all spies - 007 James Bond. His name? Frederick Forest Yeo-Thomas. As part of the S.O.E (Special Operations Executive, a section of the British intelligence services) Yeo-Thomas was first parachuted into this area on February 26th 1943 with Andre Dewavrin DSO, an officer of the Free French Forces. The two of them spent the first night with Roger Vinay, the pharmacist, and his wife in their home in Lyons-La-Forêt. According to Forest's reports, that night they were treated to a true feast fit for a king. The following morning both were on their way to Paris to forge links with the resistance. He was later caught in 1944 in Paris by the Gestapo when on a mission to save his friend, the resistant Pierre Brossolette, who had previously been caught. Frederick was tortured by the infamous Klaus Barbie (the butcher of Lyon), he was then sent to Buchenwald where he managed to escape and alerted the advancing allied forces of the airmen being held in the camp. He ended the war at the rank of Wing Commander and was awarded the George Cross, Military Cross and Bar, 1939-45 star, France and Germany Star, Defence Medal, War medal 1939-45, Légion D'honneur, Croix De Guerre 1939-45, Croix de Combatant Voluntaire 1939-1945, Croix du Combattant de la Résistance and the Queen Elizabeth II Coronation Medal. These were to lie next to the World War I Victory Medal and the Polish Gold Cross of Merit which were awarded to him for his services during the First World War. Forest later died in 1964 in Paris, France.

In 1945 Huguette Lambert, who by this time had married Alphonse Verhague and had become a widow in 1943, wrote a letter (now held in the Scottish heritage centre in Inverness) to her ex-sweetheart, Mr Sutherland, whom she lovingly called 'Duke'. This letter tells the story, in great detail, of life in the area of Lyons under the German occupation of 1940-44, a period during which she was a member of the local resistance group. In the letter she describes how her beloved forest was heavily bombed in 1940 by the enemy when the British 10th Hussars met with General Veygand and his men before being evacuated back to England in June of that year. She talks of how at times, people were so desperate they lived on nothing but nettles and grass whilst all other worthwhile crops were sent to the front to feed Hitler's armies. She describes in lurid detail the death of some of her resistant friends who were caught by the SS after a failed raid on an enemy unit, saying that they had their feet boiled, arms broken before being shot in the head just 100 metres away from her own home. She wrote of the day that she could not enter into the village of Lyons to seek medical help as the village had been cordoned off due to the visit of Feldmarschal Erwin Rommel, who spent the night in one of Lyons's hotels. She also wrote that on 30 August 1944, the day of the liberation of the area, an abandoned German landmine claimed the lives of corporal Walter Ware (aged 26) and troopers Arthur Dick (aged 19) and Aubrey Verdun Drew (aged 28) of the 53rd Welsh Reconnaissance Regiment, part of the 7th armoured division, when their vehicle, a Bren Gun carrier, mounted the device.

Madame Huguette, second from left in front row, with crewmen.

The history of Madame Verhague, née Lambert, during the war is still partly shrouded in mystery at present, however, it is known that whilst she lived in a small holding on the outskirts of the grounds at Mortemer after her parents sold the abbaye in 1940, she hid at least seven allied service men. During the summer of 1944, the summer of hope for France, Flying Officer Phillip Derek Hemmens (of 49 squadron), Air Gunner Sgt. Ronald Leverington, Air Gunner Sgt. Reginald Joyce, Flight Engineer Donald Lesley, Douglas Eagle from 102 squadron, USAF co-pilot Theodore Basket of 457 bomber group and RCAF pilot Hugh Nixon were all hidden by Madame Huguette after their planes had been shot down at different times.

Don Lesley.

Madame Huguette in front of the wreckage of a Handley Paige Halifax aircraft.

Hiding place used by airmen.

So fond was Huguette of the RAF and RCAF boys that she helped that she called them her little 'Bluebirds' due to the colour of their uniform. On August 23rd, seven days before the liberation of the area by the 53rd Welsh Reconnaissance Regiment her 'Bluebirds' were collected by what appeared to be a Red Cross driver. The driver was in fact Jacques Desoubrie, a Belgian who, reportedly, was responsible for handing over 147 of the 168 allied bomber boys to the Gestapo. They almost met their death after Hitler's orders were sent out to execute all those that he considered to be "terror fliers". All 168 lives were spared 24 hours before their execution date thanks to the orders of Hermann Goering, who issued instructions for all allied airmen being held at Buchenwald to be handed over to the Luftwaffe.

After the order was issued Ron Leverington, Donald Lesley, Douglas Eagle and Reginald Joyce were transferred to Stalag Luft III famed for the story of the "Great Escape". Phillip Hemmens unfortunately did not survive in Buchenwald as a result of contracting the fatal blood disease septicaemia. Reginald Joyce returned several times to Lyons after the war and in 1949 married a young local girl Janine Colzy whose father helped with local resistance forces.

LES BELLES ÉPOUSAILLES D'UN OFFICIER DE LA R. A. F.

avec une jeune fille de Lyons-la-Forêt

par Jehan LE POVREMOYNE

REGINALD WILLIAM JOYCE n'avait pas vingt ans lorsque dans la nuit du 25 au 26 juin 1944, il tomba du ciel avec son Halifax et trois compagnons, près de Goupillières, à 23 km. de Caen.

Mais il en avait vingt et un lorsqu'il revint à Mortemer remercier l'héroïque Mme Verhague de l'avoir caché et hébergé pendant plusieurs semaines.

Et parce que la guerre était finie et qu'à 21 ans on n'a pas les yeux dans ses poches, Reginald William Joyce s'aperçut que Jeanine Colzy, de Lyons-la-Forêt, était jolie comme un cœur.

Alors il lui a donné le sien.

Et elle aussi.

Il avait 21 ans. Elle n'en avait que 18.

Ils ont attendu trois ans... Lui, en Angleterre, à Walthamstone, Londres, 22 Exeter Road. Elle à Lyons-la-Forêt, où papa est électricien.

C'est là que le samedi 16 juillet 1949, Reginald William Joyce, 24 ans, et Jeanine Colzy, 18 ans, se sont donc épousés.

Par devant M. Ulysse Holbé, croix de guerre 1914-1918, maire de la ville, et M. l'abbé Poirson, curé de la paroisse.

En présence de MM. Jacques Courtaud, radio-navigateur à Air-France, domicilié à Paris, et Georges Traich, radio-électricien, de Walthamstone, Londres.

En présence encore d'un groupe d'amis dont Douglas Eagle, qui était tombé du ciel en même temps que Reginald avec le Halifax, avait été, de même recueilli par Mme Verhague, à Mortemer, mais n'avait pas dû rencontrer Jeanine... C'est Reginald qui a été favorisé dans l'histoire.

Ne manquaient que Donald Leslie, mais il habite Vancouver et tout récemment il a entrepris, avec sa jeune femme, un voyage de 10.000 kilomètres à travers les Etats-Unis pour trouver une situation à son goût, et Ronald Lederrington, quatrième coéquipier, resté en Angleterre.

Eh! oui, ainsi va la vie.

C'était, samedi, à Lyons-la-Forêt, un beau roman d'amour qui s'épanouissait en une fête de profonde et précieuse amitié.

Car on ne vous a pas tout dit et l'on a même une grande émotion à le raconter.

Cette adorable petite mariée en robe blanche, dans ses dentelles, ses voiles et ses fleurs et ce si jeune officier de la R.A.F. n'illustrent pas seulement un roman d'amour.

Ils illustrent les pages d'un héroïsme secret.

Si secret que lorsque vous en parlez autour de vous, les gens répondent :

Les jeunes époux devant l'église de Lyons

— On n'a jamais bien su ce qui s'était passé.

Ce qui s'était passé ?

Voici :

Lorsque Reginald, Douglas, Donald et Ronald tombèrent à Goupillières, ils furent tout d'abord camouflés par des paysans du coin qui leur donnèrent des habits civils.

Se croyant suffisamment protégés, les quatre jeunes gens décidèrent de gagner Caen pour tenter de rejoindre les lignes anglaises.

Ils furent fort heureusement rencontrés sur la route par un membre des réseaux d'accueil et amenés à Mortemer, chez Mme Verhague.

Ils demeurèrent là jusqu'au 7 août.

Ce jour-là, Mme Verhague reçut l'ordre de les confier à une autre personne. C'était le processus habituel des chaînes de rapatriement.

Hélas! c'était là un guet-apens. Un certain Jean-Jacques qui s'était introduit dans la Résistance, était en réalité à la solde de la Gestapo.

Il livra les quatre aviateurs.

Reginald, Douglas, Donald et Ronald furent donc faits prisonniers et déportés à Buchenwald. Ils gardèrent fièrement et fidèlement le secret sur les noms et les lieux de résidence de ceux qui les avaient aidés.

Mme Verhague, qui, naturellement, ignorait tout de la trahison, les croyait retournés en Angleterre.

L'odyssée était tout autre.

Ils ne furent délivrés que le 18 octobre !

Reginald William Joyce raconta cette triste histoire à Jeanine.

Mais Jeanine Colzy lui en raconta une autre, non moins triste et non moins belle.

Son père à elle appartenait au Réseau Notre-Dame-de-Castille que dirigeait le colonel Rémy. Il avait, Lyons, pour compagnon, Lucien Lanoy et tous deux étaient en relations avec Mazouy et Jacques Courtaud, dit Jacot.

Le 19 août 1943, ils furent arrêtés et conduits à Paris.

M. Colzy, dit Olaf, subit avec Mazouy le supplice de la baignoire. Mazouy fut condamné à mort et les autres déportés.

Lucien Lanoy mourut au camp d'Elrich.

M. Colzy connut Buchenwald, la Laura, Daura, Elrich et Saxa-Hansen où les Russes le libérèrent le 22 avril 1945. Il pesait, alors, 40 kilogs !

Comprenez-vous maintenant pourquoi, samedi, à Lyons-la-Forêt, ce mariage de Reginald William Joyce, officier de la R.A.F., maintenant chronométreur dans une usine anglaise de matières plastiques, avec Jeanine Colzy, était le roman d'amour de la guerre et de la Résistance ?

... Mille vœux de bonheur, les amoureux !

Article which appeared in the newspaper l'Impartial about RAF airman Reginald Joyce's marriage to Janine Colzy in Lyons La Foret dated 1949

Reginald Joyce died in 2014 back in his beloved England. Ronald Leverington passed away at the age of 96 in 2016 after having returned on several occasions to visit Madame Verhague and the people who risked their lives for him and his crewmates. His last visit being in September 1997 for the annual ceremony of Mortemer. The annual ceremony at Mortemer is where homage is given in honour of the memories of Huguette and her eight resistance friends who were executed by the SS. Huguette herself died in 1961, penniless and blind. A plaque on the side of her house, bears the names "Huggy, Don, Ron and Doug", Huggy being the name given affectionately to her by her bluebirds.

Jacques Ernest Dumas and Francoise Dumas (grandparents of the author).

The beauty of the village of Lyons has not only inspired the artistic minds of artists such as the American painter Frederick Arthur Bridgeman, the French surrealist painter André Masson, Claude Monet and his friend Camille Pissaro, it was also the holiday home of the famous French Cartoonist, my grandfather, Jacques Ernest Dumas under the pseudonym 'Marijac' creator of Nano Nanette, Far Ouest and Frimousse. His most famous comic strip *'Les Trois Mousquetaire du Maquis'* was created after he received a request by a resistance leader during the war of 1939-1945 to create something to boost morale in resistance groups.

Resistance Card of the Mouvement Liberation Nationale of Jacques Dumas.

Lyons is also the place that inspired Gustave Flaubert to write *"Madame Bovary"*, the famous French romance novel. The village has in the past paid host to film crews that used the village for film adaptations of monsieur Flaubert's work and it is still regularly used today as a film location by film and TV companies. The last major project was a Franco/British production. Anne Fontaine's *'Gemma Bovery'* the big screen's adaptation of Posy Simmonds' graphic novel of the same name starring Fabrice Luchini and Britain's own ex "Bond Girl", Gemma Arterton, was filmed primarily in Lyons-La-Forêt. The village though small, has also been the subject of many TV programmes and in 2015 was voted 19 by viewers of France 2's '*Les Villages Préféré des Français*'. In 2017 Lyons hosted the 1st Festival Internationale de la Peinture dans le Berceau de L'impressionnisme where artists from all over Europe descended upon the village for a four-day competition.

Every summer, Lyons-La- Forêt's village population increases from 800, when thousands of tourists visit to experience the stunning forest, its beautiful countryside, artisanal markets situated under the 17th century 'Halle' and to admire the beauty of its timber framed buildings from the same period. The magnificent ancient beamed courtroom and the ancient prison cell which dates from the time of the French revolution can be found in the Mairie (Town Hall). One can sample the locally sourced delights in the restaurants. How many people meandering through the streets realise that they are walking through a award winning village of historical importance? Why not come to discover the beauty and the history of this tiny Norman village for yourself? 1

---

1   The author of this article would be keen to hear from anyone who passed through Lyons, during either of the World Wars, as he is looking to find relatives of airmen and soldiers who were there.

He can be contacted at lesherosalyons@gmail.com.

Remember

by Elysa

Remember the courageous soldiers who gave their lives for us
Evermore will we thank them for their sacrifice, that
Made it possible that we live in freedom and safety.

Evermore we will honour them by
Making sure that we live in peace with one another and
Believe in a better world.

Every year we will pause and
Reflect on a war that changed the world.

George Keely Monkhouse M.C. – 1884 -1957

Stephen Morris

Regimental Badge of the Royal Dragoons

It is one hundred years since the commencement of the First Word War and many of us have embarked in research of our ancestors who took part in The Great War. I have found that none of my relatives in the immediate family, or that of my wife's, fully recovered from this World conflict and carried the trauma of it throughout their lives. I believe that their stories should be told and not be forgotten. My research includes a large contribution from Claire Thorndike who by her efforts made my task of research much easier. She is related to George on his maternal side, she covers most of George's life and I have added in more detail regarding his later life when he came to be a part of my wife's family and other information concerning George's military service.

I first became aware of George Keely Monkhouse when carrying out some work in my father and mother-in-law's house in Dartford, Kent. Sitting on a shelf I found a rather tarnished and dirty presentation tankard. I could see an inscription on it which read "Presented to Major G Monkhouse MC with Appreciation from Officer and Men of C Coy 17thBn KHG 1943". I turned to my wife and said "who is this?" She said "That's my mum's Dad. I did not know him. He died before I was born. He was her step-dad but the only father she knew". And so from that point my research into George began.

George Keely Monkhouse was born to Martin and Laura (née Thorndike) Monkhouse on the 20th February 1884 in Cliffe, near Rochester in Kent. George was the oldest living son, the previous four children of Laura and Martin having died in infancy and early childhood. He was baptised in St Helens Church at Cliffe on the 4th of March 1884. The area of Cliffe was a favourite haunt of Charles Dickens and it was around this Thames marshland village and surrounding area that Dickens wrote *Great Expectations*. Many infants and children of the time fell Ill and died of Marsh Fever (A form of malaria) and it is possible that this might account for George's younger siblings.

In 1901 aged 17 George was living with his growing family at 14 Bramble Tree Cottage, Cliffe, the Parish of St Margaret, Rochester, in Kent where his Father was a cooper by trade, possibly carrying out work in connection with the Royal Dockyard at Chatham. As well as with his mother Laura, he also lived with his younger siblings Major, Bishop, Frank, Rose and Martin with May yet to be born in May 1901. As with many families of the time it was tough living and the family moved from Kent to Aston in Birmingham possibly in line with his Fathers work.

George remained in Kent and took the *King's Shilling* enlisting in the 1st Royal Dragoon Guards, Service no 1593. The Regiment was sent to South Africa and took part in quelling the Joburg Riots of 1913, while stationed at Potchefstroom. The Regiment remained there until the outbreak of WW1. And was sent back to the UK landing at Southampton on the 19thof September 1914.

The regiment was sent to Luggershall to join the newly formed 6th Cavalry Brigade of the 3rd Cavalry Division, and at this point George had attained the rank of Corporal. After training the Royals were sent to Belgium arriving at Ostend and Zeebrugge on the 7thof October 1914.

The regiment took part in the first battle of Ypres in October 1914, the second battle of Ypres in 1915, the battle of Loos in September of 1915, and the advance on the Hindenburg Line in 1917. During the first battle of Ypres in October 1914 George received a gunshot wound to his right arm. It is not clear at this point if he remained in theatre or was sent back home to recover. However on the 3rd of April 1915 he married Olive Gray at St Marys Church, Greenhithe in Kent. They had two children – George Thomas born 2ndApril 1916 and Kenneth Martin born 21st December 1917. Sadly, Kenneth died at the end of 1918, the Family Home at this time being 62 High Street, Greenhithe in Kent. He continued to serve with the Regiment up to the 5thof October 1917 and he must have attained advancement in the ranks because at this time he took a commission as a second Lieutenant in the Royal Field Artillery.

Artillery Regiment Badge

George met up with his uncle, Frank Thorndike, during this time in April 1918. A photo (opposite) was taken to mark the event. Frank had migrated to Australia in 1911; judging by the photo, I would imagine they were about the same age, showing Frank in his Australian uniform and George with his newly commissioned Lieutenant uniform.

In 1918 during action in the field George was awarded the Military Cross for gallantry (I am still researching where this took place) and the following citation was printed in the *London Gazette* on the 16th September 1918:

> **2nd Lt George Keely Monkhouse R.F.A.**
> **For conspicuous gallantry and devotion to duty.**
> When a gun pit received a direct hit setting the ammunition on fire, this officer rushed up and found an officer with his clothes on fire and two men wounded. He put out the flames and removed him to a place of safety, then returned and assisted the two wounded men to a dugout. Meanwhile the battery commander having been wounded, he took command of the battery and though suffering from the effects of gas remained in an exposed position superintending the dressing and evacuation of the wounded.

George remained in the Army until he retired in 1921, the London Gazette states:

> Lt G.K. Monkhouse, MC retires receiving a gratuity, 9th September 1921.

George Monkhouse and his uncle, Frank Thorndike

Dartford Park Old Contemptibles

The Old Contemptibles

Upon retirement George returned to Greenhithe and started up in business as a coal merchant under the name of Greenhithe Coal and Coke Merchant, based at the Wharf in Greenhithe. Having spoken to my father-in-law, Mr Charles Wells, at some length he informs me that George was possibly suffering what we now call Post Traumatic Stress Disorder (PTSD). It is possible that this and some bad judgement calls in business were contributory factors in the failing of the business which led to bankruptcy. George took work as a chauffeur for the Everard family who ran a shipping line from Greenhithe and would have been business neighbours of George when he ran the coal merchants. I am reliably informed that Everards supplied George with the coal and coke via their shipping line. George continued to take part in local life and is shown in the 1930's as the Secretary of the Greenhithe Conservative Working Man's club. He was a regular at Remembrance Parades, on Armistice Day and outings with the Old Contemptibles.

George's only son, George Thomas Monkhouse, followed in his father's footsteps and joined the Army enlisting in the Royal Scots Greys. Prior to 1940 he moved to Redford Barracks, Edinburgh with his Regiment, and took part in actions of WWII. He met and married Pauline Mcnally; they raised a large family of their own and adopted children, and to this day the family flourish in Scotland.

On the 15th of September 1940, Olive Monkhouse died in West Hill Hospital aged 52. She is buried in Stone Cemetery grave T4832. This of course was war time and George, ever the stalwart, once again in 1941 found himself in uniform as a Lieutenant with the Home Guard (Dads Army!), 17th Kent Northfleet Battalion Home Guard, from whom he received the presentation tankard in 1943 that I refer to.

As I have already stated, George, at 58 years of age, was working for Everards as their chauffeur and handyman. Also working as their Housekeeper was Lucy Olive Smith, who had also been widowed and was bringing up her young daughter Elizabeth Rose Smith (Betty). Despite the obvious age difference, Lucy and George married in 1942, and set up home at 44 Carlton Avenue, Stone in Kent. Elizabeth did not know her biological father and saw George as her father and always referred to him as "Dad" and as such he gave her away to her future husband when she married Charles Albert Wells. They thrived as a family unit and George took Betty on occasions to meet his son George T in Scotland.

George continued through his life to suffer from the effects of the gas attack during the First World War and as such succumbed to this on the 15th July, 1957, aged 75. It was his wish that he be buried with his first wife Olive in Stone Cemetery and now lies with her in grave T4832. The funeral was attended by George T. Monkhouse, Lucy, Betty, and her husband Charles. Not far away is their son Kenneth Martin in grave W3751 and also close by is George's brother Major who died in 1933 and is buried in grave T1845. None of the graves are marked and remain so to this day.

Lucy Olive Monkhouse died in May 1984 aged 77, still living at 44 Carlton Grove, and was cremated at Falconwood Crematorium. Her ashes were then scattered on the unmarked grave of George.

When you look back at the life and times of George, you realise how tough it was – the personal tragedy of loss of loved ones, the full horrors of war, disappointment of a failed business. When I spoke to my father-in-law about George, he said that George always did his pools in his wife's maiden name of Smith in case he had a big win – he was afraid that as a bankrupt, the powers-that-be would take away his money.

He liked a drink but was not a drunk and it was believed by the family that Lucy kept him on the right path. It was a sort of marriage of convenience – it suited them both but when you look at the family photos of weddings and outings to the coast you can see the affection of a shared love and mutual respect. He cared enough to show his annoyance when Betty married Charlie – it was in a Registry Office and not the local church. He told Charlie, "I want to give away my girl in church" and threatened to boycott the wedding. Lucy soon brought him around – apparently she told him not to be so pompous. When I look back on all this information found I reflect that it all started with a sentiment on an old tarnished presentation tankard.

Remember World War I

by Matilda

Remember that day, so much blood spilled,
The guilt of the soldiers who lived.
Remember their words,
"We'll be back by Christmas"!
They were wrong, oh so wrong.

Remember the sorrow in the soldiers' hearts,
As their comrades fell and cried.
Remember their determination, though oh so many died.

Remember the happiness at the end of the bloody war.
Remember the miserable families of the slaughtered men.

Remember that they did it for us, for our future to be bright.
Now it's our turn to hold the flame to help the next generations get it right.

Remember

by Natalie

Forget the suffering,
Forget the killing.
In Flanders Fields
A weary soldier kneels
To pray.

One day we heard birds,
And the next only gun shots.
Until the whistle blows
For King and country,
My wife and future.

Remember...
Remember...
In an English Town,
A lonely wife kneels
To pray.

Part 2 – World War II

Frederick Cardozo

Frederick Cardozo, 1916 – 2011

Geoffrey Cardozo

Frederick Cardozo, who died on 7th October, 2011 aged 94, played a key role in the organisation and operations of the French Resistance in the Massif Central immediately before and after D-Day.

An officer with Special Operations Executive (SOE), Cardozo was parachuted on to the snow-clad Mont Mouchet, some 50 miles south of Clermont-Ferrand, on the night of 8-9 May 1944, together with two Frenchmen and an American. His brief was to report to London on the strength and location of the Resistance in the area, to make recommendations about the types of arms required, and to integrate Maquis activity with the forthcoming Allied invasion of Normandy.

Cardozo's first challenge was to overcome the suspicions of Emile Coulaudon, better known by his code-name, Colonel Gaspard, who was the socialist leader of some 2,000 Maquis in the area, many of them Communists wary of SOE's connection with de Gaulle's Free French. Gaspard's doubts, however, were dissipated after Cardozo arranged for 28 plane-loads of arms and ammunition to be parachuted in between May 26 and June 9.

Cardozo's natural affability, allied to his perfect French, meant that he was invariably warmly welcomed by the Resistance. He found it harder, however, to appease the rivalries and jealousies of the Maquis chiefs, who were often reluctant to unite in the common cause.

With the Allied invasion of France clearly imminent, volunteers flooded into the Resistance, so that by the end of May Gaspard commanded some 4,000 well-trained and well-armed men. The problem was that an equal number of potential Maquis in the region was neither trained nor armed. It was hard enough simply to vet and feed the new arrivals, and to find them blankets. But Cardozo failed to convince Gaspard that there was no point in taking on new volunteers while equipment for them was lacking.

He soon, however, distinguished himself in action. When the Germans attacked Mont Mouchet on June 2, he took part in a well-executed movement in their rear, which inflicted some 40 casualties on the enemy, and forced them into a hasty retreat.

The Resistance leader in Clermont-Ferrand warned that another, more formidable German onslaught was forthcoming. Anticipating his own arrest, he asked Cardozo to assure the appointment of his replacement – an extraordinary testimony to the esteem in which the British officer was held.

When the Germans again attacked Mont Mouchet on June 10, Cardozo's skilful use of Browning machine-guns took a heavy toll. Next morning though, there was no alternative to retreat, and, thanks to the rear-guard making the Germans fight for every yard, the main column reached safety some 17 miles to the west at Truyiere. Frustrated, the Germans began murdering and terrorising civilians. In the village of Ruynes-en-Margeride alone, 27 men were shot.

In mid-June Cardozo ensured the drop of a further 25 plane-loads of arms and ammunition. Subsequently he led a successful ambush in which 10 German soldiers, together with two officers, were captured. The Maquis wanted to kill them, but Cardozo's more merciful counsels prevailed.

Travelling by car on minor roads, Cardozo found his way as far west as Argentat in La Correze to co-ordinate Resistance groups, and to arrange for arms drops in that area.

On his return to Truyiere on June 20 he found the village being shelled by a heavy German force. Again, it was necessary to beat a retreat; this time, though, some 100 Maquis were killed in the process. The Germans also murdered 60 wounded men on stretchers. Cardozo and his wireless operator hid in the woods near St. Martial, and on June 21 watched helpless as the Germans set that village ablaze. Subsequently they managed to escape north-west through enemy lines to Cezens.

Still bent upon uniting the various elements of the Resistance, Cardozo had another narrow escape when he turned up for a meeting with two leaders who, unknown to him, had been arrested. Fortunately he sensed that something was wrong with the rendezvous, and managed to get away.

Finally, on July 13 at a meeting at the Barrage de l'Aigle on the Dordogne west of Mauriac, in La Correze, Cardozo achieved his purpose when it was agreed to amalgamate the disparate Maquis forces under the titular leadership of Gaspard and the effective command of Colonel Fayard. On the morrow, Bastille Day, 36 Fortresses parachuted in some 430 containers of equipment.

Thereafter the Germans were under increasing pressure in the area. In August, when they retreated east from Aurillac, Cardozo led a group of Maquis to harry them, to such effect that it took them four days to accomplish a march normally completed in three hours. Meanwhile the German garrison guarding the dam nearby at Mur de Barres was surrounded by the Maquis. Cardozo reinforced the cordon, and insisted on negotiations which were responsible for the dam being taken intact.

In September Cardozo moved north to join Colonel Fayard, who succeeded in cutting off a force of 5,000 Germans south of Nevers, virtually ending the German occupation of central France. His mission more than accomplished, Cardozo returned to London. He was awarded the MC in 1945, and in France the Chevalier de la Legion d'honneur and Croix de Guerre avec Palme.

Sixty years later Cardozo was still revered for the courage and *sang froid Britannique* he had shown in France, as well as for his humour and humility. To the end of his life he was invited every year to address the village fete, La Forestie, in Chalvignac, where he had been based while seeking to unite the Resistance in July 1944.

Frederick Henry Cardozo was born on December 1 1916 at Newhaven in Sussex, where his father was commanding a garrison after being wounded the previous year at the battle of Loos.

The Cardozos, of Portuguese descent, established themselves in the London tobacco trade at the end of the 17th century. From the end of the 18th century, however, Frederick's ancestors, including his father, were East India Company merchants in Madras.

Frederick's mother was the daughter of Henry Daniell, who ran the family china and antiques business from Wigmore Street, and helped to organise both the Wallace Collection in Manchester Square and the Pierpont Morgan Collection at Princes Gate.

Frederick Cardozo's early years were spent in Devon, where his father had bought a farm, but when, in 1922, the government stopped subsidies for farming, the family moved to St. Remo, and then, after a spell in Geneva, to the Loire Valley in France. Frederick went to Jesuit schools in Geneva and Tours, and then to Prior Park in Bath, where he excelled at games. The hockey team actually won the European Schools Hockey Tournament in Koblenz, where they refused to give the Nazi salute. The Fuhrer unamused, left before the prize-giving ceremony.

Cardozo began his career as a bank trainee, but soon opted for a military career. He passed through the Supplementary Reserve Officers Scheme at Sandhurst, before being commissioned into the South Lancashire Regiment. His youthful bonhomie made him immensely popular with his men, who christened him *"The Kid"* on account of his short and wiry stature.

Shortly after the beginning of the Second World War, the regiment was sent to France, only to be forced back from Brussels to Dunkirk by the German blitzkrieg of May 1940. Cardozo was wounded in the bottom by some shrapnel, which his orderly extracted with a pen-knife.

After a protracted and uneventful period of home defence, Cardozo's battalion moved to Scotland to train for D-Day. There, in the lull between bawdy songs after a gruelling exercise, he heard a voice intoning similarly crude ditties in French. Cardozo took up the refrain, and, the duet over, went to introduce himself. His fellow-singer turned out to be Henry Thackthwaite, who worked with the Free French in SOE. In no time, Cardozo found himself recruited.

After his return from France in the autumn of 1944, Cardozo was sent to the Udine area of north-eastern Italy, where he helped to stabilise the region and demobilise the Italian Maquis. He was also involved with the repatriation of German prisoners through Vienna.

Later Cardozo attended Staff College at Quetta, in India, and was posted to intelligence appointments in Karachi and Haifa with the Airbourne Division, before rejoining his regiment at Trieste. After a spell as British instructor at the Ecole de Guerre in Paris, he returned to England in 1955 to command a wing at the Royal Military Academy, Sandhurst.

During the Suez Crisis, in 1956, Cardozo was sent out to Cyprus to the headquarters of Brigadier 'Tubby' Butler's 16th Independent Parachute Brigade, with orders to ensure close liaison between the Parachute Regiment and their French equivalents, battle-hardened veterans of Indochina. When operations began, Cardozo was a member of the force dropped into Egypt to secure key positions before the surface troops arrived. He saw some brisk fighting as the Egyptians attempted to regain a captured water-works.

When the French were told that Anthony Eden, rattled both by American pressure and opposition at home, had ordered the British to pull out, they were aghast. Not until a full British colonel was dispatched with formal written orders that the French too should halt did they accept the position.

General Hugh Stockwell, in command of British surface forces, contrived to interpret the 'cease-fire at midnight' order to his advantage by recalling that midnight in London was 2 am in *his* war zone. He ordered Butler to get as far down the canal as possible. Butler, accompanied by Cardozo, duly led 2nd Parachute Battalion at speed down the 300-yard tarmac causeway between the Canal and Lake Manzala. By the time they halted, at 2.10 a.m. on November 7, they were only 23 miles from Port Said.

Shortly after the Suez fiasco Cardozo left the Army, and for the next ten years worked from France as press attaché for the Americans. After de Gaulle took France out of NATO, and the organisation's headquarters were transferred from Paris to Brussels at the end of 1966, Cardozo moved to London, where he joined the Latin Mass Society as secretary to its president, the broadcaster Harmon Grisewood, his first cousin. He soon left, however, when he discovered that many members were more Catholic than the Pope.

Later, he worked for the Save the Children Fund in Morocco, and for De Beers in Sierra Leone before retiring to Bath, and finally, after a short time in London, to his beloved Loire valley in France. He remained an excellent tennis player, and continued to play the violin to the end of his days.

Gordon Bastian

Caroline Clopet

Gordon Love Bastian, GC, MBE (30 March 1902 – November 1987) was an engineering officer in the British Merchant Navy who was awarded the Albert Medal for risking his own life to save other members of the crew of SS Empire Bowman after it was torpedoed on 31 March 1943. In 1971, living recipients of the Albert Medal and Edward Medal were instructed to return their medal and were instead issued with the George Cross, the highest decoration for gallantry awarded to civilians or to military personnel for actions "not in the face of the enemy" in the United Kingdom and Commonwealth.

Early Life and Career

Bastian was born in Barry, Vale of Glamorgan in south Wales on 30 March 1902. In 1927, he first travelled to Canada. He joined the Merchant Navy and became an engineering officer. With the outbreak of the Second World War most British merchant shipping was organised into convoys, but German U-boats and surface raiders still inflicted considerable losses during the Battle of the Atlantic. Bastian was appointed Member of the Order of the British Empire for his convoy service on 1 January 1942.

By 12 March 1942, Bastian was second engineer officer on SS *Empire Bowman*, which was departing Freetown, Sierra Leone as part of Convoy SL 126, due to arrive in Liverpool at the beginning of April. On 30 March 1942 (coincidentally Bastian's 41st birthday). She was torpedoed by *U-404* in the Atlantic Ocean some 425 nautical miles (787 km) north west of Cape Finisterre. At great personal risk, Bastian rescued two stokers from the sinking ship, for which he was awarded the Albert Medal (AM) on 17 August 1943, the citation read:

> *Ministry of War Transport, Berkeley Square, W.1. 17th August, 1943.*
> The King has been graciously pleased to make the following award: —
> *The Albert Medal.*
> Gordon Love Bastian, Esq., M.B.E., Second Engineer Officer, Merchant Navy.
> The ship in which Mr. Bastian was serving was torpedoed and sustained severe damage. Mr. Bastian was on watch in the engine-room when the ship was struck. He at once shut off the engines. He

then remembered that two firemen were on watch in the stokehold. The engineroom was in darkness and water was already pouring into it. Although there was grave risk of disastrous flooding in opening the watertight door between the stokehold and engineroom, Mr. Bastian did not hesitate but groped his way to the door and opened it. The two firemen were swept into the engine-room with the inrush of water. One man had a broken arm and injured feet and the other was badly bruised and shaken. Mr. Bastian made efforts to hold them both but lost one, so he dragged the other to the escape ladder and helped him on deck. He then returned for the other and helped him to safety. The more seriously injured man had practically to be lifted up the ladder by Mr. Bastian, who was himself half choked by cordite fumes.

Second Engineer Officer Bastian took a very great risk in opening the watertight door into the already flooded and darkened engine-room of the sinking ship and both men undoubtedly owe their lives to his exceptional bravery, strength and presence of mind.

In 1944, Bastian was also awarded the Lloyd's War Medal for Bravery at sea for his actions.

Later Life and Legacy

Soon after receiving his Albert Medal, Bastian was invalided out of the Merchant Navy as a result of the damage caused to his lungs by the cordite smoke he inhaled during the rescue. In 1947, he settled in Canada, living in Montreal.

The high status of the Albert Medal was not generally understood by the public, and in 1971, Queen Elizabeth II instructed all living recipients to exchange their original medal for the George Cross (GC). The medal had been created by her father, King George VI, in 1940, in recognition of the hazards faced by the civilian population, and by merchant seamen such as Bastian. It was intended to have a similar status for civilian acts of gallantry, or for acts performed by members of the armed forces but which were not "in the face of the enemy", as the Victoria Cross does for acts of gallantry in combat. On its creation, holders of the Empire Gallantry Medal (EGM) were immediately instructed to exchange their medal for the GC, but holders of the Albert Medal and Edward Medal were not, despite these being higher in the order of wear than the Empire Gallantry Medal.

Bastian received his George Cross in a presentation made by the Governor of Canada on 27 November 1973. He presented his Albert

Medal and Lloyd's Medal to the National Museum Wales. He died in Canada in November 1987, survived by his wife, Mary, and a son and a daughter. Soon after the award of the Albert Medal, Bastian's portrait was painted by war artist Bernard Hailstone: the painting now forms part of the Government Art Collection. In 1990, a new road in his hometown of Barry was named "*Bastian Close*" in his honour.

Gordon Bastian

James Edward Luen

James (Jim) Edward Luen

Caroline Clopet

James Edward Luen, a son of Albert Edward and Rebecca Luen of Barry, South Wales, was a Chief Officer within the British Merchant Navy. Known locally as Jim, he had attended High Street School in Barry. Apparently, in 1910 after an argument with a tutor Jim departed via a school classroom window and ran away to sea. He reappeared at Cardiff two years later, when someone contacted his mother saying he was in Cardiff and needed some shoes.

Jim is noted as having served in the Royal Naval Reserve during WWI. Still a mystery is that he is also recorded as joining the Canadian Overseas Expeditionary Force. Jim survived WWI, only to commence going through it all again in WWII.

Between wars he spent some time in Australia. Jim and his wife Violet married in Australia, the day after she arrived in Sydney from Barry. The couple left Australia in 1927 before the birth of their first daughter.

A keen artist, Jim Luen held a exhibition of his work in the County Hall, London during 1937-1938. He wrote copiously all the years he was at sea. Jim was also involved with The British Ship Adoption Society, an organisation which enabled schools in Britain to "adopt" merchant ships. The main school with whom Jim corresponded with was the Archbishop's Temple School in Lambeth in London.

At one time at sea Jim cared for an albatross that landed on deck suffering from exhaustion, but which recovered. There is a campaign to save the Albatross, spear headed by Ellen MacCarthy. So impressed with his kind act, they asked permission to use the photograph in a brochure. A picture of Jim was taken off the Straits of Magellan, off of Cape Horn in 1937 on board the *Harlingen*.

During the last voyage he saved the lives of two people, by performing an appendix operation on a fellow sailor on the wireless instructions of a doctor on another ship. Jim died at the age of 43 on November 25, 1939 off the coast of Newfoundland, Nova Scotia when a wave crashed into the ship and he was washed overboard.

EXAMINATION ON OATH – Relating to the death of James Edward Luen on the *Harlingen*

I was on the bridge on the morning of 25th November 1939. There was a high sea and E.N.E. Gale. At about 09.35am, the vessel shipped into a heavy sea, and directly afterwards, I heard the First Mate, Mr. Luen, shouting for help, and could see him in the water about 100 feet to starboard. Four lifebuoys were thrown to him, and a raft was heaved over the ship's side at once, and I saw him grasp a buoy and get into it. The ship was kept as near to him as possible and on one occasion sighted. It was difficult for the look-outs to see him on account of the heavy seas, and I wanted to swim to him with a line attached to a [buoyancy aid] which had been thrown to him and which fell short. It was impossible on account of the seas and the distance and I was restrained. At 11.35am, we came quite close to Mr. Luen and I could see he was unconscious. I volunteered again to go to his assistance and went over to the side to him. The water was extremely cold and owing to the ship rolling and the heavy seas it was difficult to reach him. As he was in a buoy and I was on a swimming bowline he was more buoyant than I was and although I managed to grasp the buoy twice I was unable to hold it. When those at the other end of the line saw that I myself was in distress and that Mr. Luen was by the time out of my reach they hauled me aboard and I was taken to the stewards room for treatment. I saw no more of Mr. Luen who was undoubtedly lost by now. I am satisfied that every possible effort was made to rescue him.

Signed: Roy Dudley Cresser, 29th December 1939

"There are no graves: no crosses: nowhere a loved one can shed a tear: We should remember them".

Jim Luen is one of over 600 names on the Merchant Navy Monument at Barry and in the towns Roll of Honour – little is known of many on all Merchant Navy monuments, hence we record that known of a few in tribute and remembrance of the many.

A small tribute in remembering Jim: From the scroll commemorating him – the words are *"This scroll commemorates J.E. Luen, Chief Officer Merchant Navy held in honour as one who served King and Country in the World War of 1939-1945 and gave his life to save mankind from tyranny. May his sacrifice help to bring the peace and freedom for which he died"*.

Chief Officer, James Edward Luen, *SS. Harlingen* (London). Merchant Navy. 25th November 1939. Age 43.

SS Harlingen was sunk just under two years later by U-75 on 5th August 1941.

Remembrance

by Juliette

We did not ask to go to war,
But they said we had to go,
We left our families and our lives,
In mud and blood and sorrow.

So many years have passed by,
The world forgets our pain,
But poppies help remember,
It was not all in vain.

The 42nd Infantry Division (42ID) - Rainbow Division

Robert Martinson

The 42nd Infantry Division – Rainbow Division – is a division of the United States Army National Guard. The 42nd Infantry Division has served in World War I, World War II and the Global War on Terrorism. The division is currently headquartered at the Glenmore Road Armoury in Troy, New York.

The Division adopted a shoulder patch and unit crests acknowledging the nickname (Rainbow Division). The original version of the patch symbolized a half arc rainbow and contained thin bands in multiple colours. During the latter part of World War I and post war occupation duty in Germany, Rainbow Division soldiers modified the patch to a quarter arc, removing half the symbol to memorialize the half of the division's soldiers who became casualties (killed or wounded) during the war. They also reduced the number of colours to just red, gold and blue bordered in green, in order to standardize the design and make the patch easier to reproduce.

World War I

The 42nd Division was activated in August 1917, four months after the American entry into WWI drawing men from 26 states and the District of Columbia.

The 42nd went overseas to the Western Front of Belgium and France in November 1917, one of the first divisions of the American Expeditionary Force (AEF) to do so. The AEF was commanded by General John Joseph Pershing. Upon arrival there the 42nd Division began intensive training with the British and French armies in learning the basics of trench warfare which had, for the past three years, dominated strategy on the Western Front, with neither side advancing much further than they had in 1914. The following year, the division took part in four major operations: the Champagne-Marne, the Aisne-Marne, the Battle of Saint-Mihiel and the Meuse-Argonne Offensive. In total, it saw 264 days of combat. While in France, the division was placed under French control for a time, commanded by various French commanders, including Henri Gouraud and Georges de Bazelaire, of the French VII Army Corps.

Notable Commanders were: Maj. Gen. W.A. Mann – September 1917, Brig. Gen. Charles T. Menoher – December 1917, Maj. Gen. Charles D. Rhodes – November 1918, Brig. Gen. Douglas MacArthur – November

IN HONOR OF 42ND RAINBOW DIVISION
AND OTHER U.S. 7TH ARMY LIBERATORS
OF DACHAU CONCENTRATION CAMP
APRIL 29, 1945 AND IN EVERLASTING
MEMORY OF THE VICTIMS OF NAZI
BARBARISM, THIS TABLET IS
DEDICATED MAY 3, 1992.

EN L'HONNEUR DE LA 42ème DIVISION
"ARC-EN-CIEL" ET DES AUTRES ELEMENTS DE LA
7ème ARMEE AMERICAINE QUI ONT LIBERE LE CAMP
DE CONCENTRATION DE DACHAU LE 29 AVRIL 1945
ET A LA MEMOIRE INEFFAÇABLE DES VICTIMES DE LA
BARBARIE NAZIE CE MEMORIAL A ETE INAUGURE LE
3 MAI 1992.

ZU EHREN DER 42, REGENBOGEN · DIVISION UND ALLER
ANGEHÖRIGER DER 7.US ARMEE, DIE DAS
KONZENTRATIONSLAGER DACHAU AM 29.APRIL 1945
BEFREIT HABEN UND DEM FORTWÄHRENDEN GEDENKEN
AN DIE OPFER DER NAZI BARBAREI GEWIDMET
AM 3.MAI 1992

RAINBOW DIVISION
VETERANS MEMORIAL FOUNDATION INC.

Memorial Plaque at Dachau

1918, Maj. Gen. C.A.F. Flagler – November 1918, Maj. Gen. George Windle Read – April 1919 to the division's deactivation on 9th May 1919.

World War II

When reformed and activated for World War II on 14th July 1943, the 42nd was a unique unit, although it was a reconstitution of the Rainbow Division from World War I. Except for the division headquarters, none of its earlier elements had reformed in the interwar period, so the Army Ground Forces filled its new units with personnel from every state. From the division standup at Camp Gruber until the division stood down in Austria, at every formal assembly, the division displayed not only the National and Divisional Colours, but all 48 state colours (State Flags). To emphasize the 42nd lineage from the 42nd of WWI, Maj. Gen. Harry J. Collins activated the unit on 14th July, the eve of the twenty-fifth anniversary of the Champagne-Marne campaign in France.

Here is one story from Robert Martinson who was in the 42nd Infantry, Rainbow Division.

"I left New York City in November of 1944 and landed in Marseille in December. We moved to Strasbourg and the Alsace region of France and we went on line Christmas Eve. Because of the movement of the allied troops to the sector of the "Bulge" our division was put on the line to replace them before we were supposed to be there. Our division's tank, artillery and special units were still in the United States. When the Germans were defeated in the Bulge, they swung around and tried to come through our area, beginning January 2, 1945."

Our division was outmanned, outgunned and inexperienced, but with the help of the artillery and tanks of other units we held the Germans until January 22, 1945. On that date, in the middle of a snowstorm, at 22h00 hours our units pulled back some 15 miles to better defensive positions. When the Germans attacked again, they suffered very high casualties, and that ended the final German offensive attempt of the war on the Western Front.

However, the cost of the January battle was very high to our division. We lost over 50% of our front line troops, including well over 1,000 men who were captured by the enemy.

We were relieved by the 101st Airborne Division and were sent to the rear for "R and R". The division tanks, artillery and special units arrived from the States and we were again a full division.

On about February 14, 1945, the division was ordered to take front line positions once more. On March 15 we attacked the Hartz Mountains and Germany. On Easter Sunday, April 1, 1945, we crossed the Rhine at Worms and continued into Germany. For the next 54 days the division attacked and captured the following cities: Wertheim, Wurtzburg, Schweinfurt, Furth, part of Nurenberg, Donaworth, the Dachau Concentration Camp, Munich and Salzburg, plus smaller villages in between the larger ones.

Our division was in occupation in Salzburg, in several Tyrolean Alps villages and in Vienna, which was a four-nation occupation city like Berlin.

On April 29, 1945 my division arrived at Dachau and liberated the camp. Shortly after liberation, I arrived and the guards were gone; they had either fled, surrendered, been wounded or killed. The shooting had ceased.

I arrived at the south side of the camp which was fenced off with electrified wire. There were many dead bodies lying around the camp and many, many inmates milling around or sitting/laying against the barracks' walls. There was a railroad siding next to the moat beside the fence. There were many boxcars on the tracks holding about 1,500 dead prisoners in them. They had been shipped from Buchenwald and had died from starvation, dysentery and the cold weather. Some of the dead were naked because after they had died the live prisoners took their clothing to keep warm. The scene was horrible, as was the stench of the dead bodies. I later learned that the medics found one prisoner alive.

The camp held about 33,000 prisoners at that time. After viewing the scene for about half an hour or more, we moved out and drove into Munich which was in the process of being captured or liberated as it became known".

On the 65th anniversary of the closing of the last concentration camp, the "liberators" were honoured guests of the Holocaust Memorial Museum in Washington D.C.

On May 3rd 1992 a Memorial was unveiled in honour of 42nd Rainbow Division and the other US 7th Army Liberators of Dachau Concentration Camp. The plaque on the Memorial is ilustrated on page 83.

Royal Canadian Air Force Wellington bomber crash, Marly-le-Roi, France April 2nd 1942

Patrick Gautier-Lynham

RCAF Squadron 405 Emblem

In 1993 I was deputy Mayor in Marly-le-Roi, a small town 15 miles west of Paris and among my duties I was in charge of the ex-servicemen. One day, I was in my office when some one knocked at the door, and I welcomed Mr André Duchemin, who lived in l'Etang-la-Ville, a nearby town. He was a WWII Resistance fighter veteran, he had belonged to the FTP, *Francs-Tireurs et Partisans* (linked to the Communist party) in the Eure department. He dropped on my desk a few photographs of some dead soldiers asking me: '*Why don't you do something for these airmen who died in Marly-le-Roi?*' I replied that I had never heard anything about these men. On these photographs you could see five dead allied airmen. Mr Duchemin told me that German soldiers had taken the photographs and copies had been passed on to one of their French girl friends.

It was for me the beginning of a long research, which began in Marly-le-Roi and went on in Versailles, Canada, Australia and back to Marly-le-

Wellington wreckage, Marly-le-Roi, 1942

Roi. I started my investigation by questioning some old people in Marly-le-Roi and soon I was able to meet an eyewitness, Colonel Roger Manaut, a lieutenant in 1944. He was at the window of his house in rue de Saint Cyr on that night of 2nd April 1942. He told me the story of a British aircraft, which had crashed, in the Royal Park of Marly. He had written down all the details of the crash in a small booklet in which he used to write down the events he had witnessed all along the war. On that day he had written: *'Tonight, at 4 a.m. I saw a British bomber plane crash, it was an incredible sight'.* He saw a ball of fire falling towards the "*Tapis Vert*", a long stretch of lawn in the middle of the Royal Park. The plane had already launched its bombs on the Ford car factory in Poissy. No doubt these young airmen did their best till the last minute to avoid the village and its inhabitants. Roger Manaut went in the park and managed to bring back some parts of the aircraft without being caught by the German soldiers. He brought back a piece of the frame, some canvas and the bulletproof plate, which protected the pilot's head and chest.

The plane was a Vickers Wellington bomber. The Wellington was nicknamed the "*Wimpey*" and it was the Royal Air Force's night bomber. Sir Barnes Wallis had designed it in 1935; one of its characteristics was its geodetic structure design, made of aluminium girders, which made a wire-mesh airframe.

Mr Gross was another witness: *'I was on my balcony when I saw this plane flying low over the Saint-Germain-en Laye chateau: it flew between 40m and 50m above my house. It was on fire, a ball of fire'.*

Among other witnesses, Mr Azaïs gave me more information, *'I know these photographs. On one of them we can see the breast wall, today covered with ivy.*

It is the park approach road retaining wall. We can distinctly see the entrance to the park through the stone door and opposite the President's residence. We can also see the vegetable garden of the Forestry Commission boys. I spent some time on the spot; I went back when the Germans had left the premises. At the car park entrance I found a lighting bomb in the ground. I knew that there should be a parachute at the tip of the rocket.

I took my penknife, removed the lid and found the parachute, but hard luck, it was a huge one. I found myself in an awkward situation, the Germans were not far away, I was behind a tree, I wound the parachute round my waist and rushed back home. I also recovered an electromagnet that was on the dashboard."

Mr Azaïs carried on: *"parts of the plane were in the trees, above the old guardroom, which proves that the aircraft did turn round; one engine was on the car park. The plane was in pieces, she had exploded before* the crash. Laurel Burgoyne was at the rear of the plane when he was ejected then he landed in a tree, I saw him hanging".

Mr Charles Grégoire, another witness, showed me copies of leaflets he had found on the spot.

Mr Azais added: *"Such leaflets were often found in the Marly forest. In those days I was working in Paris, I used to collect them on Saturdays and Sundays, filling my briefcase, taking them to Paris on Mondays, and passing them on to Parisians, probably making people believe they were Resistance heroes handing out British leaflets".*

Mr Manaut: *"At that time we were so glad to bring back those leaflets".*

Mr Azaïs: *"The planes were fitted with shell shape drop tanks as they were short range aircrafts. And I think that the people of Marly realized what was going on when one of these fuel tanks fell on a garden hut, which immediately took fire".*

The high street baker, Mrs Lucienne Hankenne went on the spot of the crash with other onlookers: *"I only saw a young lad his arms outstretched in the shape of a cross, we were almost immediately driven away by the Germans, we had never been so close to the war, on that day we imagined that it was the end of the world, it was terrible. The next day, marks of the tragedy could still be seen in the soil, especially a dreadful body print. It was the season of violets, people laid sprig of flowers, in the hollow where his arms, legs, and body had been".*

Charles Grégoire: *"I was sleeping in the forest when the plane crashed, the Germans were everywhere, one had to be careful not be machine-gunned. I was so close, I saw the crash".* He managed to retrieve a leaflet from the charred fuselage, which he kept preciously.

Mr Chatel, a fireman went on site with Mr Leguen the Louveciennes rural policeman, when they reached the *"Le Bon Gite"* inn on the Versailles road something was burning on the roadway: *"It was a canvas first-aid kit, I extinguished the fire and brought the item back home, inside I found a pair of scissors engraved with the English Crown, there was also a phial with a syringe".*

A few days later, in the night of April 5th to April 6th five bombs fell on Marly, the church stained glass windows were blown up. Marly was on the path of air raids over Paris, Saint Cyr and Versailles.

Mr Azaïs: *"we were showered with anti aircraft shrapnel. The anti aircraft batteries were fitted on wagons located on the Puteaux station siding".*

Now I had to look for the graves of these airmen, Mr Cahouet told me: *"At first the dead were buried in Louveciennes we looked for them everywhere till we found them. Today they are buried in the Gonards Cemetery, Versailles".*

Flight Sergeant AG Howsan, 1941

It is in the CWGC plot where 181 WWI and WWII casualties are buried
that I found the following 5 graves:

Flight Sergeant Moneddeen A.G. Howsan RAAF, first pilot, 22.
Pilot officer James G. Mackinon RAF, rear gunner.
Sergeant William P. Ashun RAF, second air gunner, 26.
Flight Sergeant Martin Charles Howe RCAF, second pilot, 22.
Flight Sergeant Raoul Omer Joseph Page RCAF, first air gunner, 20.

Thanks to the British Embassy and the Royal Air Force Historical Branch, I obtained the plane's identification. It was a Vickers Wellington, serial number Z8527 LQ-L, attached to squadron 405 (Vancouver squadron) RCAF, air based in Pocklington, North Yorkshire. Four planes had for target the Ford motor factory in Poissy. There were 4 groups of Wellingtons in the squadron. 405 Squadron was formed in England on 3rd April 1941 and carried out 522 operations and lost 20 aircraft.

The plane that crashed on April 2nd 1942 at 4 am in Marly-le-Roi Park, near today's car park, was the only one lost that night by 405 Squadron. Her crew, six airmen all in their twenties – the eldest was only 26 years old – and several Commonwealth nationalities on this RCAF aircraft.

My next task was to find the 6th member of the crew. The Ministry of Defence, Air Historical Branch had given me the information: "*Unfortunately the Aircraft was hit by flack and crashed killing all but one of the crew.... Surviving crew member Pilot Officer Burgoyne...*"

I asked for help from Marlow-on-Thames Council and Royal British Legion branch, the Royal Air Force Association, and the British Embassy in Paris. One Marlow staff member had been in the RAF for 12 years, including WWII; he had been severely burnt in a crash and was a member of the "*Guinea Pig Club*" a group of mostly RAF aircrew who underwent reconstructive plastic surgery after suffering burn injuries during the Second World War. He advised me to get in touch with the National Archives of Canada in Ottawa. On 17th September I had the information that Laurel Burgoyne was still alive and living in Canada!

My letter had been forwarded to the surviving crew member. In the meantime I had got in touch with the Mayor of Mahon Bay (Nova Scotia) Mr Joe Feeney.

At last I was in touch with the surviving crew member, we exchanged a few letters. Pilot Officer Laurel Burgoyne was Air Observer and Gunner. He remembered the crash: "*On our last and fatal trip on April 1/42, we were sent to bomb a special target, for which the best crews were chosen from each Squadron. Our crew had a good record, with all trips being successful, and that is why we were chosen. We had to bomb from a low altitude, and that is why we were shot down. Our aircraft was set on fire just after bombing, and I started to make it out, after reporting it to Bob (Pilot) and the rest of the crew. .... My parachute was starting to burn* in its rack, so I made that out, and put it on, and resumed fighting the fire in the aircraft, which was increasing. I then went up to the pilot's control, and was immediately thrown from the aircraft. I landed in a treetop, and saw our aircraft crash to the ground. I was captured almost at once, and a few hours later I was shown the bodies of the rest of the crew. None of the bodies were burned but all were killed instantly in the crash. The bodies were given a military burial by the Germans".

Pilot Officer Laurel G. Burgoyne

The tree where Laurel Burgoyne had landed was in the grounds of the Count of Paris, in his Coeur Volant mansion in Louveciennes where the Germans had their headquarters. Laurel Burgoyne was released 3 years later, on 13th May 1945.

In support of these testimonies and at my request Mr Yves Guibert, Mayor, and the Town Council awarded Laurel Burgoyne the Honorary Town Medal. Unfortunately his health condition didn't enable him to come over to Marly so it was posted to him. He wrote to me: *"Thanks for what you have done for the memory of the crew and myself"*. A few weeks later Laurel Burgoyne was interviewed by Canadian Television.

In Marly-le-Roi Mr Yves Guibert and I took the decision to erect a memorial on the site of the crash. Unfortunately we did not get the permission from the Elysée Palace in charge of the park, so it was built in the cemetery in the forest a few hundred yards away.

The money to build the memorial was collected thanks to fund-raising in Marlow-on-Thames, Marly le Roi and also thanks to a contribution of the Souvenir Français and Marly-le-Roi Council. A local artist who had been a prisoner of war and who had worked at Dassault Aviation, a French aerospace company where he was in charge of plane paint schemes, did the design of the memorial. The memorial is in the shape of a wing, 3m high, and at the top, the 405 Squadron badge. The wing is fitted in a small pyramid where a plaque reads the names of the aircrew. The memorial was unveiled on November 11th 1994, by French, British, Australian and Canadian officials.

But this is not the end of the story! On 2nd November 1994, a German citizen knocked at the door of my office in the town hall. Mr Helmut Majer, who was in the army during the war and in 1942 was posted to Marly-le-Roi. He told me how he had taken part in the arrest of the surviving crewmember. *"Mr Burgoyne's face was severely burnt"*. He also mentioned the flowers that had been laid by the inhabitants in the park where the bodies had left a print in the ground. *"Our doctor treated the man. He was suspended in a tree, his parachute stuck in a tree. The five other crew members jumped later but without a parachute they had no chance. It was our Feldwebel Christoph Heinlein, who lived near the Marly Aqueduct who saved his life"*.

He showed me on a map the house in Louveciennes where Mr Burgoyne was detained for a few days.

In June 2017, I had the chance to welcome in Marly le Roi the relatives of First Pilot Bob Howsan. They had come from Australia to see for the first time the place where their nephew had lost his life. They gave me Bob's last letter:

"31st March, 1942
Dear Mum, Dad and Family,
Here I am again feeling as fit as ever. These days I haven't very much to write about because I haven't had a letter to answer for a very

long time...I didn't think I would take to operations as I have done. I'm enjoying it very much. You know flying over enemy territory is like climbing over someone's fence to steal oranges. It's much the same feeling-because I've done both. You know yourself how lucky and confident about it all as I have plenty of faith and love and that's what we need in this game.... By the way I think I told you in my last letter that my plane was U for Uncle. I have a brand new one now L for London or L for Leather as I always call it.

We had a bit of a shaky do the other night. We raided a port in northern Germany and on the way back we got a little bit or should I say a fair bit off track. You see, they fired at us coming home and through dodging we got north of track. Couldn't very well find our way because we were above the North Sea, just out from Denmark. Anyway we thought we were down just off the English coast but when I went down under the clouds we were still over water. So, I went up again above the clouds. This went on for about an hour. By this time, we had about half an hour of petrol left. I told the navigator I was going to steer west to hit the coast somewhere.

About 10 minutes later we broke cloud and saw the coast with an aerodrome not much further along. Apparently, they knew we were stooging around off the coast so they switched on the flare path. We got down safely with 10-15 minutes of petrol left. I wasn't worried at all because I knew faith and luck would see me through okay. I will admit I was beginning to think back about all I had been taught about landing in the sea! The station we landed at was a fighter station and they made us comfortable.

It was about 4.45 am when we landed after being about one and a half hours overdue at the base. They took us into the officer's mess and gave us a good breakfast after which we slept until about 8.30 am- about two and a half hours.

Then they refuelled our plane and we took off back to base. We were very lucky over that airfield. As we circled around to land, the front gunner was coming out of his turret. He stumbled and grabbed the handles of the gun and they went off. After we landed, the duty pilot said he very nearly put the flare path lights out because he thought we were a Gerry. Fortunately, I put my navigation lights on and they knew it was okay.

By the way, last week a newspaper correspondent came up here, one night after we had come back from operations. He wanted a story for the newspaper back home. I didn't tell him much except for some of the places I'd been to in Germany and German Territory. I think that was the night I had just come back from the Rhur Valley- the happy *valley as we call it. (The Ruhr Valley is one of the most heavily defended targets in Germany). There is also going to be published a photo of all the Australians on this squadron. Keep an eye open for it. I have done a couple more trips since he was here ....*

Well I guess that's about all for now. I'll say cheerio to you all. With lots of love.

Your loving son and brother.

Bob

PS You will see by the heading I'm a Flight Sergeant. I got it last week, back dated from September".

Bob and his crew were not so lucky when they flew to France a few days later, on 2nd April 1942.

On 3rd April 1942, Squadron 405 lost another plane in the Yvelines district.

Let's not forget these brave young men who came from Britain and the Commonwealth to save our democracies. In Memory of the Commonwealth aircrew.

One School Day in Edinburgh

Joyce Gilhooley

The Headmaster had just finished morning prayers. We were all about to rush to our classrooms when he held up his hand and asked for silence. The War was now over so we didn't expect to hear any drastic news. However, we all sat down quietly and waited. He informed us that he had the honour of distributing, on behalf of The King, special certificates to all the school children.

The Headmaster hoped that we would treasure The King's message, keep it safely and always remember the sacrifices that had been made on our behalf by so many during the terrible war years. He explained that although the War had been over for almost one year, he knew that many children had suffered and were still suffering. Some of us had lost family in the services, certainly all of us had had someone who was either in the Army, Navy, Air Force or the Merchant Navy.

We in Scotland heard a great deal about the war at sea and the terrible hardships the Merchant Navy had had in the Atlantic while transporting food and ammunition throughout the world. Two of my cousins had served in the Royal Navy, and one other in the Merchant Navy.

In Edinburgh we were never really bombed, although on one memorable occasion a lone German bomber hit a local distillery. This gave great satisfaction to the residents, who promptly rushed down with buckets to catch the whisky! We were frequently awakened in the middle of the night by the awful sound of the sirens and my family and myself spent many nights in the air raid shelter as the enemy planes droned overhead looking for the shipyards.

We used to hear *"Lord Haw-Haw"* with his propaganda broadcasts from Berlin telling us the time shown on the North British Hotel's clock in Princes Street. I remember the war years but also the wonderful relief when the war ended and all the lights came on, no more blackout in the streets or houses, and the joy of seeing Edinburgh Castle lit up for the first time.

I have to thank my mother for keeping my special souvenir certificate in a safe place over the years.

My Remembrance Poem on the Second World War

by Simon

I am the ghost of an old soldier.
My side won,
But I am not gone,
I am miserably stuck,
Completely out of luck.

The beautiful poppies represent us,
It is the symbol of hope,
But there is also suffering,
With which we have to cope.

Carry on our word,
Like an Olympic torch,
Just as you have heard,
And don't lose our memory.

Continue on fighting,
Continue remembering,
Otherwise, I died for nothing.

Bombings Around Leicester During World War II

During World War II, many towns and cities were heavily bombed; often, very few escaped. Leicester was one of the towns that did not escape. Although it was lucky in many ways as they did not suffer bombing in the same way as many other cities. However they were in the direct flight path of German bombers targeting Coventry and the Black Country. Because the city had not been a specific target of bombing raids, many children from the big cities like London, were evacuated to Leicester because it was thought safe. Here are two memories from ladies who lived and were from the Leicester area.

My Memories of The Second World War

June Worth

The Luftwaffe started bombing Coventry in November 1940. At the time I was living in a village to the north of Leicester.

One memory was seeing the orange in the sky from the flames after the bombing raids, but at the age of three, I had little understanding of what had caused it – to me it was just a pretty sky.

During the bombing raids my older brother and I slept in the kitchen. My father had put a mattress under the large wooden kitchen table and there we spent our nights for as long as the bombing raids lasted. One thing that I do remember, and this may sound strange, is listening to the crickets in the fire place when the fire had died down but not the sound of the bombs.

One morning there was quite a lot of excitement amongst our neighbours. During the night a German plane had dropped a bomb which was about 500 yards away from my home. Luckily it landed in a field belonging to a farmer living just up the road. No harm was done but the bomb left a huge crater which we children were delighted to visit after it had been ascertained there was no longer any danger. The big children, mainly boys, would climb all over the crater pretending to be soldiers killing the Germans!

1940 – The Evacuation of British Troops from France

Jean Dardet

I was 15 and lived in Leicester, Midlands. I used to go by tram to work in the centre of Leicester each day. One morning as I rode pass the Victoria Park which is a very large green park, (this was actually the cricket or football pitch), I was amazed to see 100's of soldiers, sitting or lying on the grass looking exhausted and in some cases with coverings on wounds.

I asked someone what was happening and was told that these men had been brought up from the coast having been evacuated from France. This was the evacuation of Dunkirk which we had heard about only recently as it was a *hush hush* rescue of our men on the beaches. Thousands never made it back home.

From all the surrounding houses, ladies were crossing over to the park carrying jugs of hot tea with mugs and cups for these men. Some were helping with bandages or just talking to the men to keep their morale up or asking after loved ones.

This was a wonderful sight to see and showed the true British spirit which brought tears to my eyes.

An English Schoolboy In The Second World War

by Patrick Noble

War is Declared

I was five years old at the start of World War II in 1939, and eleven when it finished in 1945. During the whole duration of the war, I was living with my family in Weymouth, a seaside resort and port on the south coast of England, close to Portland Naval Base, facing Normandy on the other side of the English Channel. My pre-war memories include picnics on the beach and an excursion on an Edwardian vintage paddle steamer. This relaxed lifestyle came to an end on 3rd September 1939, when following the invasion of Poland, the United Kingdom declared war on Germany. A blackout was imposed, food was rationed, everyone, including school children, had to carry a gas mask and no access to the beach was allowed.

Suddenly during the spring of 1940 the Germans overran Denmark, Norway, The Netherlands, Belgium, Luxembourg and finally France. Thousands of tired and hungry French soldiers were landed in Weymouth. People were asked to take them in, so my parents invited two soldiers to come and stay with us for a few days, so they could take a bath, shave, eat a square meal and have a good night's sleep. We never knew what happened to them after they left us. At about the same time tens of thousands of Channel Islanders also landed in Weymouth, having fled their homes just before the arrival of the Germans. It was not to end there, for hundreds of school children arrived by train, evacuated from London to escape the Blitz. Some of them became pupils in my school. Their London accent contrasted with our Dorset (*Daarsit!*) way of speaking, but we all got on well together.

The Invasion Scare

With France invaded and occupied, everyone was asking "Is it our turn next?" Weymouth Bay would be ideal for the Germans to land troops, so frantic efforts were made to erect barbed wire barriers, place concrete tank traps and set up gun emplacements. My father had been in the Army in World War I and in the Royal Navy in the 1920s, so when he joined the Home Guard, he was putting on a uniform for the third time, but this was no "Dad's Army" comedy, it was in deadly earnest. At home in his wardrobe he kept ready a Sten sub-machine gun with 200 rounds of live ammunition; he was on guard all night once a week and Sunday mornings were taken up with sessions on the rifle range.

In 1941 when the Germans attacked the Soviet Union, our invasion scare became less urgent. This new situation led to a 180 degree turn in perceptions. Up until then, the Soviets had been presented in the media as bullies who had collaborated with the Germans to crush Poland, and had then attacked Finland. Overnight they were transformed into friends and allies. From then on, when Stalin, now referred to as "*Uncle Joe*", appeared on a newsreel, the cinema audience clapped, as they already did for Churchill and for de Gaulle.

The Air Raids

The *Luftwaffe*, now operating from airfields in Normandy, were only 20 or so minutes flying time away from Weymouth. Our defences against enemy aircraft included barrage balloons, reflecting the sunlight like silver fish in the sky, searchlights and anti-aircraft guns, familiarly known as "Ack-Ack", as well as RAF Spitfires based nearby in Warmwell. There were air raids both during daylight and at night, which were to continue until 1944. My father got a local builder to construct a concrete air raid shelter in the garden. Danger came not only from the enemy, but also from shrapnel produced by our own Ack-Ack munitions exploding in the air. So the important thing was to get under cover. A warning siren once sounded when I was walking to school, so I ran into a laundry, where a few minutes later we could hear the sound of a German plane flying low with its machine guns firing. Quite an experience!

Daylight attacks were mostly aimed at shipping and port installations. A number of ships were hit and sunk. In due course we got into the routine of night time air raids. Sometimes the prime target was Weymouth and Portland, but often the German bombers passed overhead about midnight on their way northwards to bomb Bristol, Cardiff, Birmingham, Liverpool or Manchester. On the way back to their airfields in France, the *Luftwaffe* reserved one or two bombs for us. Once, coming out of our shelter in the early hours, we saw the sky over the northern horizon lit up with a red glow, due to fires raging in Bristol some 60 miles away. With high explosive bombs, besides the direct effect of the explosion on the immediate surroundings, there was the phenomenon of the shock wave or blast propagated through the air, which could wreak havoc up to several hundred yards away. Sometimes one could see a row of houses with all the windows blown in. Occasionally the Germans dropped incendiary bombs, each about two feet long and two inches in diameter, hundreds or even thousands at a time. One of these could smash through the tiles of a roof and start a fierce fire in the loft. So to be prepared for such an eventuality, every evening we filled the bath with water and had our stirrup pump and hose handy, but we were never put to the test.

The bombing amplified anti-German feeling, which was brought home to me when one day with my brother, we found ourselves by chance at the front of a crowd before the police station waiting for some shot-down *Luftwaffe* prisoners to come out. When they appeared some people in the crowd started to shout and to boo. In reply one of the prisoners took out of his pocket a handful of coins, which with a contemptuous gesture he tossed at the feet of the crowd. We scrambled to pick up the coins, but someone else got there first! Fortunately the prisoners with their guards were quickly taken away in an army vehicle.

The air raids brought casualties, including my best friend, seven year-old Gerald, killed with his mother, which today, some seventy-five years later, still saddens me when I think about them.

The War at Sea

Right from the start, there was intense naval activity. We saw with our own eyes local aspects of the war at sea, for there were minesweepers, motor gunboats, and motor torpedo boats based in Weymouth Harbour. Some of them were manned by members of the *Forces Navales Françaises Libres,* that is to say "de Gaulle's Navy". The French sailors were very visible due to the red pompom on top of their caps. In nearby Portland Harbour we were able to watch the comings and goings of battleships, aircraft carriers, cruisers, destroyers and so on. Further afield, from time to time the news was punctuated by the sinking of a major warship. Each event generated immense emotion. The loss of H.M.S. Hood out in the Atlantic was a huge shock; there were only three survivors out of a ship's company of some 1 400. I also very clearly remember the sinking of H.M.S. Repulse and H.M.S. Prince of Wales off Malaya with heavy loss of life, including Tim, the 18 year old son of a neighbour. An ongoing worry was the never-ending attacks by German U-boats on convoys on which we were dependent for our very survival. It was the courage and determination of the British and Allied sailors, who risked, and often lost their lives in the convoys, that ensured that we did not starve.

Morale

Winston Churchill ("*Winnie*") gave an immense boost to our morale. He was everywhere, in person, in the newspapers, on the wireless and in the newsreels, with his emblematic cigar, homburg hat and "*V for victory*" finger sign. The British sense of humour was mobilized for the war effort. The main thrust of the BBC comedy programmes was to help people laugh at the everyday problems that the war had forced upon them. Then of course Hitler, with his moustache and quiff, Goering with his fat paunch, and not forgetting Mussolini, who fancied himself as a latter day Julius Caesar, were an absolute gift to the cartoonists, so that when we opened our newspapers we could all have a good laugh at their expense.

For me, World War II was full of music, all part of keeping cheerful in the face of adversity. World War I was only twenty or so years earlier, so the popular songs from that time, such as *"It's a long way to Tipperary"*, resurfaced. There were also new songs, for example "When the lights go on again all over the world", mostly of a sentimental or nostalgic nature, often sung by Vera Lynn, evoking everyone's longing for peace. I also vividly recall every Sunday evening just before the BBC nine o'clock news, when the national anthems of the occupied countries were played. The anthem I liked best was the Polish one; I still remember the tune. Then Glenn Miller and his Army Air Force Band came to Britain to boost the morale of the American troops, but they also boosted the morale of us British. We were all very upset when in December 1944 Glenn Miller disappeared in a plane lost in the English Channel (and never found). Most surprising of all was the popularity enjoyed by "Lili Marlene", broadcast to the German *Afrika Korps*, with the British Eighth Army tuned in. Soon everyone in Britain (and in Germany I suppose) was listening to or singing this song.

Build-up to D–Day

Sometime in 1943 American troops started to arrive in Weymouth, which being a seaside resort, possessed numerous hotels, which the Americans took over, but the hotels were not enough, so they pitched their tents on every available free space in town and there were also big camps on the outskirts. Our streets were full of their vehicles, identified with a white five-pointed star on each side and on the roof or engine bonnet, with a warning notice at the rear of the vehicle "Left hand drive". It was the Jeeps that took my attention. How I dreamed to drive one of them.

From about April 1944 onwards we could feel the tension building up. We all knew that the Allied landings to liberate Europe were going to happen at any moment. Weymouth and Portland were one of the bases from which the American forces were going to launch their attack, so we could see every day the massive preparations. More and more American troops were arriving with their vehicles and weapons. In parallel there was the assembly in Weymouth Harbour, Weymouth Bay and in Portland Harbour, of hundreds of ships of every size and shape, landing craft, merchant ships all painted grey and warships. Both the Royal Navy and the United States Navy were very much present.

Finally during the night of 5th/6th June, we were awakened by the deafening roar of aircraft overhead, which lasted for hours. No Ack-Ack, for they were our planes on their way to Normandy to bomb the German positions or to drop paratroops. We went out in the street with our neighbours; everyone was saying: *"This is it"*! I do not think that anyone in Weymouth had much sleep that night. The next morning on the 6th June 1944 on the way to school, I made a detour onto the seafront. Weymouth Bay was empty, the gigantic armada of hundreds of ships present the previous day had sailed. This made a huge impact on me. I was just a schoolboy of ten years of age, but I knew instinctively that I had witnessed first-hand a landmark historical event, D-Day, seen from the sending end. The destination was Omaha Beach, where the Americans suffered very heavy casualties.

Beyond D-Day

The 6th June was the start of massive troop movements; the whole American Army seemed to be on the move pouring through Weymouth, though of course we were only one of several ports concerned. (We did not see anything of the British or Canadian troops involved, as they were embarked elsewhere). Battalions of American soldiers marched from the railway station through the streets of Weymouth on the way to the harbour, and others went by train to go aboard ships in Portland. In fact our house was close to the railway line to Portland. In the morning trains passed full of American soldiers, then in the afternoon the same trains came back in the opposite direction with German prisoners of war (POWs). One of the POWs jumped out of the train. I heard a shot ring out, which killed him. Sometimes I think about him. Who was he? What was his name? Why did he jump out of the train? If he had stayed on board, he would have eventually gone back home to Germany. (After the war the German POWs were to be with us until 1948 in semi-liberty.)

Every available ship was pressed into service to transport the American troops. On one occasion I saw the previously mentioned Edwardian vintage paddle steamer of our pre-war excursion leaving Weymouth Harbour outward bound for Normandy. She had lost her peacetime colours of black, white and yellow. Instead she had been painted a uniform grey, sported a few Ack Ack machine guns and her decks were covered with American soldiers like a swarm of bees.

In addition to the troops on their way to embarkation, there were endless convoys of trucks, half-tracks, towed artillery pieces and low loaders transporting tanks, not to mention ambulances. These vehicles were to be driven aboard landing craft, the ancestor of modern roll-on roll-off car ferries. Just recently I read that some 144,000 vehicles and 550,000 American soldiers were embarked in Weymouth and Portland, so that gives some idea of the scale of the operation. After the war a monument was put in place on Weymouth seafront in remembrance of these young Americans who came to our aid in our hour of peril, in particular honouring those who lost their lives, who never went home when the war was finished.

Peace at Last

On the 8th May 1945, to become known as V-E Day, the war in Europe was over. There was an explosion of joy, relief and thanksgiving. Two days later a German U-boat surrendered in Portland Naval Base. Once the crew taken ashore as prisoners, the submarine was opened to the public. With my father I went on board. Looking at the periscope, I thought to myself that just a short while before, the German captain would have been peering through it to seek out British and Allied ships to sink.

However V-E Day, was not the end, for the war was still raging across the Pacific Ocean and in South East Asia. The newsreels showed us Japanese kamikaze planes crashing onto American aircraft carriers with devastating results. So a long and bloody path still lay ahead. However without any warning there came on the scene a fantastically powerful and mysterious new weapon, the atomic bomb, dropped on Hiroshima and Nagasaki. The nuclear age, with all its fears and uncertainties, had begun. V-J Day was declared the 15th August 1945. Everyone was happy to finish almost six years of war, but there was not quite the same spontaneous celebration, as there had been for VE Day.

I suppose I was too young to appreciate fully the sheer horror of World War II. In fact I did not suffer, for we were never occupied by the Germans, our house was not hit by a bomb, none of my family died or were injured as a result of the war, and moreover we were never really very hungry. So we have to be thankful for the way it turned out for us, but we must also remember the millions of people across the world on both sides of the conflict, for whom the war brought immense hardship, suffering and tragedy. A year after the war ended King George VI sent a message to each British schoolboy and schoolgirl, which read:

"Today, as we celebrate victory, I send this personal message to you and all other boys and girls at school. For you have shared in the dangers and hardships of a total war and you have shared no less in the triumph of the Allied Nations. I know you will always feel proud to belong to a country which was capable of such supreme effort; proud too of parents and elder brothers and sisters who by their courage, endurance and enterprise brought victory. May these qualities be yours as you grow up and join in the common effort to establish among the nations of the world unity and peace. George R.I."

Daylight Murder At Sandhurst Road School

Richard Neave

Introduction, and what led me to write about the following story

At the beginning of World War II my late mother was a Red Cross Nursing Sister, later she rose to the rank of Matron and Deputy Commandant. After the war, she continued to work for the Red Cross becoming Divisional Commander for West Suffolk. A post she held from 1945 until 1960.

I used to help her from the age of eight in 1955 until 1960 when I was home from boarding school. I would help her at garden fetes in aid of the Red Cross as well serving teas to the disabled at a club that she set up. I also helped prepare the Red Cross collection tins and boxes, which she delivered to the various collectors throughout West Suffolk. Like my late father, my mother never really talked much about her experiences during the war.

However, one afternoon when we were preparing the Red Cross collection boxes, and tins, to my surprise she did tell me some things about her duties during the war.

My mother told she served for most of the War at Himley Hall, Dudley, in the West Midlands. Himley Hall was at that time the home of the 3rd Earl of Dudley, MC.,TD, known as Viscount Ednam. The Earl and his family continued to live and entertain their guests in one part of the Hall while the Red Cross used the rest of the hall for the treatment and convalescence of servicemen who having spent time in hospitals needed time to recover from their wounds. There could be as many as a hundred patients being looked after by a staff consisting of a Commandant, Matron, my mother as a Sister, five Nurses, cooks and domestic helpers. Quite a number of the patients at the beginning of the war were Royal Air Force aircrew who had come from Barnsley Hall Hospital, Royal Wolverhampton Hospital, and Queen Victoria Hospital in East Grinstead, Sussex. Many had suffered severe burns and undergone plastic surgery by the famous plastic surgeon Sir Archibald Mcindoe who frequently came to visit them at Himley Hall. They were known as members of '*The Guinea Pig Club*'.

On the night that Coventry was all but flattened by German bombers, my mother was asked to drive the one ambulance they had at the hall up to Coventry, to pick up casualties and take them to the nearest hospitals in

Coventry. She said it was the most terrifying experience she had, had up until that time, driving through the streets, whilst the bombs were falling, knowing that at any moment she could be blown to bits. Everywhere there were massive fires and buildings were crashing down blocking streets, which meant her having to find alternative routes to the hospitals. At one point she was close to the famous Cathedral and watched in horror as it disintegrated in balls of fire. Owing to so many fires there was insufficient water for all of the fire engines to be fully operative, and a number of fire engines were destroyed. She said that the gutters of the streets and roads were awash with blood from those who had been either killed or wounded.

After having had to spend many nights continuing to help as best she could in Coventry she was then asked to do the same in Birmingham, which again she said was a terrifying experience. She would return in the early hours of the mornings, grab a couple of hours sleep, then go on duty in the Hall.

Later in the war whilst at Himley Hall, my mother looked after soldiers who had been wounded in the D-Day landings; some had been Parachutists who had been shot as they were descending, others suffered severe burns, and quite a number had received terrible leg and spine injuries due to having landed badly because their parachutes had been torn by gun fire and shrapnel.

Whilst she was telling me this, she brought out a box of photos that had been taken during the War. They included photos of my mother when she was deputy Commandant at Tudor Grange in Solihull, home of Lady Bird of the Bird's Custard family — Tudor Grange being a Red Cross auxiliary hospital. My mother became a good friend of Lady Bird who was a Red Cross Commandant.

There were photos taken while she was at Himley Hall. Photos of my mother with the then Commandant, group photos of her with the nurses and some of the patients, as well as photos of the Hall and grounds. There were also photos of her with groups of children, which included a photo taken of the children sitting at tables in the dining hall and being overseen by the Commandant, Matron, Nurses and my mother. Another photo of my mother with the children working on completing a jigsaw puzzle. Another one showed the children sitting on a long wall all waving their arms. There was a newspaper cutting showing some of the children playing a game of football in the grounds at the hall. On asking her who the children were and why they were at Himley Hall, my mother promptly gathered up all the photos, put them back in the box saying, "The children had come from London to stay at the hall. It was all a long time ago. You don't need to know who they were, and why they were there. So, don't ever ask me about them, it's to upsetting for me to talk about". Tears began to appear in her eyes and it was clear that having seen the photos of the children again it upset her deeply.

I never asked her about the children in the photos again. I assumed that they had been evacuees, and that my mother would tell me about them when and if she chose to do so. However, she never did.

My mother died in 1992, and it was whilst I was sorting through her things that I came across the box of photos. Having not seen the box for nearly thirty years I thought she had thrown it out, but no she had kept the box hidden away for all that time. Seeing the photos again, my curiosity was once again aroused as to why the children in the photos had been sent to stay at Himley Hall.

I had never been to Himley Hall because I assumed that there was an Earl of Dudley still living there but he wouldn't want me pestering him with questions about the past. So, I did nothing until some years later when by chance I came across a rare book which listed all the private homes, most of which were or had been owned by titled families who during WWII had given over parts of their homes to be used by the Red Cross or Saints Johns as either hospitals or auxiliary homes for wounded service personnel. The book hadn't been published until after the war, because during the War it had been decided that the list of homes used were to be kept secret, for fear that the Germans might decide to bomb the homes, thus killing not only service personnel, but also the titled people who owned them — which could have had serious consequences. The majority of the British public and the Germans didn't know of the houses' existence during the war, and probably still don't know. Over 470 homes were used.

I decided to find out more about the homes used by contacting the Red Cross branches near to each of the homes to see if it was possible to get information about life in the homes during the war from those who had served in them with the Red Cross. I thought it might prove to be an interesting book.

Having written to the heads of the Red Cross branch's explaining what I was wanting to do, I was to discover it was ill timed, because the Red Cross Headquarters in London had at the time requested all branches to send their War archives, which would have contained information about all of those private homes used by the Red Cross to them in London.

However, I did manage to obtain a lot of useful information from a number of the branches who hadn't yet sent off their war time archives; regretfully not enough for what I had set out to do.

I contacted British Red Cross, London Headquarters and told them about what I was trying to do, and they agreed that I could go to their offices and trawl through all the archive material they had received, which they had not had time to put into any proper order. However, I would have to pay them for the time I spent there even though I had said that I was prepared to give them a percentage of the money I raised from the sale of the finished book.

Needless to say, I put the idea on hold, and decided instead to contact Himley Hall to see if I could find out about the children in my late mother's photos.

Himley Hall, I discovered, is now owned by Dudley Council and is used for conferences, Wedding receptions, tours of the interior which includes a talk about the history of the Earls of Dudley family and the Hall. This includes information about how the hall was used by the Red Cross during the War, and they have a book of photos taken at that time, which can be viewed by the visitors. Also, in the hall there is a large area displaying fine interesting glassware that continues to be produced in the surrounding areas. In the grounds there is a large lake, extensive gardens, and a golf course. The gardens are open to the public.

When I contacted the hall by phone I spoke to the then 'keeper of Himley Hall', and introduced myself, explaining that my late mother had spent time at the hall during the war with the Red Cross. I mentioned the photos that I had from my mother's time there and what I was endeavouring to do. Much to my surprise the keeper responded by saying that she knew of my mother and how she had come to work there. She informed me that my late grandfather, Mr. Robert Neave — who was at that time the Political agent for the local Conservative MP for Dudley — had been a friend of the 3rd Earl of Dudley, who had also been an MP at one time. And it was my grandfather who had asked the Earl if he would be prepared to loan out part of the Hall to the Red Cross. The Earl agreed, and it was not long before my mother was soon in post at Himley Hall with the Red Cross.

Needless to say, I was invited to visit the Hall and to bring the photos for the keeper to look at to see if they matched photos that she had in the halls collection. On visiting the hall and meeting the keeper she kindly gave me an extensive tour of the inside and grounds whilst telling me about the Earl of Dudley's family and his family history. She mentioned that he had been a close friend of the late King Edward, Mrs Simpson, King George VI and our present Queens mother all of whom had been regular visitors to the Hall to attend parties. I also discovered that my mother, grandfather and grandmother had been invited to some of the same parties and my mother had danced on a number of occasions with King George VI. I was shown the room that my mother had as her bedroom. Asking the keeper how she knew about my mother and grandfather, she explained that she had been informed by the then Commandant, who was now dead, as well as some of the staff who had worked at the hall during my mother's time there. She showed me several plans of the hall, one of which showed the area used during the War by the Red Cross, which showed the rooms that were converted into wards as well as the rooms used by the nurses and staff. She also gave me a booklet detailing the hall's history.

On showing her my mother's collection of photos, I was surprised to discover that the Hall had some of the same photos. The keeper requested that I send her copies of the photos that they didn't have. I agreed to send her copies including copies of photos of the children which she also didn't have. I asked her if she knew who the children were and why they had been sent to the Hall, she said that as far as she knew they had come from Catford in South East London to recuperate because their school had been bombed. However, she was not aware of all the details, but would be grateful if I would let her know if I found out any information so she could include it within the Red Cross history at the Hall. I agreed to get back to her as soon as I discovered anything more.

On returning home I had made the copies of the photos the keeper had requested made and posted them to her. I also contacted the *Lewisham Mercury* newspaper which covers the Catford area, and spoke to a very helpful reporter and told her about the photos of the children and why I was trying to find out the full story as to why they had been sent to Himley Hall. The reporter asked me to send her copies of the photos, which I did. On receiving the photos from me she phoned me back a few days later to say that she had made some enquiries about the photos and had discovered that the reason that the children in the photos had been sent to Himley Hall was because the school that they were attending at that time, namely Sandhurst Road School, Catford in the borough of Lewisham had been bombed in a daylight raid. Those children who survived the bombing were suffering from shock, and some were recovering from injuries sustained as well. As all of them needed treatment and time to get away from London, to stay in a secure environment, the local council decided to find somewhere for them to stay. The Earl of Dudley, having read of their plight offered to let them stay at the Hall under the care of the Red Cross.

The reporter kindly sent me photocopies of the local newspapers coverage at the time of the bombing. Having read the newspaper cuttings and seen the photos in the cuttings I was eager to hear from those who might still be around and who had survived the bombing. So, I asked the reporter if she would kindly publish two of the photos of the children taken at Himley Hall, along with a request for any of those who were in the photo to contact me, as I was keen to hear their accounts of the bombing of their school. She agreed to do this.

Sandhurst Road School as it was before it was bombed

Sandhurst Road School after bombing in 1943

There was quite a good response from the newspaper article. I received letters not only from survivors still living within the area, but also from survivors who had moved as far away as Canada, Australia, and Spain. They had received a copy of the newspaper article from friends in Lewisham. I also received from some of those who contacted me copies of photos taken at the time and published in both the local and national newspapers, along with extracts from books that had mentioned the bombing.

Having read the letters, I received. I wanted to find out even more about the bombing of the school. I wanted to know why the school had been targeted, and who was the pilot responsible for bombing the school, was he still alive, if so I was determined to track him down.

The results of my research into the daylight murder at Sandhurst Road School, Catford, South East London

On Wednesday 20th January 1943 the sky over South East London was clear with bright sunlight. The barrage balloons like a large number of barrage balloons across London had been lowered to assist in the calibration of the gun laying radars, which was a reassuring sign that everything was ok. The balloons would only be put up to full height if air raids were expected. On that day no one was expecting the German Luftwaffe to risk attacking London in broad daylight like they had done in 1940.

However, the air crews of the 10th (Jabo) Staffel of Jagdgeschwader 26 having recently been re-equipped with the first of the new Focke-Wulfs FW 190A-s and operating from several air bases in Northern France were given orders that morning by their newly appointed Kommodore - Oberst Josef Priller to go and bomb specific targets across London. The squadrons set off accompanied by Bf 109s fighter planes and crossed the channel without interception crossing the coast between Beachy Head and Rye just before midday. The formations then split up, a diversionary force headed towards Maidstone in Kent while the main body continued flying very low towards London.

A misunderstanding between the adjacent Observer Corps areas led Fighter command to believe that all the German aircraft were heading for Maidstone. When the full implications of the raid were realised the bombers were nearing their targets in South-east London. At 12.30 p.m. the Focke-Wulfs swept in flying just above the roof tops with the sky to themselves. None of the air raid sirens went off until it was too late. Some of the bombers targeted and shot up four RAF balloon sites in Lewisham, one set a gasholder alight at the South Suburban Gas Company at

Sydenham. While another one accurately bombed the President's House at the Royal Naval College at Greenwich. Other bombers scored direct hits on Deptford West Power Station as well as Surry Commercial Docks.

Rescue workers attempting to uncover those buried under the rubble at the school

The Mass Grave in Hither Green cemetery, where thirty-two of the children and one teacher are buried. Parents and relatives still come regularly to lay flowers and pay respects.

Some of the children from Sandhurst Road School who went to Himley Hall.

Himley Hall, Dudley. Of those who survived, many were treated in hospital before being sent for convalescence. Large numbers went to the Earl of Dudley's home Himley Hall, Dudley, Worcestershire. Others went to a Nunnery, or to private homes in Shropshire.

The photo of Sister Neave with some of the surviving children, taken at Himley Hall in 1943, that was published in the Lewisham newspaper years later. This resulted in some of those present coming forward with their stories of what happened on the day their school was bombed.

Matron, Sister Neave, Nurse, Commandant, Nurse, Nurse with some of the children in the dining room at Himley Hall.

One of the bombers also flying at roof top level flew over Catford and began firing its machine guns at adults and children walking through the streets before it approached the LCC school in Sandhurst Road. Where children were playing in the playground. One of the children, a little girl aged around seven, was skipping merrily by herself when she heard the roar of an engine overhead, she stopped skipping to wave, assuming the swooping plane was an RAF bomber.

The pilot waved back, smiling, as she turned her little face upwards returning a smile.

She couldn't have had time to spot the swastikas under the wing, before he fired his machine guns slicing the little girl in half. He then pressed the bomb release button dropping a 1100 lb bomb right into the heart of the four-story school building.

Thirty-one children and six members of staff were killed at the scene of the attack. Five further children died in hospital. Sixty others were buried under rubble for many hours and suffered devastating life changing injuries. The youngest child killed was aged 5 and the oldest was aged 15½. Reporting restrictions were lifted at the time, and the news spread across the country and the world, as this was seen as the worst killing of innocent children in the UK at that time.

Thirty-two of the children killed along with one of the teachers were buried in a Civilian War Dead Plot at Hither Green Cemetery, South East London. The children were buried on the 27th January 1943, in white coffins; the teacher was buried in the centre in a black coffin.

Over seven thousand mourners attended the service, which was conducted by the then Bishop of Southwark. The flower-laden hearses seemed to stretch for miles. The graves each had a brass plaque with the child's name on along with their photo.

The remaining children and teachers killed had private burials.

Some weeks after the mass burials, a lorry drove in to the cemetery and parked up alongside the mass grave. The driver, along with his accomplice, got out of the lorry and proceeded to rip the brass plaques off the graves and put them in the lorry before driving off. They were never caught. They had no doubt taken the plaques and sold them for scrap, as brass was fetching a good price at the time.

Individual Accounts From Some of the Survivors, Parents of Children and Witness Accounts of the Tragedy That I Managed to Obtain

Doreen Fidler (née Westbourne).

Tuesday, January 19th 1943, was a special day. My Aunt Alice had got permission from the school to take my mother and me to see 'Cinderella' at the Stoll theatre, it was a late birthday treat for me, and my first visit to a London theatre. While we were waiting for the doors to open, I saw Pamela, one of my sister Mary's school friends, walking with another school friend who, like my sister, had left the school the previous term. Little did I know this was to be the last day of Pamela's life.

Wednesday, January 20th 1943, was just another school day. Once the Blitz was over the continuous anxiety we lived with at that time had subsided and only returned when the siren sounded.

My friend Alma who lived on the other side of my road, called for me as usual. Alma was a tall, slender girl very much like my mother. How I envied her ability to do handstands, cartwheels and backbends. My efforts were very clumsy by comparison. She also stayed to school dinners and I pestered my mother to let me stay, but she always refused. On the way to school I told Alma about the pantomime and also seeing Pamela.

Our teacher was Mrs. Smith who had a formidable reputation for the number of Junior County Scholarships her pupils achieved. The exam was set for March 3rd so there was no time to waste.

When the bell rang at the end of the morning, Alma went downstairs for school dinner and I hurried home. It was the day I had to buy our cat's fish from the fishmonger's in Sandhurst Road.

Fortunately, my mother's friend, Mrs. Smith who lived in Sandhurst Road, had already brought it round. I decided to go to the Library instead, but remembered just as I was about to open the front door that the Library had recently started closing at mid-day on a Wednesday. I went back into the living-room and settled down to read that week's copy of "*War Illustrated*".

I had just opened the magazine when I heard a terrible roaring noise. As the siren had not sounded I thought it was a plane crashing. I dived for shelter under the dining-room table and I could see our tabby cat Tim, rushing back and forth across the room in terror. As the roar of the plane's engine increased I felt the floor shake.

The noise gradually subsided and then we heard the wail of the siren next to the Library. My mother called from the kitchen, "It's a bit late for that. Let's get down to the shelter in case there are any more about".

Feathers were floating down as we ran along the garden path. We thought they were from someone's mattress, but it transpired that they were the feathers from the dozens of pigeons that roosted on the roof of the school.

Fright made me stumble with the shelter door and I fell into the shelter badly bruising my shins. No more aircraft came over and we could hear shouting. At the same time, someone was banging on our front door. Coming out of the shelter, we saw our next door but one neighbour comforting a teen-age girl who was covered in dust and crying hysterically. Our neighbour had gone out the front of her house and intercepted one of the central schoolgirls running down the road. Our neighbour called to us and said, "She says the school's been bombed". We could hardly believe it, but when we opened our front door my Uncle George stood there. On catching sight of me he said, "Thank God, she's safe, her school has been bombed".

It was then that I thought of my friend Alma. My mother decided we would go to the school and find her.

When we turned the corner of Glenfarg Road into Torridon Road we saw a lorry parked outside the Library. One of our infants was sitting in the driver's cabin. She looked like a broken doll. She had been dressed in a red jumper with a red plaid kilt. She was grey with dust from head to toe. The only red was the blood from a wound on her head running down her face on to her chest.

Suddenly, nerves got the better of me and I told my mother, "I can't stand this". She told me to go around to Mrs. Smith's house while she went to look for Alma. Alma was the only child and her mother worked in one of the Ministries in London and would not be able to get home for at least an hour. Her father was in the army.

I spent the afternoon at Mrs. Smith's house waiting for my mother to return. We watched the endless stream of ambulances going to and fro from the school to the hospital.

Eventually, my sister came home from work. Finding the house empty, she started to cry. Our next-door neighbour told her I was safe and sent her round to Mrs. Smith's house. We returned home and sometime later my mother returned home. Her coat was covered in dust and blood-stained. She had not found Alma, but had helped two motorists take injured children to hospital and had nursed and comforted the children until the nurses could dress their wounds and their parents arrived. Later in the evening Alma's mother came to tell us that Alma had been blown into one of the fireplaces at the end of the Hall and had suffered serious burns to her face, and had undergone a long operation to save her sight.

It was decided that I should not go to see Alma in hospital. I never did see her again because as soon as she was well enough to leave hospital she and her parents moved to Bournemouth where her father was posted. We didn't have her new address and I have often wondered what became of her.

Exactly a week after the bombing the mass funeral took place in the morning. Not all the victims were buried at that time. My mother decided not to go to the ceremony. She could not bear to watch the relative's misery. Later in the afternoon, when the crowds had gone home, we did walk to Hither Green Cemetery. The grave had been left open and I can still see the long row of small white coffins with the one dark coffin of the teacher, Miss Langdon, in the middle.

It was so sad and ironic that several of the children in my class had not been pupils in the school for very long. Malcolm who sat in the desk in front of me had come from Scotland just over a year previously. Eunice came from Wales. Tony and his family had not lived in the district long. Only Dennis had been in the Reception class with me before the War. Had they not moved into the district they may have lived to become a grandparent as I have done. The words of the Remembrance service:

"They grow not old as we that are left grow old",

have a particular meaning for me. By September 1943, the horror of the bombing receded somewhat although it was several years before I could bring myself to walk within sight of the school. Also, during June 1944, the flying bomb attacks started followed by the V2 rockets which made bombing by piloted aircraft seem almost civilized. I still visit the children's grave and spend a few, quiet, reflective moments there.

Keith Mills

My sister and two of my brothers, (myself included) were remarkably lucky to escape with our lives on that eventful day in 1943.

The attack which occurred at dinner time, was by a lone aeroplane, and its timing, enabled my elder sister of 12 years old, to go home to dinner, she didn't like the school dinners (perhaps it was the greens or the custard).

My older brother Raymond who was 10 years old, was sitting at the dinner table in the school hall, just about at its central point, and immediately below where the bomb actually fell, demolishing this part of the main building. He ended up underneath the rubble unconscious, for a few hours before he was found and dug out.

Rodney Jarrett, the little boy of 6, who was at his side and whom he used to look after, was killed.

My younger brother Colin, who was only 5 years old, would have been sitting at Raymond's other side, but on that fateful day he had a cold, and being of such a tender age our mother had wisely kept him at home.

Raymond suffered fairly badly, with a fractured leg and a wound to his head, which left a scar, two inches long and where his hair wouldn't grow from, thereafter. He also had a fractured arm.

I was lucky too. I was 8 years old and was sitting at the dinner table with my friends near the end of the school hall at what you might call the Brown Hill Road end. I was to experience the horror of it all, like many others. We heard the plane coming overhead and the teachers shouting in urgent haste to get under the tables and pull the chairs in behind us. Then one teacher called out to us, "Run into the classroom". I remember it was one of the classrooms on the Minard Road side, which was nearest to us. The teacher had instructed us, probably feeling it would be safer to go there because the classrooms had a smaller ceiling span and because the windows had a brick wall built two feet away from them, to stop the blast from nearby explosions ripping into the shattered glass and injuring its young occupants. In the few seconds left, we obediently did as she bade us, and most likely saved some of us from serious injuries and even our lives.

As the bomb exploded, those of us in the classroom, had two walls between us and death and destruction, then the clouds of dust and debris arose in the air around us, we heard the teacher, who deservedly should have been awarded a medal for her rapid decision making. Urged us to get out of the school and seek shelter in people's houses. We felt our way out of the classroom and saw dim daylight through the obscuring dust which was choking us, we scrambled through the broken tables and debris and I remember climbing over the windowsill of the school hall where the windows and their frames had been blown out, running across the littered with debris playground and into Ardgowan Road where we ran in panic to the houses that were opposite, banging on doors for protection but getting no answers at the first few, then eventually someone heard our calls for help, and let us in until the all clear siren sounded. We were then taken by the family along Sandhurst Road to Saint Andrews Church Hall on the corner of Ardgowan Road, which was hastily being opened as a central point in the emergency.

Grownups made cups of tea to dry our parched and dust filled mouths, then people with cars were asked to convey those of less serious injuries to take us to Lewisham hospital, so that ambulances could be kept back for the more serious cases.

I remember being wrapped in a blanket and being taken by one of these cars and a kind man and his wife to the hospital.

Meantime, my sister June, had tried to go back to school for the afternoon tuition, from our home and was stopped on the way there by a policeman who informed her that the school had been bombed and that she should return home. He asked her if she had any brothers and sisters at the school at that time. She replied saying, "Yes my two brothers are there, they stayed at school lunch". "Then you must go back home as quickly as you can and tell your mum and dad to come back up to the school to make sure that they are safe".

When our mother heard of the disaster, she hurried in distress to the school, leaving my sister to look after my two younger brothers one of them only two years old. When our mother reached the school, she was horrified at the sight of thinking the worst especially for us two but even for the other children also. She was shown along to Saint Andrews Hall, where a roll call of the children who had passed through its doors, as safe. She saw my name was on the list but no news of Raymond at that time, however hearing that I had been transferred to Lewisham hospital decided to make her way there to see what state I was in. She arrived at the hospital about half-an-hour after I arrived, and having been looked over by nurses who noted that I had only a bruised arm and leg and with shock, having registered the day's events, I was in the waiting room ready for collection. She threw her arms around me in great emotion, being thankful that I had at least been spared.

As I looked decidedly unwell she said that she would take me home and put me to bed, with my sister June to look after me, while she would go back to the school to find out if there was any news of Raymond yet.

I remember travelling home on the bus which we got outside the hospital. All the passengers soon heard that I had been in the school when it was bombed, and all expressed their sympathy to me. I was glad to get home.

Our dad was at work and hadn't managed to be contacted just yet, so mother went back to the school to hear if there was any news yet about Raymond, it was a few hours yet before he would be dug out from underneath the rubble, when he was eventually found alive, but badly injured he would have to stay in hospital for a few weeks.

It was a few days later at the hospital, that the Queen (our present Queen Elizabeth's mother) came to see the most badly injured children. She and her husband King George had already visited the bombed school within a day or so to see the destruction of it and hear at first-hand accounts from local inhabitants.

At the hospital, the Queen brought with her a basketful of bananas for the bombed school children. These had been brought back from Casablanca by Lord Louis Mountbatten, Chief of Combined Operations, to give to the two Princesses, our present Queen Elizabeth and the late Princess Margaret.

When the two Princesses had heard about the plight of the bombed school children, they asked their mother to give them instead to the most severely injured children. (Nowadays bananas are in abundance in the shops, but in 1943, they were non-existent and were indeed a luxury at that period of time).

Out of about twelve children that were in the ward, all but my brother Raymond were girls. My brother being shy hid his head under the covers when the Queen approached.

A few weeks after the bombing of the school, a letter arrived at the Lewisham Council Chambers, from the Earl of Dudley of Himley Hall at Dudley, Staffordshire, inviting about twenty at a time of the bombed school children to visit him and his wife in the quiet of the countryside and away from the bombing of London. The Earl of Dudley had naturally read of the bombing in the national newspapers, and having been in conversation with the Red Cross Commandant at the Hall it was agreed the children should convalesce there. Sister Neave was to be put in charge of their care and wellbeing. This was agreed to, and a date was set for a first batch of children. I found that I was included in this first lot. We were instructed to assemble on a certain day at one of the council offices.

While we were assembling, someone noticed that I wasn't wearing an overcoat, in the cold wintry weather, so I said that I hadn't got one, and without further ado, I was hastily taken to a nearby tailors and fitted out with one. I remember a photograph was taken of this incident, also another one taken with a group of the children being handed a sweet each, from a basket held by the Mayors wife who was there with her husband to see the children off on their way by coach which was to take us to one of the major railway stations for the trip to Dudley. Photographs were taken by the newspapers of our departure, with even more newspaper photographs taken whilst we were at Himley Hall.

Whilst at Himley Hall we all still needed to be educated so we were sent to the local village school, where the teachers managed to fit us all in. It's not every day a village school suddenly has twenty or so pupils turning up out of the blue on their doorstep. We even got daily bottles of milk to drink, even though they were ice cold, because of the time of the year.

It was a nice respite at Himley Hall to breathe the fresh country air and to be able to sleep at night without the continual sirens going off to warn us to go to our air raid shelters and the bangs which could be our last. Some people used to sleep in their air raid shelters but they were damp and cold and nothing better than your own warm bed, to sleep in.

Sister Neave and the nurses were brilliant in the way that they took care of all of us. We were all well fed with more food than we received back home. When not at school we had space to play football in a large field behind the Hall. We would be taken for walks in the large grounds which were fabulous and we were entertained in the evenings with stories read to us as well as having games and huge jig saw puzzles to complete. It helped us enormously to put behind us the horrors we had left behind in London.

Sadly, after about three weeks we had to return back to our homes, to make way for the other children to come and have their time to enjoy the peace of the countryside. We said our goodbyes, and thanked Earl and Countess Dudley as well as Sister Neave and the staff for all the kindness that they had shown us, then we were soon on our way home by train to face whatever was to be befall us back in London.

Raymond Mills (Keith's brother)

I was ten years old at the time the school was bombed. I was in the school hall on the ground floor, which was used as a dining room at midday for school dinners. We were sitting on forms around large strong wooden tables.

Suddenly we heard the sound of low-flying aircraft; the lady teacher in charge, whose name I can't remember, looked through the window and immediately turned around and told us to get under the tables. This we did and then everything went black as the school collapsed around us.

The next thing I recall is waking up in Lewisham Hospital about three days later. I found myself with a broken leg, a fractured head with fourteen stitches in it, and cuts and abrasions all over.

I was in hospital for the next four months, and a further four months in a convalescent home. I always thought that I was lucky to survive and I am sure that it was only through the quick action and supreme calmness of the teacher that got us under the tables, speedily and orderly, that saved the lives of those that didn't get killed. I believe that she was one of the casualties.

My younger brother Keith who was eight at the time was also in the school hall when the bomb fell, but he wasn't knocked out and managed to climb out through a window. Though not badly hurt, he did suffer from bad nerves for years. I also had an older sister June who was twelve, and another brother Colin who was five, that attended the school, but they were both home at the time. One very exciting thing that happened to us while we were in hospital was a visit from the Queen who brought us bananas.

Fred Greenstreet

The school was a mass of fire. The houses in Ardgowan Road had their doors and windows blasted off and the curtains hung in shreds. Worst of all were the children. The youngsters, many of them hurt, were running in and out of the front gardens, crying and screaming. There were children everywhere. A quarter of an hour after the search began I found my son Norman, aged 8. He was dead. I lifted him in my arms and laid him down in the playground. We carried on and then someone said: "Your other boy is safe".

When I got home, neighbours kept coming around asking if I had any news of their children. I answered all the questions I could. I then returned to the school.

Jack Threadgold

At the time of the bombing of the school I was eight and attending Downberry Road School which was approximately 50-100 yards away from Sandhurst Road school. It was lunchtime and we were outside the school gate when we heard aircraft overhead. We looked up, expecting to see our own aircraft, and then the sirens sounded so we all ran.

I ran up Shroffold Road in the direction of my home. Halfway up the road I heard a loud explosion and gunfire and took cover in a nearby garden. After a short while I carried on up the road and an air-raid warden took me into his home. I can remember his son vividly describing seeing the bomb being dropped from the aircraft.

On returning to school the following day, one of the teachers told us that one of our classmates had been killed. The teacher was in tears when she told us.

Brian Robinson

I lost two of my cousins Judith and Anne Biddle both aged five, they were twins, in the bombing. They were found clung together. Another of my cousins Maureen had a cold that day and didn't go to school, otherwise the total could have been three.

Maureen Watkins (née New)

I am Brian Robinson's cousin, and as he says I missed being killed thanks to a cold. However, I can still vividly see in my mind's eye the plane, with a swastika on the side, flying low over where I lived. I was six years old at the time. My mother went to the school to look for her nieces in the rubble. I don't think she ever recovered from that and who could blame her. The twins mother Edith died in December 1943. My mother said it was of a broken heart.

Charles Allford

I was a veteran of the First War and signed up as a gunner in WWII. I was on leave the day the school was bombed. I lived just around the corner from the school. I had two daughters at the school, Brenda aged five and Lorina aged seven. When I heard the explosion, I rushed round to the school and saw that the central part of the school had collapsed into a pile of rubble. I frantically started digging through the rubble and eventually I found Brenda. Her forehead and cheek were cut badly. Her little arm lay over her face as if she had tried to protect herself. I am glad that it was me who found her. I continued to search for the rest of the day and night for Lorina. I was grief stricken I just felt I could not leave. However tired and worn out I went home the following morning to comfort my wife. Later Lorina was found. Both my daughters were dead.

Mrs Embelin

On hearing the explosion my first thoughts were for my mother and grandfather who lived in Minard Road, which was the playground side of the school. I grabbed my bike and cycled up Brownhill Road, and turned left in to Minard Road and was greeted by smoke from the school. As I approached the last few houses before the playground I dismounted because of the rubble which was strewn across the road. Then, to my horror, I saw several children's bodies and limbs of the ones that had been playing in the playground. An ARP Warden ushered me away despite my saying I was a qualified St John's nurse. I finally reached my mothers and grandfathers who were in a state of shock so I stayed with them for the rest of the day. St Andrew's church hall nearby was used to take the slightly injured while ambulances transported the more serious cases to Lewisham and Hither Green Hospitals. As bodies were discovered they were taken to St Andrew's Hall to await identification.

Margaret Clarke, Headmistress of the school, 1943

I was in my room on the top floor when I heard a distant siren. I went into the hall outside where I found the top class lunching and another class preparing to leave for a special visit to 'A Midsummer Night's Dream'. The next I remember was a tearing, rending sound and I realised half the hall had gone. About six feet from where I was standing there was empty space.

I joined some children who were going down the stairs and on reaching the ground floor started getting the children out. Before the rescue workers, soldiers on leave and civilians who were passing came into help us dig amid the stifling fumes of the fire in the debris. It was not until later that I noticed my own arm injuries for which I had an operation in Farnborough Hospital.

The only question the children were asking was "How can we help Miss?" They took home the younger ones, tore up their clothes to bind the injuries and even helped the rescue work—a particularly grim job for youngsters of 14 and 15.

Eric Brady

I was aged 9 and Kitty, my big sister was aged 14. She was upstairs talking to the headmistress, Miss Clarke, when they heard a distant air-raid warning. Miss Clarke told Kitty to go to the dining hall and get the children into the shelters, but just as she reached the dining room door, the aircraft swooped. Kitty called out and ran towards me when the bomb dropped.

I remember scrabbling to get under the table as the roof cascaded down. A lump of masonry pinned down my left arm. Another lump landed on my left ankle and I was hit on the side of my head.

My right side was uninjured, and many years later my mother told me that Kitty had been found lying on my right side-killed by a piece of the rubble which would have killed me.

I was in hospital for eighteen months, and kept asking for Kitty. I broke down in tears when they told me. Because I was in hospital for so long, my father and I became strangers. I also remember refusing to change out of my hospital gown in front of the strange boy who was with my mother. She said, "He isn't a strange boy – he's your brother".

Molly Linn

We had made shepherd's pie in cookery class that morning, but I was too excited to eat because we were going to the theatre to see 'A Midsummer Night's Dream'. I was 12 at the time, it had been my birthday eleven days earlier, and I had a new coat in royal blue, which made me feel grown up.

We were chatting excitedly when someone ran in and said the air raid siren had sounded. I thought, 'I'd better get my purse and gloves from my desk to take to the shelter', and walked across to my classroom.

I saw other children hanging out of the window, and Betty, the head girl, was telling them to get to the shelter. As she spoke, I looked out of the window and saw a plane. The pilot was wearing a leather helmet and googles, but it didn't occur to me that he was German. His mouth was draw back and for a few seconds I thought he was grinning. Then I realised he was snarling, and I saw him reach forward and do something with the controls. He was probably releasing the bomb at that very second.

The next thing I knew, I was buried. Betty, who had been standing next to me, had been killed.

I was eventually rescued and taken to Lewisham Hospital. I remember my clothes being cut away, which upset me. I thought, 'It's my new coat, what are my parents going to say?'

I had two broken arms and two badly mangled legs. My legs were operated on, and while I recovered, the Queen came to visit. She brought bananas, and told me that her daughters had been sent them, but insisted they came to us instead. Some children tried to eat them with the skins on.

I was transformed to hospital in Roehampton at the end of July, and in October 1944, my left leg was amputated. I had endured so many operations that I just accepted it. In March 1945, my other leg was amputated. I finally came home in October 1945, and the following year I started work as a telephonist. I married in 1958, and just got on with life and my prosthetic limbs.

Mary Burch

I was five years old and had been off school with an illness until the day before the bombing. On the day of the bombing I begged my mother to stay at school for lunch. I had become friendly with three other little girls, and I wanted to sit with them while I ate. My mother said no, but my brother, John who was ten said, 'Go on, Mum, let her stay. I'll stay with her and look after her". Reluctantly my mother agreed to let me stay.

At the lunchtime I was sitting with my friends at the table and we had just been given jam tarts for dessert when the plane flew past the window. We saw the pilot and he waved at us. We waved back, but as we did I saw the German markings on the wing. Someone shouted for us to dive under the tables, and as I jumped down my jam tart fell. I picked it up and put it into my mouth-and I've never been able to eat jam tarts since. I saw my brother running past the table and I called his name. As he turned the bomb fell and I was buried. I couldn't breath or move, and I remember trying to call for help. I remember the relief of the bricks being lifted from my face.

The next thing I knew, I was lying on the cold hard pavement outside, and someone was saying, "She hasn't got long'. I didn't know what that meant.

My jaw was fractured and there was wood protruding from my head and my back. I was transferred to Queen Mary's Hospital in Sidcup, and I remember seeing my father by my bed, dressed in black. I asked for John, and was told my brother had gone to live in the countryside.

I remained in hospital for nearly two years, and I still didn't realise that John was dead. When I returned home, everything he had owned was gone. It was as if he had never existed.

I convinced myself that the German had picked John up in the plane and had taken him to Germany. I imagined he would walk back through the door, smiling one day.

It was only when I heard two women talking, saying, "It was her brother who was killed", that I learnt the truth. His body was found three days after the bombing.

For years afterwards, if I was naughty my mother would say, 'The wrong one lived". She never forgave me, and the night before my own son's christening, she took the baby from my arms and said, "You don't deserve a son because you killed mine".

I have two children and three grandchildren, but I have missed John every day of my life. The image of him turning to look at me that one last time is frozen in my mind forever. I visit his graveside at 12.30pm on January 20th every single year.

Brenda Ward (née Parker)

I was ten years old, and was eating my dinner in the dining room at the school when I heard a loud noise. I went to the window and saw the plane. Then one of the teachers screamed at us to get under the tables.

I peeped out from under the table and saw the walls starting to fall in. I got up and ran as fast as I could to the other end of the room. Suddenly I was buried and I could just see a tiny spot of light. That terror has stayed with me all my life, and I still can't go underground.

Two men dug me out, and carried me across the road to someone's front room. I lay on the floor and asked the woman to clear my eyes, because I couldn't see. I asked, "Why do Germans bomb children?" The poor woman burst into tears and said, "I don't know dear".

My blouse and blond hair were stained red with blood from the terrible injuries to my face. When I was taken to hospital, my own mother walked past three times without recognising me.

A week later, I was transferred to East Grinstead hospital where the plastic surgeon, Archibald McIndoe, who did pioneering work on pilots from the Battle of Britain, helped repair my face.

No one allowed me a mirror, but one day I polished a spoon with my sheet and saw my reflection. I was so shocked at the damage to my eye and my nose that I fell into a brief depression.

I am still having operations to repair the damage done to my face and leg. But the memories of those who dug us out of the rubble, my friends at the hospital and my incredible mother who just kept going through it all, remain with me as much as any evil.

Joyce Kruger (née Parker)

I am Brenda's sister. Who as you know suffered very badly from the bombing. I was nearly fourteen at the time and was due to go to see a performance of "A Midsummers Night Dream" in the afternoon. I never got to see it, and until this day I have never seen it performed. I was lucky in so far as that I survived without getting any physical injuries, unlike my poor sister. My father was an Air Raid warden based at St Swithins Churchyard in Hither Green Lane, he was on duty when he heard of the bombing of the school so immediately made his way to the school. He didn't stop digging into the rubble until after midnight the same day, also checking when possible children coming out of the debris for my sister and myself.

Audrey Cutts (née Bull)

My recollections are of standing in the school corridor along with other children, behind a pair of large double doors. We were waiting to go into the school dining hall for lunch. Our reason for queuing up was that lunch was held in two sittings and we were part of the second session waiting to go in. After the bomb dropped there was a lot of confusion and I remember climbing out of an open window. After which I ran home. (A distance of about half a mile). As my mother was at work at the time I went to the home of my Aunt who lived in the same street. She recalls my arrival on her doorstep covered from head to toe in dust from the debris of the bomb blast. I seem to have recollections that the barrage balloon which was sited in the school grounds was not up at the time.

I was later sent to Himley Hall, and remember sleeping in a room like a dormitory. Being visited by the Princess Royal, who was shown around by the Earl of Dudley and your mother Sister Neave. I remember looking down from the Hall at the panorama of the vale and seeing a steam locomotive wending its way across the countryside like a miniature train. I remember going for walks in the grounds and seeing wild daffodils in abundance. We were always well fed, better than back home, and the staff were always very kind and supportive.

On returning to London I found that the bombing experience had made me frightened of sleeping in a room on my own, and also much more nervous during subsequent air raids, one of which demolished our house during one of our short breaks away in the country.

Kathleen Anderson-Wigley (née Roberts)

It had been arranged for our class, central 6, to go to see a performance of "A Midsummer Night's Dream" at 2.00 p.m. on Monday, January 20th. We were to have second lunch that day in order to be ready to leave for the show. A group of us girls were in the playground awaiting our turn to go in to lunch when we heard a distant air raid warning. We decided to go into the school to see what we should do, passed through the dining hall and told the teacher on duty that we had heard a warning and she said to continue as usual. We left the dinning hall and made our way up the staircase to the top floor where our classroom was located and went via the assembly room where one of our teachers, Miss Hawswell, was cutting out a dress for a needlework class. Miss Hawswell wanted to know what we were doing in school when we should be outside awaiting lunch and we told her that we had heard an air raid warning and she said to make our way downstairs, which we did, using the staircase on the other side of the hall. When we reached the ground floor we again made our way through the dining hall to the other side of the building and had just got through the doors when we heard the most hideous sound of grinding, whistling and whooshing and about six of us were blown through the door of a bomb proof classroom that was located next to the dining hall and then there was a colossal explosion and it seemed that the whole world had collapsed on top of us. We were all screaming by that time, picking ourselves up from the walls and floor against which we had been thrown and the air was thick with dust, smoke and debris that we were all choking and coughing – we could smell fire by then and started to scream for help and tried to clamber out from the masonry and bricks that were piled up against the classroom walls. Eventually we got through and there were bodies of children laying in distorted positions and covered in blood – the school was cut in half by the bomb and we scrambled into the playground. We were just crossing the playground as the plane returned and started to dive and machine gun us as we made our way from the rubble. Our screams and the screeching of the plane and the whirr of the bullets is a sound that we have never forgotten. We saw one of the older girls, an Edith Wilson, sitting in the playground with her legs and arms outstretched and she seemed to be bleeding from every part of her body. (Edith eventually became our Head Girl in 1944 when we were relocated in Holbeach Road School). By this time there were dozens of A.R.P. wardens, Civil Defence and other people helping to get the bodies from the debris and we were ushered into one of the houses on the other side of the street – the front of the house had been blown out but the lady was offering us glasses of water but as soon as we put it to our lips it turned the dust and smoke in our mouths into mud which made us wretch; we were all sobbing and crying.

Eventually we were taken around the corner to an air raid shelter in Torrindon Road and then on to St. Andrews Hall where the wardens comforted us and tried to make us less scared.

After some time had passed the "All Clear" siren was sounded and they told us to make our way home and report back to the school grounds the next day.

We made our way to the bus stop on Brownhill Road and I eventually arrived home and my mother nearly collapsed when she saw me – she had been in the garden when the air plane passed over and she said it was so low she could see the pilot adjusting his goggles – and knew by the direction it was flying that it was going towards Catford.

My sister arrived home almost simultaneously with me – she was relieved to see me because she had heard people saying on the bus that Catford Central had received a direct hit and she was petrified to tell my mother when she reached home.

We heard later that day that they were still digging in the debris for bodies and eventually the death toll was 48 children and 3 teachers killed. Our head girl, Betty Barley, was one of the girls killed and so was Kathleen Brazier and Winnie Cornell who were in our class. Brenda, the little sister of a friend Joyce Parker, was one of the younger children who were having an early lunch and was in the dining hall when the bomb dropped. She was severely burned and spent weeks in hospital at St. Mary Cray where she had plastic surgery. Another friend Mavis Russell was also injured badly and spent a long time in hospital. I went with her mother to see her a few weeks after the bombing and her face was still in a terrible mess when I saw her.

Luckily for us, we group of girls that were outside the dinner hall when the bomb started coming down and were blown into the bomb proof shelter, managed to get out of the bombing with just minor injuries to our bodies and limbs, but I do believe that most of us had problems with our ears afterwards as a result of the blast from the bomb.

For a few days we reported to the school and on the first day I was greeted at the bus stop by some girls who grabbed hold of me and said that they had heard that I had been killed but they had mixed me up with Kathleen Brazier who was in our class. In what had been our playground the A.R.P. had started putting clothes, books and other belongings from the school and we were told to look and see if anything belonging to any of us was amongst them. I personally found all my outdoor clothes, coat, scarf, hat and school satchel. The following Monday, January 25th we girls went to St. Andrews Hall and were told our school would be housed in Holbeach Road School and we were to report there the next day.

Although we were doing these mundane things it was a very traumatic time for us girls, we were petrified every time we heard an air raid warning and were on the ready to run anywhere just so we could hide away and if we heard the sound of airplanes we were paralyzed with fear.

We were told at school that the children who were in the school when it was bombed and were able would be going away for three weeks and on Friday, February 19th a group of us including Barbara Robinson, Mavis Russell, Betty Gray, Megan Davis and myself met at the Citizen's Advise Bureau along with another group of children and left for Worcestershire. By the time we had arrived at Paddington Station we had been photographed more than twenty times. We arrived at Himley Hall, Dudley in Worcestershire at 5.30 in the late afternoon to be greeted by the Matron who was dressed completely in white which seemed to match her very pallid complexion and we girls were more than a little intimidated. The Matron then took us to Sister Neave who greeted us with a big smile and cheerfully showed us the different rooms we would be using as well as the dormitories where we would be sleeping. After that she took us back to the dining hall where she along with the Matron and nurses served us our dinner which to us was huge. After we had finished eating we were instructed to go quietly to our dormitories. So, like every day it was to be early to bed with no fuss or excitement. We were quite excited at seeing how big the Himley Hall Estate was until we realized that we were considered to be invalids and were to be treated as such. We were informed that we would have to attend school in the nearby village which didn't go down well with us all. We went to see the Commandant and explained to her that we didn't think that we should go to school because we had been told we were going on a holiday, however this didn't make any difference, we still had to go to school.

The following Friday another group of children arrived amongst them June Jarret, who had lost her little brother Rodney in the school, Kathleen Emerson, Iris Green and Corrine Fisset. We were all in the same dormitory, that is, twelve of us girls, six beds each side of the room quite close to each other which was comforting because we could stretch out our arms and hold hands during the night if we were scared which was quite often the case because we could hear airplanes all the time.

One-night June Jarret had us scared to death, she woke us in the middle of the night crying out loud and said that her little brother Rodney was sitting on the bottom of her bed, we were all really scared and not many of us had much more sleep that night.

We were still endeavouring to get out of going to school and one morning we all complained of being sick and Matron made us go back to bed. The doctor was called and after examining us we were put on a diet of Bovril and a dose of caster oil so I guess he didn't believe too much that we were sick.

Eventually some people from the Citizens Advice Bureau came to Himley Hall to see how we were faring and informed the matron and doctor that we should not be sent to school so we eventually got our way.

The Lord Mayor of Birmingham (Councillor W.S. Lewis) and the Mayor and Mayoress of Dudley (Alderman and Mrs H.C. Whitehouse) came to visit us on Sunday, March 7th and again more photographs were taken.

We were still being continually photographed by journalists from the local and national newspapers and even from abroad and commandant had a word with us one morning to tell us that although we might think we were important because of being photographed so much we were not to let it go to our heads!

It was arranged for all the children to go to see the pantomime "Little Miss Muffet" in Birmingham on Tuesday, March 9th and afterwards we had tea with the Mayor. Again, more photographs were taken.

The next day Lady Patricia, the sister of the Earl of Dudley along with Sister Neave, took us for a walk in the grounds and it was suggested that we put on a concert as Lady Patricia would like to attend. We were quite excited about this and rehearsed all the next day with the help of Sister

Neave and the nurses to put on the show. I can remember that a group of us sang "There were ten in the bed and the little one said, roll over, roll over" it was quite hilarious because we all wore ill matched pyjamas and had our hair in curlers.

On the morning of Friday, March 12th Lady Dudley took us for a walk to collect some daffodils prior to our returning home to London in the afternoon. We left at 2:00 in great jubilation very excited to be going home to our parents.

Overall, we enjoyed our time at Himley Hall, and were very grateful to Lord and Lady Dudley and the Red Cross Staff who helped us to try and put away in our minds what we had experienced on that horrendous day when our school had been bombed, and we had witnessed our friends being either killed or severely injured.

Mavis Hall (née Russell)

I was aged twelve and a half on the day of the bombing, and was in the school playground with my friends Betty, Barbara, Katy, Megan and others. We were waiting to go in for our lunch, when suddenly we heard a distant siren go off, so we rushed into the school and into the dining room and asked one of the teachers what we should do. She told us to carry on and ignore it. So, we went upstairs to the top floor and spoke to another teacher who wanted to know why we were in school when we should be outside in the playground. We told her we had come in because we had heard a distant siren. She told us to go back down and wait in the playground for our lunch. So, we went back down and went through the dining hall and having gone through we suddenly heard a horrendous noise followed by an explosion, we were all blown through a bomb classroom shelter door. I was knocked unconscious and buried under rubble. I was buried for quite some time. When I came around I was in Lewisham Hospital. My Mother and Father like other parents had spent hours searching through the rubble at the school trying to find missing and buried children. When my parents heard that I had been found and was in Lewisham Hospital, they immediately came to find me, only they walked past me as they didn't recognise me. I called out to them, and they were beside themselves with shock at seeing that my face was bandaged up. Later I was moved to Orpington Hospital where I spent several weeks. I was not allowed to have a mirror to look at my face, because the nurses and doctors didn't want me to see the extent of the damage.

When I came out of hospital I and my friends were sent to Himley Hall, to convalesce. That's where I met your Mother. (I have her autograph which she kindly put into my autograph book). She and all the staff were so very kind to us, and did all they could to take our minds off what we had been through.

Himley Hall, was a most beautiful stately home, and as it was spring time the grounds were full of Daffodils, primroses and bluebells. I shall never forget it as long as I live.

I remember seeing Countess Dudley and her daughter Sarah Long, riding out in the grounds, dressed in their smart riding clothes.

I have always wanted to go back to visit, but have been kept busy over the years looking after my husband and son, and my health has not been good. I have had to have lots of operations on my face.

However, I mustn't complain, I am one of the lucky ones who survived that unforgettable day back in 1943, and have had a life, not like those poor children who were so tragically killed, and never had the chance to have a family and live a life.

Betty Etches (née Gray)

I was one of the lucky ones to have survived the bombing of the school, and remember going to Himley Hall, with my friends Barbara, Katy, Mavis, and Megan.

By an unfortunate stroke of fate my father died at 8.30 am on the 20TH January 1943. The day the school was bombed.

Imagine how I felt that day, first losing my father then losing some of my friends, and seeing others suffer terribly.

However, when I got to Himley Hall I distinctly remember the Sister who was responsible for looking after us. (Sister Neave) Your mother. I used to talk to her about my trauma and she helped me a great deal. She took us all for walks (crocodile fashion) to the right of the building up a slope under trees where hundreds of wild daffodils grew – it was balm to my mind and heart.

I remember having to go to the local school which I enjoyed apart from hockey lessons when the local girls used to thunder down the pitch, farmers daughters I imagine, with big red rosy cheeks and sturdy bodies and full of confidence, against us puny Londoners who had never played hockey before!

The whole experience on 20th January 1943 has shaped my life, I feel passionately for the children of wars, having suffered from panic attacks ever since and knowing that although I escaped with my life and a few scratches, the mental scars are forever.

(From the Left) Betty Gray, Barbara Robinson, Kathleen Roberts, Mavis Russel, Megan Davies. At the front is Keith Mills.

June Pack (née Jarrett)

On the 20th January 1943, around lunch time, my class had just finished PE and we were getting the sewing machines out ready for needlework in the afternoon.

The infants school had their lunch first and the central school for girls, as we were then known, had their lunch after the little ones. (I should mention that the infants school being in the same building was only a temporary arrangement; as their school had previously been bombed so they were housed in the lower part of the central school).

I was upstairs in the hall near the window and saw a German plane fly so low past the window that I saw the crosses on its wings. I called to our teacher and said "Miss that was a German aeroplane". As I spoke there was a most terrifying noise of machine – gun fire. With that I felt a sting at the top of my leg, but I took no notice as we started towards the stairs as the teacher called us to run. We got about half way down when everything seemed to just fall and we went with it. The school had been bombed and the building was collapsing. I was lucky – I was saved by a beam above my head. I crawled out and my first thoughts were for my brother in the infant's school. I was very shocked and dazed but at that time I did not realise this - I was more intent on looking for my brother.

I spent ages looking for him, asking adults to help me. They were pulling the children out from the rubble, laying them in the playground and covering them with whatever was at hand, sheets etc.

Pulling the children out from the rubble

People from houses opposite and ARP Wardens all arrived and were helping. It was terrible. I lifted up the sheets looking for my brother and was horrified by what I was seeing. I suddenly went very, very cold and realised that all I was wearing were my gym knickers and a blouse.

With that I went to a public call box, reversed the charges, and telephoned my mother. All I said to her was "Mum, the school has been bombed and I cannot find Rodney".

At this stage I only remember my mother coming down in a terrible state, also trying to look for Rodney, but without success, so she took me home and then to the doctor's. I had been hit in the leg with a bullet, which had ricochet off something. Fortunately, it did not do any damage, but it was a bad flesh wound. It was dressed and I was ok and all I have to remember is a nasty scar.

My parents eventually had to identify my brother. He had been blown into the fire by the blast and was burnt (in those days we had fires in the classrooms and, in this case, in the dining room where he was found). The dreadful outcome of this air – raid was that 38 children and 6 teachers were killed.

All I can remember of the funeral were the hundreds of people lining the streets and the small white coffins being carried to Hither Green Cemetery and the terrible crying of the victims' parents and relations. It really was an awful day, one that I do not wish to remember.

To help us recover we were sent to the Earl of Dudley's home at Himley Hall in Dudley, Worcestershire, were we spent three weeks and met the late Duke of Kent and Sir Malcolm Sergeant of the London Philharmonic Orchestra, although he was not a "Sir" then. He played the piano to us, which was beautiful and which I can still remember.

There were several other celebrities, who came to visit us including George Formby, Gracie Fields and Frances Day.

We met our host, Earl of Dudley and Countess Laura (Lady Lang). I have lasting memories of the house with the fine rooms and the enormous staircase which we had to climb up every night to get to bed. Also, the gardens with the thousands of daffodils on the estate which were in bloom when we were there.

I remember the Kindness of the Red Cross staff, especially your mother Sister Neave with whom I and others spent considerable time with talking through our experiences of the bombing of the school. Your mother was a good listener and very sympathetic towards all of us. She would take us for walks, read to us, and would keep us occupied and amused to try and help take our minds off what we had been through.

Brian Jarrett (Brother of June Pack, née Jarrett)

I, too, went to Himley Hall for recuperation, though I didn't attend Sandhurst Road School, like my sister and younger brother Rodney who as June explained was tragically killed in the bombing.

I guess I was included to give my parents a chance to come to terms with the tragedy.

My memories of Himley Hall are similar to June's. I was ten at the time and June was fourteen. I certainly remember what seemed like endless press photographs and, indeed, there is a picture of pupils sitting at dining tables with nurses standing behind them in which my sister and I appear. I remember the wonderful grounds and the daffodils in the woodlands in full bloom – these are never forgotten. I also recollect an organ standing at the top of one of the staircases which, to me, as a choirboy at that time, seemed a strange place to have one. Lastly, I remember receiving a Red Cross parcel from the United States containing several wonderful items – my lasting memory being of a green US airplane model/pencil sharpener.

There were further photographs taken in the grounds of Himley Hall and I clearly remember a photograph of myself and several other children running through the grounds; I am fairly sure that this photograph appeared on the front page of the *Daily Mirror*.

Robert Loader (extreme left) and Keith Mills (second left) along with some of the other children playing football in the grounds of Himley Hall.

Robert Loader

I am a friend of Keith Mills, we were at school together on the day that our school was bombed. Keith and I went to Himley Hall for convalescence and we were very well looked after by your mother and the nurses and staff. We were always being photographed as I remember, and there's a photo of Keith and myself along with others playing football in the grounds of Himley Hall.

Lydia Coxhead (née Blackmore)

"Auld Lang Syne" is a song often sung at the beginning of a new year - January- as it was then, in 1943. I was playing it on the piano in the recreation room of the part of Himley Hall, Dudley, Worcestershire, which had been generously loaned to the British Red Cross as a convalescent home by the Earl of Dudley. Having learned the song just a few months previously in time for Christmas and the new year was just begun, it seemed a fitting song for myself and those who were in the room. But suddenly, one girl walked quietly out of the room, tears running down her cheeks, and another told me – "Please don't play that anymore, her little brother who was killed used to sing that song......"

Now I rarely fail to hear or join in the singing of that song without I remember those words and the little boy, who was five years old and who had not long started at the school.

Remember, remember – yes, I remember how it happened. That day, January 20th, 1943, though now far away, will never be forgotten. To me, as a child of twelve, it was the most terrible day of my life. Yet I think I learnt a lot on that day about how brave and self-sacrificing people can be.

The bell at Sandhurst Road School, Catford, South East London, had just gone for home time. It was the dinner break, and as it was a cold wintry day, I had taken sandwiches which I was eagerly 'tucking into' around the classroom fire in the company of about half a dozen classmates. Suddenly, one of the girls said "Ssh! – isn't that the siren?" We didn't take any notice at first, as we thought she was joking, then there was silence. It was the siren after all – but a distant one. Our first thought was to go to the shelter, as we had been instructed to do. We went out of the room quite calmly, but not too slowly as we were told we were not to linger about after the siren had gone. I remembered that I had left my sandwiches in the classroom, so I told the others I would catch them up whilst I went back to get them. I soon caught them up on their way down to the shelter, munching at my sandwiches.

The shelter was a bricked-up classroom on the second floor of the building. We soon settled ourselves, thinking more of our tummies than any danger which might be at hand! Then – the whirr and screech of a diving aeroplane right above us. My friend, Edna, and myself clung together, our hearts thumping very rapidly. "It's alright," we tried to console ourselves. "It's only one of our fighters." Then two girls rushed into the shelter – "the plane," they said, "it's got black crosses on it!" We all looked at each other, the silence being shattered by a tremendous thud which shook everything and everyone in the shelter.

There was a split second's silence – the moment between life and death. It was all over. Our school, which I loved, and where I had attended since I was four years old, had been laid to ruin by one man, in one plane, by one evil bomb, during an evil World War.

One man, whose leader afterwards broadcast to the German people of his remarkable day's achievements. With pride in his voice, he said – "It was a most interesting raid- you might call it a special treat...." One Nazi – did he have children at home, who loved their school and their teachers and chums?

Now many years later, if he is still alive, perhaps he is enjoying the comfort of a home and family, as I am, as it should be. There is so much that is good in life, in peace. He perhaps knew no better. Perhaps Nazism made him that way. Perhaps he was to be pitied.

But those children who died knew no better – no better than to enjoy their fun in the playground, their lessons, the friendship of their schoolmates. Everything was natural to them except the awful news that came over the wireless and the things their Mums and Dads talked about – the houses down the road which were no more. The sweets which were rationed. The being wakened up in the middle of the night- "Come on love, wrap yourself up, we've all got to go down the shelter, the siren's gone. War is not a child's game, not in reality.

And so, to us in that shelter, it somehow was not real. We were transformed from neatly dressed school girls into ghastly frightening creatures, covered all over in dust which was choking us too and some of us bleeding from cuts, one girl was particularly very badly cut. Yet somehow, there was no panic – just bewilderment.

Choking, bleeding and with tears streaming down our faces, we made our way out of the shelter, over girders, plaster, bricks, wood, glass. Was this our school?

Then, through the debris we gasped as only a matter of a few yards away from where we had been in that classroom shelter, there was a huge smouldering gap, like a severed limb, where the bomb had dropped. Where below us, about ten minutes previously those that had the school dinners were assembled. Right on the target – oh God! – those cries and screams. There below us were the bodies of those children, some dead, some dying, some in terrible pain.

Stunned by the sight, we made our way down the remains of the steps to the ground floor. I shall never forget the bloody sights which were all around. One of the teachers was thrown back onto the stairs and holding her eye, her hand covered in blood from it. I tripped over a board and fell on some glass which cut my knees and hands, but I felt no pain. Then another teacher joined us downstairs, I remember how wonderfully calm and concerned she was. She was badly cut, but soothing us with comforting words. Then I cried. Sobbed. I realised what had happened. The teacher, who herself was now crying and bleeding, wiped my eyes with her blood-stained handkerchief. Then I was calm again. We started digging at the debris. I heard a soft whimper. Amidst the rubble in a corner was a friend, June, in a sitting position, one of her eyes hanging on her cheek. "June, June" I screamed, but all she did was whimper. Then I saw a little arm and hand. Heard the screams and cries. By now, one of my classmates who was with me in the shelter, was sobbing hysterically. "We must get out". I thought I must take her home, I must go home to Mummy, where's Betty, oh Betty, where are you? (Betty Barley was my brother's sweetheart at the same school, she was the school captain, a lovely sweet girl of 15½).

Somehow, we found our way out into the playground. There, we heard that before the bomb had been dropped, the pilot machine-gunned some children who were in it. I did not hear if they were killed. Now my thoughts were on getting home and telling Joe to find Betty. I do not know what my Mother felt when she saw me coming down the road, my dress splattered with blood and dust, which was also in my hair. She had only just heard that the school had been hit and was on her way. I remember she said "Oh my baby". And fainted. Then I was at home, in my favourite chair, alive, but where was Betty, June, June? Those bodies, those screams!

By the evening, it seemed that every available man in the locality was there, digging, some with their bare hands, as was my brother, frantically searching for loved ones, hearts and hands torn. Boys in the services home on leave, digging, searching, all through the night. The Red Cross, the women in the church hall just across the road making tea, tending those brought into the hut, even the vicar in his shirt sleeves had been there since the search had begun. All with one motive, even if it meant constant danger from falling rubble - to get those little mites out.

The next morning, my father and brothers, pale and worn had many heart rendering tales to tell. My brother Joe came home only for a brief spell – he had to find Betty.

She was found, as were many others – dead. She died whilst taking some smaller children down to one of the shelters. The staircase was demolished. The head mistress of the junior section of the school, our headmistress, was killed. Teachers were killed; one was never found.

A day or so afterwards I went back. I know my Mother didn't want me to, but I had to! I was joined by a couple of other girls, we hardly spoke, we were content to stand staring, thinking, watching the rescue work going on. Wondering why it had happened. What had we and our school done to deserve the death and destruction that was before us? Not long after we had been standing there, a kindly lady reporter came up to us and asked me to tell her all about it.

There were many newspaper stories about that fateful day, many of us had our pictures in the papers. I think a lot of other countries heard about it too. We had books and sweets and other gifts from commonwealth countries. We had three lovely weeks convalescence on that beautiful estate in Dudley, Where the Earl and countess of Dudley came to several times to see us. We all talked about the countess of Dudley. She was very beautiful and spoke so sweetly to us. We would meet her when she and her daughter were out riding. The fact that a countess a beautiful one at that, spoke to us, made a big impression on us all.

We went to tea in Birmingham Town Hall where we met the Mayor and Mayoress, and on to a pantomime, where we were treated as "guests of honour", - yes, it did a lot to make us forget for a while.

Sister Neave, nurses and staff at Himley Hall were all so helpful and cheerful. We enjoyed the lovely walks across the hills, picking bunches of wild daffodils. Good clean fresh air, away from war, being children once again, enjoying life as children should. Forgetting during the day, enjoying our convalescence from the recent shock, enjoying the fuss and attention, and above all, enjoying our meals at Himley Hall – those country walks certainly made us hungry!

We were alive to enjoy all this, but what of those who were dead, our friends, brothers, sisters? What of those in hospital, suffering, some of their little bodies badly maimed? During the night in our dormitory, we could hear someone crying, as I myself did. Then it would come back, the realisation of it all, and that we would not see those that we knew, again. The little boy, not long at the school, who loved to sing "Auld Lang Syne"!

In one of my newspaper cuttings, now yellowing with age, there is a short poem which was written for the Washington Star soon after the episode. I should like to quote the last few lines:-

That God shall help men set aright
The tragic world!.... revealing light
Streams from a school at Zion's portal.
Shining, tear-jewelled and immortal.

Mrs Shoebridge (née Mathews)

I was eleven years old at the time of the bombing of Sandhurst Road School. I shall never forget that day.

I shouldn't have gone to school that day, my Mother and sister were full of flue, and I at that age was capable of looking after them, which is what I wanted to do. I was a good cook and able to look after the house. However, my Mother said "No, you go off and do your thing, go to school". So, reluctantly I did so, worrying about leaving them at home.

Once I got to school I had to go right to the top class, near the science class. Later suddenly all hell broke loose there were children running to the windows which I remember were sash windows. Some of the children had opened the windows and were looking out. As I was walking down the steps to the bottom of the class, I could see over the children's heads and saw two aeroplanes, and in the nearest one I could see clearly the pilot who threw back the hood of the cockpit, the flaps of his flying helmet were blowing in the wind. I remember seeing that he had blond hair.

Suddenly the head girl Betty Barley appeared and grabbed my hand saying "Come on we have to go down stairs to the shelter. Which consisted of class rooms which had tall brick walls directly outside of the windows to take the blast from bombs that might land nearby. We got to the top of the stairs. The school was built with stairs, stairs, halls, halls and as we got to the level of the stairs by the class room I saw a split appear of the hall where one half took it and the other half didn't. There was an instance and I crashed down, blacking out totally. When I came around I could smell burning and there was dust everywhere. I could hear screaming, screaming, crying, panic, shouting, machines, engines running and more screams. I could not see anything my eyes were clogged up with dust and dirt, and I could not move as there was heavy pressure, everything seemed to be on top of me. I couldn't breathe properly, I was gasping for breath. I didn't know it at the time but I had a collapsed lung, plus broken ribs which had punctured my other lung. I struggled to clear some of the dirt from my eyes and when I managed to open them I saw a small round opening where daylight was coming through. As I lay there I thought I will be found soon, and this must be what it's like at the worlds end, but at least I'm alive.

Suddenly bricks started to come down through the opening above me, and I thought I have to do something because my little bit of air space would be gone and I would be filled in. So, I started to yell out "Help, help" and I heard a man's voice say "We will be with you in a minute son, boy". I thought I'm not a boy, I'm a girl. They started to move the bricks and rubble and I heard a man say "Don't throw the bricks, take them away, you will put them on top of people who you don't know". Of course, by throwing the bricks they were uncovering someone, but quite possibly covering up someone else. I went unconscious again, and when I came to again I found myself being carried on a stretcher.

Meanwhile my parents, my father came home and with my mother they went around to the church hall to look at the bodies laid out, none of which had names on. They just had to pull back the covers to see if it was there child lying there dead. When they saw that I wasn't there they went home and started to play cards to take their minds off what might have become of me. Then they decided to visit the different hospitals to look for me, and finally found me.

I lost a number of friends in the bombing including Doreen Thorn who was aged twelve. Betty Barley the head girl who had grabbed my hand was also killed.

Whilst in hospital the late Queen Mother came to visit and gave me a bunch of bananas.

I didn't go to Himley Hall, I was sent to a Nunnery to convalesce.

Conclusion

Having read of what happened that fateful day, and having been fortunate enough to have met and talked to some of those who were children at the time in the school who survived, as well as researching other survivor's stories, I now understand why my late mother didn't want to talk to me about it. It must have been a very upsetting experience for her, especially as she had been partly responsible for looking after a large number of the surviving children whilst they were at Himley Hall, and having talked to and listened to what they had been through.

There were a number of inquiries held after the bombing as to why the sirens weren't sounded in time to give warnings, but, alas, nothing was ever concluded.

The East Lewisham's MP, at that time, Sir Assherton Pownall, demanded the German pilot's head as a war criminal.

So, what happened to the bombers that came over? Again, there have been a number of accounts written as to what happened to them. Accounts written by people who claimed they shot down the pilot responsible for machine gunning children at the school and dropping the fatal bomb on the school.

The pilot responsible was not shot down on his return to France that day. JG26 lost three of their Focke-Wulfs, and four of the escorting fighters which were shot down by either Spitfires or coastal anti-aircraft batteries as they returned across the coast.

Heinz Schumann

So, who was the pilot responsible. He was Hauptmann Heinz Schumann, who was at the time aged 28, and had recently been appointed Staffelkapitan of 10(Jabo)/JG2 which took part in the raid. On his return to France he made a bold statement, broadcast on German radio on the 21st January 1943, a day after the bombing. He said:

"We have recently been harassing the English quite a lot on their southern coast. The low-level attack on London in daylight will probably remain for all of our airmen an experience which they will remember for a long time. We reached our objectives and dropped our bombs where they were to be dropped. The British flak was active but bad, and the Spitfires which were in the air took no notice of us. While flying away we saw barrage balloons slowly going up and used the moment to make a diving attack against them."

Interviewer: " I understand you also attacked industrial buildings with machine gun fire?"

"Quite right. We shot, in London, two gas reservoirs into flames and at a railway station an engine under fire. We also attacked some other things as well".

Major Krueller, second in command who took part in the raid said.

Our escorting fighters were soon engaged in combat. It was quite a jolly enterprise.

William Joyce, Lord Haw-Haw, the Englishman who continually broadcast lots of propaganda on German radio during the War, was heard to say on the radio at the time in answer to why German bombers attacked the school:

If you put military personnel and firefighting equipment in schools, you expect to get them bombed.

There was no military personnel or firefighting equipment in the school.

Heinz Schumann was awarded the Knight's Cross on March 18th 1943 for 18 war flights over the Soviet Union and against England. He was shot down and killed near to the city of Charleroi in Belgium seven months after bombing the school. His second-in-command Krueller was killed earlier.

Oberst Josef Priller, nicknamed (Pips) due to his short height, born 27/07/1915, was the Kommodore of JG26 that ordered the raid. He survived the war as one of Germanys top air aces, and was awarded Knight's Cross of the Iron Cross with Oak leaves and Swords. He went on to become the general manager of a brewery. He was one of several D-day combatants to advise on the making of the film "The Longest Day". He was also featured in the film. He died aged 46 in 1961.

After the bombing of the school there was much publicity as the story was printed in the English newspapers as well as foreign newspapers across the world. At the time there was furious reaction resulting in bitter hatred against the Germans. From as far away as Mexico people were convinced that the school had been deliberately bombed and, more than any other single incident to date – and more than any other throughout the war – it raised a wave of hatred and bitterness towards the enemy. Letters of sympathy and good wishes flooded into the borough from home and abroad.

In Mexico a group of school children having heard the story paid for a memorial tablet to be placed in the cemetery chapel.

The part of the school that was damaged was not rebuilt until 1950. Today there is a garden of remembrance in the playground and a stained-glass window of memorial inside the school.

The children who now attend the school will never forget what happened, as will the families and relatives of those who suffered.

Many believe that Hitler ordered the bombings in retaliation for us and our allies bombing German cities.

If Heinz Schumann had been married with children and not brainwashed into the Nazi philosophies would he have machined gunned children and bombed a school full of children? That we will never know.

In the times that we are now living in, with all the wars, terrorist attacks which continue to see hundreds of children and adult civilians killed at one time, it might not seem that the Sandhurst Road School bombing back in 1943 compares.

However, we should remember that if the school hadn't been bombed those children, the same as all those children who are continually killed by war and terrorism, would like us have had the opportunity to finish their education, get work and have families of their own. This is why all children should be educated to be aware that all acts of war and terrorism result in the killing of children. Killing is not the answer. Children across the world need to learn this, that it is better to live in peace and harmony, which requires understanding of other religions and ideologies and learn to accept and live with them by peaceful means. Those children who die are the adults of future generations.

My mother was aware that this was not a reality, and told me in my early youth.

"It's time you learnt, that for thousands of years there have been wars, and there will always be wars. Wars keep population numbers down, creates work for those not working, takes away people from their work to fight in one of the armed forces or caring fields, and creates vast profits for lots of industries. Civilians also suffer through rationing, and loss of loved ones. God knows, I have lived through two world wars this century, and seen the suffering they have caused".

Sadly, as my mother grew old she suffered with her health, and longed for the day when she would die. She had made her contribution to helping others throughout her life, and looked forward to a better and peaceful life in Heaven. Hopefully she has found that.

"We Will Remember Them".

Do Not Forget

by Victor

You, the dead
Maybe living some days ago;
Do not feel betrayed,
You haven't fought for nothing.

We're hanging on to the torch
You threw to us;
And we're holding on it tight,
Never going to let it fall.

We thank you a lot
For fighting without wanting to;
For dying to protect your country,
You will never be forgotten.

Part 3 – More Recent Times of Conflict

National Service Days

by Edward George Stannard

I was born in 1939 and as such I was one of the last group of young men to be 'called up' for National Service. I reported to Aldershot to begin my basic training and army life on 21st May, 1959. My trade in civilian life was that of a labourer, but in the army I became one of the most important servicemen, that of the Cook; an Army marches on its stomach and all that!

British Armed Forces vouchers

National Service was cut short as the government of the day decided to abolish this and so I only served one year and forty-five weeks. During this time I was given a posting to Cyprus but this was cancelled. I was

STATEMENT
OF
ACCOUNT
(For key to abbreviations see reverse)

PERIOD OF ACCOUNT
REGIMENTAL PAYMASTER

31.12.60 - 31.3.61
RPO WOLVERLEY No 02

96606

CTANNARD.E.G

23624423

Date and Nature of Casualty	Balance b/forward	Weekly Rate	Debit	Credit	Balance	Remark Entry No.
JAN 27		3. 6.10		13. 7.4 -		CR
DEC 30 JAN	13. 7.4 - 18.14.5 -		23.18.0	5. 7.1 - 4. 6.4 -	18.14.5 17.3	*
FEB 24		3. 6.10		13. 7.4 -		CR
JAN 27 FEB	13. 7.4 - 12.10.1 -		17.3 6.12.0		12.10.1 5.18.1	CR FP
MAR 31 FEB 24	16.14.2 -	3. 6.10		16.14.2 - 5.18.1 -	22.12.3	CR

£15.14.4 TRAFALGAR ROAD, GORLESTON

Form N 1559

STATEMENT
OF
ACCOUNT
(For key to abbreviations see reverse)

PERIOD OF ACCOUNT
REGIMENTAL PAYMASTER

RPO WOLVERLEY No 02
1-4-61-30-50-6-61

96606

CTANNARD.E.G

23624423

Date and Nature of Casualty	Balance b/forward	Weekly Rate	Debit	Credit	Balance	Remark Entry No.
PA APR 28		3. 6.10		13. 7.4 -		
MAR 31 APR	13. 7.4 - 35.19.7 -		20. 5.3	22.12.3 -	35.19.7 15.14.4	CR CR

Statements of Account

then given another posting, this time to Northern Ireland, but, that was also cancelled. The Army then sent me to The Queen Alexandras Royal Army Nursing Corps depot at Hinhead, Surrey, I was surrounded by women. Not bad you might think, but some of those women were worse than the male NCOs. I was still the cook and had to know my place.

When I worked in the Officers Mess, one of the Officers asked me to open the front doors. I had never done this before and hoped I was going the correct way as there were loads of doors. I walked through a passage to two wooden doors, I opened both only to find two more wooden doors, so I opened these and found two half glazed doors. Now there was a story in the camp about a ghost. As I opened the second pair of wooden doors, I saw this white figure in front of me. My heart must have stopped for a second or so until I realised it was the white marble bust of Queen Alexandra behind me which was showing in the glass doors. So much for the ghost!

Whilst in the army I passed trade qualification courses, amongst these were P.E. Test, Cook 'B' II and Cook 'B' III.

When I first joined the Army, my wage was £1.00 a week but this rose to £3.6s.10p; not mega bucks, but this was the army in those days.

I include a couple of my Statement of Accounts, illustrated overleaf, for my wages plus other documents from my time in the Army.

My eldest brother, Bill, was in the Army just before the Second World War ended and he had given me a British Armed Forces special voucher to the value of 3d (about 1¼p). It was quite a good deal of money in those days, but would buy nothing today.

Once I left the army, I was put on the Army General Reservist List. In the case of an Emergency which threatened our country, I and many others, would be called back to Service in the army. Thankfully nothing happened. We were all given an Army General Reservist's Instruction Book when we left National Service.

When I left the army I was given all sorts of papers, some of which are here in my story. These included information of what I was entitled to once I returned to civilian life. I was entitled to all services related to the National Health Service. I add various letters and papers that were sent to me after I had completed my National Service. Some are a bit faded so they have been re-typed. Amongst these letters is a notice that my name on the Army General Reservist List had now been cancelled.

Here are the Notes on the Army Emergency Reserve that I received.

1. General
You will shortly commence your 24 days Terminal Leave, and on completion of this you will be deemed to be enlisted into the

O.F. 3624

MR. E.G. STANNARD.

....

....

Dear Sir,

Subject: Questionnaire - Army Form D.427

I am directed to refer to the questionnaire (Notice to a Member of the Army General Reserve - Army Form D.427).

The object in requiring you to answer the questions in the form and in asking you to obtain the counter-signature of your employer (if any) to the main items is to enable the Government to decide whether you ought to be recalled to Army Service in a future national emergency, should such arise, or to remain in your civilian employment.

You will appreciate that, however remote a large scale national emergency may appear, it is essential that detailed plans should exist for such an eventuality and that these should be completed and up to date. So long as the information asked for in this questionnaire is withheld, these plans remain incomplete.

Will you therefore complete the enclosed A.F. D.427 at Part I and send it to this office at your very earliest convenience.

Yours faithfully,

Officer IC R.A.S.C. and A.C.C. Records.

/HM

PLEASE NOTE:-
1. Part ii of the form must be retained by you.
2. Ensure that employer signs certificate after paragraph 11.
3. Ensure that you sign certificate after paragraph 10.

These pages should be entirely free from erasure.

THIS IS TO CERTIFY THAT:—

Christian or
Fore Name(s) EDWARD GEORGE

Surname STANNARD.

Army No. 23644443 Rank Pte

was discharged from* AER

on 20-11-64 in consequence of

PARA. 118 (xviii)(b) AER. Regs.

TERMINATION OF PART TIME SERVICE

ARMY CATERING CORPS
Corps from which discharged

He also served during this engagement in (Corps)

THE PARTICULARS WHICH FOLLOW
REFER ONLY TO THE ENGAGEMENT
FROM WHICH HE/SHE IS NOW
BEING DISCHARGED

DEEMED TO
BE Enlisted { at
on 22-4-61 19

He/She has served:—
(a) In Army Service years
days

b) in* AER
THREE years TWO HUNDRED
and TWELVE days

* Here insert "Army Emergency Reserve," or "Territorial Army," as the case may be.

CHARACTER CERTIFICATE

(Only to be completed in cases of service with the Colours, i.e. mobilised or embodied service).

THE FOLLOWING TESTIMONIAL IS BASED ON
THE SOLDIER'S CONDUCT DURING SERVICE
WITH THE COLOURS.

Signature in person and Rank
for 1/c R.A.S.C. & ACC

* O.C./Officer i/c RECORDS
Date Place HASTINGS

Here insert H.Q.A.E.R. or T.A. Unit or Officer i/c Records as the case may be.

[P.T.O.

157

CERTIFICATE OF DISCHARGE (*To be retained by the soldier*)

Having completed whole-time service under the National Service Acts, 1948 to 1955, you are liable to further part-time service in the AER/TA unit to which you are posted until you have completed a total of five and a half years' service in all.

If this certificate is lost or mislaid no duplicate can be obtained.

Any unauthorized alterations of the particulars in this certificate m render the holder liable to prosecution under the Seamen's and Soldi False Characters Act, 1906.

ARMY NO. **23624423**   RANK **PRIVATE**

SURNAME (Block Capitals) **STANNARD**

CHRISTIAN OR FORE NAME(S) (Block Capitals) **EDWARD GEORGE**

UNIT, REGT. OR CORPS for which enlisted **ARMY CATERING CORPS**

from which discharged **ARMY CATERING CORPS**

Service began on **21.5.59** at **ALDERSHOT**

Effective date of discharge from whole-time service **30 MARCH 1961**

Total amount of full-time reckonable service **1 YEAR 45 WEEK**

Reason for discharge **COMPLETION OF NATIONAL SERVICE**

Description of Soldier on Completion of Whole-time Service

Date of birth **2.6.39**   Height **5** ft. **4** i

Complexion **FRESH**   Eyes **BLUE**   Hair **BROW**

Marks and Scars (visible) **R/SHIN. L/SIDE/NECK**

Trade Qualifications

CIVILIAN TRADE **LABOURER**

SERVICE TRADE **COOK**

FINAL EMPLOYMENT **COOK**

Courses and Tests passed **COOK 'B' III**

COOK 'B' II

P.E. TEST

Army Emergency Reserve of the Army Catering Corps. You have been/will be issued with various forms and Booklets etc., which will explain the responsibilities whilst in the AER and so, these notes must now be regarded as an authority for any particular course of action, but as enlarging and emphasising some of the more important points. They are also intended to provide you with a clear idea of your rights etc., during the transition period.

2. Pamphlets Issued on Release

You have been/will be issued with the following pamphlets for your information and guidance :-

(a) National Health pamphlet EC13, the last page of which must be filled in by you and handed to your Civilian Doctor during leave. This enrolls you into the National Health Service.

(b) National Insurance pamphlets (Leaflet NI.53) which explains the contributions and benefits received under the National Insurance scheme.

(c) Leaflet 'Re-instatement Civil Employer' REL2 (NS) detailing your rights re-instatement to civil employment.

(d) Leaflet REL (NS) 'Application for NSM return to his former employer'.

(e) Pamphlet handed 'For Your Guidance' which may answer some of your queries on return to civilian life.

(f) Booklet 'Your Service in the Army Emergency Reserve or Territorial Army'.

3. Rail Travel

During release leave you are entitled to concessional rates of Rail Travel on production of your Release Book at the Booking Office. Similarly, if you are married your wife will receive the same concessional rates of Rail Travel on production of her Allowance Book.

4. Medical and Dental Treatment

You are entitled to Medical and Dental Treatment during leave, from the nearest Military Hospital or Army Dental Centre.

5. National Insurance Cards

Your National Insurance Card will be sent to you direct by the Ministry of National Insurance before the end of your leave. If you take up employment during leave you will not have to pay National Insurance Contributions as these have already been paid for the period of leave. You and your employer will, however, be liable to pay Industrial Injury Contributions until final leave ends and you should hand your card to your employer for stamping.

6. Release Book AB111

Your Release Book cannot be replaced if lost. Keep it safe as it :
(a) proves you have completed your full-time National Service
(b) contains your testimonial
(c) is your authority to leave

7. Pay and Allowances

(a) Ration Allowance at the current rate is credited to your account for your 24 days leave. On receipt of the Part 11/111 Order striking you off strength for terminal leave; the Regiment will close your account and despatch many balance of pay credits direct to you at your home by the 15th day of your leave.

(b) Marriage Allowance is admissible during leave.

(c) Any allotment or deductions in respect of Army Savings will be made and adjusted up to the last day of your leave.

8. Clothing and Equipment

Under regulations at present in force all clothing and equipment (with the exception of certain items which you are allowed to keep or purchase) are withdrawn before you proceed on terminal leave.

Should you be recalled to the Active Army, to be called to attend training, or become a Volunteer, clothing and equipment will be issued under the arrangements then in force, which will be notified to you.

8a. BAOR Personnel Only

If released from a Unit stationed in BAOR you will be required to retain certain items of clothing etc., until your arrival in U.K. You will be given a Railway Carrier label and instructions as to how to use it, and you will return the item in question at the earliest opportunity to HQ AER/ACC, Tournai Barracks, Aldershot, Hants. This also applies to any Documents (ie AB64 Part 1, Identity Discs and AF B 2603/4) that you are required to retain for your journey home.

9. Rank On Enlistment into AER

Irrespective of any rank which you now hold, whether substantive or acting, and regardless of trade, you will revert to the rank of

Army Form O 1836 (Revised)

KEEP THIS FORM WITH YOUR MOBILIZATION INSTRUCTIONS

IF YOU ARE CALLED OUT TO ARMY SERVICE, LEAVE IT WITH YOUR WIFE TO USE AS DESCRIBED BELOW

To be completed by Record Office/ TA Unit before issue.

Army Number ....23624423.... Name ....*SANNARD. E 9*....

Regt./Corps .......**A.C.C.**.......

FOR USE BY SOLDIER'S WIFE

If you have not received a notice 7 days after your husband was called out to Army service, telling you to obtain your Allowance Order Book from the Post Office, fill in the following particulars: —

To be completed by the payee

PRESENT ADDRESS ....

ADDRESS OF NEAREST POST OFFICE ....

Then put this form in an envelope and post it to: —

THE REGIMENTAL PAYMASTER

To be completed by Record Office/ TA Unit

.......**A.C.C.** ARMY GENERAL RESERVE...........

.......*DROITWICH*...........

DO NOT SEND THIS FORM if you HAVE received the Notice

to collect your ALLOWANCE ORDER BOOK

(987) Dd.102470. 300M. 11/65. K.C.N. Gp.616/1.

ARMY GENERAL RESERVE **Army Form W 3045**

ARMY RESERVE ACT, 1950
~~ADDRESS~~/CHANGE OF ADDRESS OF A RESERVIST

To be filled in by the Officer issuing this form.	Number 23624423	Rank
	Name & Initials STANNARD . E . G	
	Reg./ Corps **ACC**	

NOTES

1. This form should be used by a ~~Regular~~ Reservist ~~or a volunteer in the Army Emergency Reserve~~ for notifying change of address to the Officer IC Records.
2. In the case of a man transferred to the Regular Reserve, this form should be completed within 14 days of transfer to the reserve.
3. A reservist who:—
   (a) fails to notify his address or change of address within 14 days of his transfer to the reserve or,
   (b) fails to notify any subsequent change of address within a period of 14 days
   is liable to be proceeded against for failing to comply with Regulations made under the Army Reserve Act, 1950.

Sir,*
My ~~address~~/new address is as follows:—

To be completed in BLOCK CAPITALS	

The home address of my next-of-kin is *as above/unchanged. Please provide a further copy of this form.

_____   _____
(Date)   (Signature of Reservist)

*Delete whichever is inapplicable.

4574 Wt. 122—D2441 50 M 8/61 L. (D) Ltd. Gp. 786

OF 384.1.

RCT & ACC Records
Ore Place
HASTINGS
Sussex

Reference:
3R/26.

HASTINGS 51351 Ext

MR. G. R. STANNARD

Date: 18   Nov. 65

....

....

<u>AF D7254 (NOTICE OF POSTING FOR MOBILIZATION)</u>

1.   AF D7254 dated 26/4/65   at present held by you is cancelled and
should be destroyed.

2.   Please <u>do not destroy</u> Reservist's Instruction Book (AD 571). This <u>must</u> be
kept in your possession.

3.   The question of your posting is held in abeyance for the time being.

LAS/HD

OIC RCT & ACC Records.

Army Form D 401
(Revised 1964)

NOTICE TO BE GIVEN TO A MAN COMPLETING SERVICE IN THE REGULAR, RESERVE, OR AUXILIARY FORCES WHO WILL BECOME A MAN OF THE ARMY RESERVE UNDER THE NAVY, ARMY AND AIR FORCE RESERVES ACTS, 1954 AND 1964

To:

No. 23624423 Rank P/C Surname STANNARD

Christian or Fore Name(s) EDWARD GEORGE Regt./ Corps ARMY CATERING CORPS

You are hereby notified that on completing your engagement of N/S

in the AER you will become a member of

the Army Reserve, Class I (Army General Reserve) by virtue of the provisions of the Navy, Army and Air Force Reserves Acts, 1954 and 1964, and that, unless previously discharged from that Reserve, you will remain a member of that Reserve until 30th June, 1969, or until you attain the age of forty-five years, whichever is the earlier.

You are hereby warned that as a man of the Army General Reserve you will be subject to the following liabilities:—

(1) To be called out on permanent service by proclamation of Her Majesty in Council under Section 5 of the Army Reserve Act, 1950, in case of imminent national danger or great emergency; when so called out you will be liable to serve in the United Kingdom or elsewhere.

(2) To be called out on permanent service by the direction of a Secretary of State under Section 6 (1) (a) of the Army Reserve Act, 1950, for service at any place in the United Kingdom in defence of the United Kingdom against actual or apprehended attack.

*(3) To notify to the authority stated within fourteen days of being required to do so by notice in writing sent to you by or on behalf of the Defence Council, your name and address and certain particulars relating to your occupation or qualifications which will be specified in the notice.

You will not be liable to be called out in aid of the civil power under Section 10 of the Army Reserve Act, 1950, nor for any form of training.

You will not be entitled to receive any pay during your service in the Army General Reserve unless you are called out on permanent service.

*You are requested to inform the Officer in charge of your Record Office of any change in your permanent address.

Official Stamp

R. A. S. C. RECORD OFFICE

ORE PLACE
HASTINGS

(70110) 1154/5843 180m 2/48 HTC 616

STANNARD E. G.

23624423

5910

Discharge from Whole-time and Entry upon Part-time
Military Service of a National Service Soldier

Designation of HQ, AER, or TA Unit to which the soldier is posted
for part-time service :—

HS AER ACC (II A POOL)

OUDENARDE BARRACKS

ALDERSHOT. HANTS.

Army Form N.1558 (40 Sets)

PAYMASTER'S ADJUSTMENT SLIP

NOTES FOR THE GUIDANCE OF COMMANDING OFFICERS ARE SHOWN ON THE REVERSE OF THIS FORM

NAME (BLOCK CAPITALS) STANNARD

ARMY No. 23624425   RANK PTE

UNIT

AUTHORITY R/96606

SERIAL No. **B165560**

WEEKLY RATE W.E.F.	PAY SCALE		Adjustments for period From 23.4 To 28.4							
			VOTE	DEBITS £ s. d.			CREDITS £ s. d.			
£ s. d.	GRADE									
	PAY			3	6					
	ADDL. PAY									
	MARRIAGE ALLCE.									
	RA						7	1	10	
	TOTAL TAXABLE CREDITS		—	—	—	—	—	—	—	
	CLOTHING ALLCE.				4	10				
	LOCAL O/S ALLCE.									
	O/S FAM. ALLCE.									
	C.O.L. ADDITION									
	A/Rolls			2	7	6				
	TOTAL CREDITS		—	—	—	—	—	—	—	
	INSURANCE							6	1	
	P.A.Y.E. (Code No.)									
	SAVINGS BANK (No.)									
	QUARTERING CHARGES									
	ISSUED BY PAYMASTER							—	6	—
	P 1954					10				
	TOTAL DEBITS	TOTALS	27	19	2		7	13	11	
	← NET WEEKLY RATE									

REASON FOR ADJUSTMENT: ....
.... Re'd duly ....

RECKONABLE MANS SERVICE DATE

NET ADJUSTMENT DEBITED £ s. d.	REMARK ENTRY NO.	NET ADJUSTMENT CREDITED £ s. d.
20 : 5 : 3	7	: :

FOR USE BY UNIT

PAYMASTER'S AUTHG. STAMP

The Net Weekly Rate of Pay shown above has been compared with the soldier's A.B.61 Part II and A.F.O. 1875, and any necessary adjustments have been made.

Date .... Initials..................

52-3118

Private with effect from the date of your enlistment into the AER. This is regrettable, but there are not enough vacancies to absorb all NCO's coming into the AER. Opportunities for promotion do however exist, dependant on previous rank hold, and capabilities etc., during training.

Any NSM who becomes a Volunteer during his first 12 months of part time service will almost invariably be granted his former rank. And again, dependent on his showing during Annual Training, promoted up to the rank of WO, subject to vacancies and qualifications etc.

10. Occupational Screening

Approximately 8 weeks after release from whole time service you will receive from HQ AER Army Form B 2764 which you are required to complete, sign, have your employer sign, and return to this Headquarter. This information is for record purposes by the Ministry of Labour and it is in your own interests, and in the interests of you employer, if you have one, that you should complete the form correctly and return it as soon as possible.

11. Organization of the AER/ACC

Except for certain OR's who are permanently attached to other arms, NSM allocated to the AER/ACC are posted to AER Pool 11a, Catering or General Duties Section. Unlike other AER's the ACC are not formed into Units, but as in the Regular Army provide the Catering Contingent for all Units. It, therefore, follows that during an Emergency, or Training, should it be reintroduced, all cooks would be attached to other AER etc. Units, and General Dutymen recalled to this Headquarters and then allocated to C.I.C.'s as required.

12. Part Time Liability

Under the National Service Act 1948, you have a liability for 3½ years Part Time Service including 60 days training. At present, training is not taking place but it may recommence at any time.

13. Issue Of Training Notices

Should training be re-introduced, and you are required to train, a Combined Training Notice and Rail Warrant, AF/E636A, together with detailed joining instructions will be issued as early as possible in each year, and in any case at least 50 days before your reporting date.

As much warning as possible is given so that you may inform your employer and make private arrangements.

14. Penalties under the National Service Act 1948 for Absence Without Leave

For failing to report for Training, unless covered by a Medical Certificate or Deferment Authority from this Headquarters, normal absentee action will be taken, ie authority obtained from Command HQ for your arrest by the Civil Police who will hand you over to HQ, AER Aldershot for trial. If found guilty, you may be dealt with similarly by Commander HQ AER or remanded for a Court Martial which may award you up to two years imprisonment.

15. Official Secrets Act

During your full time service you may have seen or handled secret stores etc. You have signed Declaration B and C regarding the Official Secrets Acts and have been warned from time to time during your service of the danger and penalties for disclosing secrets to unauthorised persons. You are still bound by the Official Secrets Acts during your Part-Time Service and are warned not to divulge or discuss secret military matters with unauthorised persons.

I am not sure if the Army still give young people leaving the Services this type of letter or if they are still subject to being put on the Reserve List in case of hostilities. If so, some things never change! I do not think I have divulged any secrets after all these years.

159th Medical Detachment (Helicopter Ambulance)

Colonel Douglas Moore

This is my recollection of some of the time I spent with the 159th Medical Detachment (Helicopter Ambulance), otherwise known by the call sign of Dust Off. It was a great assignment where I served with some of the best people I have ever met and the job they performed was extraordinary. As a result of their courageous efforts, thousands of badly wounded American and Vietnamese soldiers went on living or had limbs saved as did many local civilians. My only problem with this effort is that I have forgotten many of the names of men who were so important to me back then. I apologize for that and chalk it up to old age. Here are some of my recollections from 1968-69..

After my first tour in Vietnam with the 57th Medical Detachment (1964-65), I returned to the States to attend the officer's career course at Fort Sam Houston, Texas. Six months later, I was sent to Japan to help organize the 587th Medical Detachment that ferried almost 65,000 patients arriving at Tachikawa and Yokota Air Force Bases to five military hospitals that were scattered in a wide arc around the greater Tokyo area.

After two years in Japan, I was sent back to Vietnam. Since a friend managed officer assignments in Vietnam, I sent a letter asking to return to the 57th as its commander. Upon arriving at the Long Binh Replacement Depot, I managed to get a supply clerk to let me use his phone to call Tom to let him know I had arrived. He sent a jeep to pick me up, so I avoided the usual 3-4 day stay at the replacement depot.

The driver dropped me off at the 45th Medical Company that controlled all medical evacuation helicopters in the southern half of the country. I was met by the executive officer who told me to take a quick shower and put on a fresh uniform because the commander wanted to see me later that afternoon. An hour or so later, I walked to a Quonset hut that served as the officer's club and bumped into the 45th commander as he was coming out. He immediately reversed course and took me to the back of the club where there was a closed-off area used for meetings.

The commander was LTC Arlie Price who was known to have extremely high standards and demanded top performance from everyone who worked for him. Arlie was a medium-sized guy with thinning blonde hair and cold-steel, blue eyes. He also had a disconcerting habit of continuously twirling cigarettes between his thumb and forefinger. At regular intervals, he would take a deep draw and then blow smoke rings at whoever he was talking with.

I had met Arlie during an earlier assignment in Germany, but never worked for him. I knew he had a reputation for quickly relieving officers who didn't meet his standards, so I knew I had to be careful. After telling me to be seated, he starred at me from across the table for what seemed like several minutes before finally beginning to speak in his usual, quiet monotone, "I understand you want to go back to the 57th, but that's not possible because the commander there is relatively new."

After stopping to twirl his cigarette several more times, he continued, "You come here with a good reputation and I intend to test you to see whether it's deserved or not. I've got a unit, the 159th Medical Detachment, at Cu Chi that needs help. It failed its Command Maintenance Management Inspection (CMMI) and I sense some personality discord within the unit. I'm going to send you there and you'll have 60 days to bring it up to my standards or else I'll find someone who can."

He then invited me to eat dinner with him at the unit's mess hall, a short walk away. During dinner, he told me to take a couple of days off to get over jet lag and become acclimated to the heat of Southeast Asia. Rather than accepting his offer, I told him I'd prefer to go to Cu Chi early the next morning because I wanted to get to work. The underlying truth was that I wanted to get away from him as soon as possible. LTC Price told the executive officer to make that happen and an aircraft from the 159th picked me up shortly after breakfast the next morning.

The commander I replaced was a friend who had been in the 57th during my earlier tour and had brought the 159th over from Fort Riley, Kansas a year earlier. I was pleasantly surprised with the commissioned and warrant officers in the unit. Several were ending their tours and new replacements were arriving, but I found them all to be eager. The only thing I noted was that most had little military experience, so I asked LTC Price to send me a captain with a supply and maintenance background in order that we could begin attacking the inspection failure he mentioned. I wanted someone with that kind of background because I wanted to concentrate on assessing pilot skills and had already told the operations officer that I intended to fly a regular schedule like everyone else in the unit.

The detachment First Sergeant was SFC George Brevaldo who was also on his second tour and we hit it off well. He told me the enlisted men were all high caliber and that I didn't have to worry about them. Over the next few weeks, First Sergeant Brevaldo and I looked into every nook and cranny and saw some things we didn't like. For example, the supply room was overflowing with survival kits and a lot of other miscellaneous items we didn't need. I was told that, when the unit left Fort Riley, they could have asked for the moon and would likely have received it, so they brought a lot of excesses that needed to be disposed of properly. The same was true in our helicopter maintenance area where I found extra helicopter doors and rotor blades that were beginning to deteriorate. I knew the commander of the aircraft maintenance unit at Cu Chi and he gladly took our excesses. Our vehicle maintenance area was a disaster, so I could tell why the unit had failed its CMMI twice earlier.

A few weeks later, LTC Price sent me Captain Walt Berry who had served with the 1st Cavalry Division during his first tour. Walt was a hard-nosed, competent supply and maintenance officer, so he went to work immediately. A month or so later, we were inspected again by the CMMI team and passed. A few days after that inspection, Walt was flying first-up duty at Tay Ninh and was called to pick up several wounded Americans at an infantry firebase that had been mortared. It was a pitch-black night and, when Walt called the firebase, he was told things were quiet with no more mortars coming in. Walt began his landing approach and, when he was about a quarter-mile out, he switched on his landing light and saw a double column of soldiers walking along a dirt road leading to the front gate of the firebase.

At that point, Walt called the firebase and asked about the soldiers he saw. The radio operator screamed over the radio, "Dust Off, we don't have anyone outside the wire!" Walt pulled in all the power he could to begin climbing, but the North Vietnamese troops he was overflying knew they had been spotted and opened up with everything they had. The helicopter took several hits including one round that hit Walt In the left shoulder. His co-pilot took control and flew him to the 45th Surgical Hospital at Tay Ninh where they found a through and through wound of his left upper shoulder.

What Walt stumbled into was the lead element of a large North Vietnamese effort to begin launching major attacks across the entire Third Corps area. The hospital where Walt was taken began filling up, so he was flown further to the rear at Long Binh and when that hospital began filling up, he was taken to Vung Tau. Along the way, Walt kept calling to tell me he would be returning soon. Then, as other hospitals began filling with casualties, he was flown onto Japan. About three weeks later, I received a cryptic postcard that said, "I'm at Fort Bragg, please send me my clothes."

Walt spent the next year receiving treatment at the Fort Bragg hospital and at Walter Reed Army Medical Center. Unfortunately, he was killed in a tragic accident in the early 90s near Woodbridge, Virginia while on his way home from work. The traffic ahead of him slowed because of congestion and an eighteen-wheeler with faulty brakes rammed his car from the rear, killing Walt instantly.

While still getting oriented to things at Cu Chi, I became concerned about the sand bags that provided blast barriers half-way up the sides of the "Southeast Asia Huts" we slept in. Many of the sand bags had rotted away and no longer provided protection. I told First Sergeant Brevaldo that we needed to replace them around both the officers and enlisted men's huts, which were built end to end. We decided to make a contest out of it rather than make it just another work detail. Since there were only about 12 officers and 35 enlisted men in the unit, I told him the officers would begin working on ours and after we had our building partially done, we would challenge the enlisted men to see who could complete the work first and whoever lost would have to buy a jeep trailer full of beer.

I explained the issue to the officers and, to camouflage our intentions, we would go out just before dark and fill a few sandbags. A couple of days later, one of the inquisitive enlisted men asked what we were doing, so the challenge was sprung. Rather than being a make-work project that everyone would complain about, it suddenly became a manhood challenge as we raced towards completion.

Needless to say, the enlisted men beat us by a few hours and proudly claimed their success. First Sergeant Brevaldo then scrounged some hamburger meat from the mess hall and the officers chipped in to buy a jeep trailer filled with iced-down beer. We began eating and drinking late that afternoon and continued on for several hours before finally rolling into our rooms about 11 PM.

I had just undressed when I heard the first rocket roar over. I quickly grabbed my trousers and began crawling across the floor because other rockets began coming in. Just as I reached the door of my room, I heard what sounded like a locomotive going past and the explosion lit up the area like mid-day. I then dashed across a small open space and dived into the officer's bunker that was made by burying steel Conex containers in the ground and then covering them with several layers of sandbags.

Several more rockets exploded and then things became quiet. We had wire running between the officer's and enlisted men's bunkers, so I tried calling them on a hand-cranked telephone, but got no response. Then I heard people laughing and shouting outside, so I peeked out of our bunker and could see several of the enlisted men standing in front of their bunker. They were obviously drunker than skunks and oblivious to danger, so I shouted for them to get back into their bunker, but they yelled back, "Hey sir, you gotta come see this!" I yelled for them to get back into their bunker, but they kept laughing and pointing at something, so I grabbed a couple of the officers and went to see what was so funny. When I got close, one of the guys said, "Sir, you won't believe what happened to our shithouse!"

I walked to the opposite end of their hut where there was a burnt-out latrine located about 20-30 yards away. The rocket that lit up our area had penetrated the roof of the latrine and hit a series of pierced steel planks (PSP) that formed the flooring for a hand-washing station out front. The only thing left standing was the two-holer frame and two halves of steel oil drums used to catch human waste in order that it could be burned later.

At that point, I began a headcount and we couldn't find First Sergeant Brevaldo. After several minutes of concern, we saw him coming through the darkness towards us. It was obvious that he had more than his share of beer too, but he was clutching his arm and mumbling something. As he approached, one of the enlisted men said, "He's bleeding!"

Later, we learned that First Sergeant Brevaldo had been taking a crap when the rockets began coming in, so he quickly hitched up his trousers and started back to his room. As he rounded the corner of the supply room where he and the supply sergeant slept, the rocket hit the latrine and blew a jagged piece of wooden 2"X4" high into the air. It went flying over the supply building and struck First Sergeant Brevaldo as he hurried along the other side. A couple of the guys took him to the aid station where he was treated for a nasty cut on his upper arm. That's one way to earn a Purple Heart!

As I mentioned earlier, I was extremely impressed with the pilots in the 159th who, although being youngsters on their first combat tour, performed in an extraordinary fashion after being given freedom to make their own decisions as pilots-in-command. One of them was a tall, thin WO1 named Stephen B. Peth who joined the Army and volunteered for the Warrant Officer Flight Training Program. Steve became one of the most skilled pilots I've flown with and his courage knew no bounds. One of his escapades that make me so proud occurred in April of 1969 when he was sent to Tay Ninh for a normal two-day standby.

After a quiet morning on the first day, Steve was called to a Special Forces unit that was attacking up the north side of what the Vietnamese called Nui Ba Den or the "Black Virgin Mountain" located about twenty miles northeast of Tay Ninh. The enemy force was well entrenched on the slopes of the mountain and was firing downward into the Special Forces' positions at the base of the mountain. Steve began taking heavy fire as he approached the landing zone, but never wavered. After several trips to that site, he managed to evacuate forty wounded Vietnamese soldiers.

That evening, a firebase located a few miles southeast of Nui Ba Den and belonging to the 1st Cavalry Division was attacked. One of their own medical evacuation helicopters was hit by enemy fire and disabled, so Steve and his crew rushed to help. As he neared the firebase, he heard other aircraft report taking heavy .50 caliber fire at 3000 feet.

Upon his arrival, another 1st Cavalry unit located about 100 meters north of the firebase requested urgent evacuation of three critically wounded soldiers. Under heavy fire, Steve spiraled down into a hole in the jungle created by a recent B-52 strike and found elements of the unit hunkered down in a large bomb crater. Unable to land inside the crater itself, Steve had to hover over the hole with his landing light on in order to maintain stability and avoid striking trees surrounding the crater. While in this precarious position, seriously wounded soldiers were being lifted up to his aircraft while gunship pilots flying overhead were screaming over the radio for him to turn off his lights before he was blown out of the air. Steve disregarded the danger and maintained a steady hover until his aircraft was loaded. After dropping those patients at the 45th Surgical Hospital at Tay Ninh, he returned for evacuate more patients from inside the beleaguered firebase.

Because of heavy enemy action in the Tay Ninh area, Steve decided that he should volunteer to stay at Tay Ninh for another two-day rotation. His rationale was that he knew the location of all the units and believed he could best serve them by staying. He called me and I reluctantly agreed to leave him there for two more days.

His decision to stay turned into an around-the-clock whirlwind of flying. The village of Ben Soi located a few miles southwest of Tay Ninh came under heavy attack during this period and was nearly destroyed. Steve rallied to their aid and flew a number of evacuation missions while dodging heavy enemy machine gun fire and incoming mortar rounds.

On his third day of hard flying, he received information that a Vietnamese Airborne unit had suffered a number of casualties in an engagement just south of Ben Soi. This led to another series of missions, all flown under heavy fire. That night, he was called back to the 1st Cavalry Division's firebase after it was hit hard again and another of their medical evacuation helicopters was damaged by enemy fire and a crewman wounded during an evacuation attempt. That did not deter Steve and his crew as they watched streams of tracers coming up all around them as they successfully landed at the firebase and loaded the wounded.

After four days of almost continuous flying, a very weary pilot stumbled into my office at Cu Chi exclaiming, "Sir, would you believe 242 patients evacuated? That set a record for the most number of patients evacuated by a single crew during a four-day period.

Steve Peth was one of those guys we called a "magnet ass" because he seemed to attract bullets. One of my more memorable days flying with him took place on December 10-11, 1968 when the 2/12th Infantry Battalion of the 25th Infantry Division sent two infantry companies to search a heavily wooded area about five miles south of their firebase.

One company walked down a dirt road and the other walked through rice paddies about three-quarters of a mile to the east of the road because they wanted to check a small wooded area where a village once stood. About 2:00 in the afternoon, we received our first call saying the company to the east had a seriously wounded soldier.

Our standard practice was to switch one of our aircraft radios to the ground unit's frequency and listen to their conversations while flying to their location. We did that to help us get a clearer picture of what was happening on the ground and not because we didn't trust the ground commanders to give us accurate information. On the way, Steve and I heard one of the company commanders talking with his battalion commander who was at their firebase, a few miles away. The company commander said he was receiving moderate sniper fire, but thought he could suppress it long enough for us to evacuate the wounded. The battalion commander began giving him some cautionary things to do and concluded with, "Be careful. You don't want to get that Dust Off aircraft shot down in your area."

Shortly thereafter, I called the company commander and told him we were about 10 miles out and asked our usual two questions, "What is your situation and what do you recommend for an approach?" The company commander told us he was still receiving light to moderate fire from a tree line located about 100 meters to his east and that he couldn't secure a landing zone for us. I told him we would hold about 5-6 miles away until he was ready for us. We orbited for several minutes before the company commander called again. He said his medic was concerned the wounded man might die unless he was evacuated right away. He went on to tell us the wounded man had an open belly wound and the medic was having difficulty keeping the intestines intact. The company commander told me he would do his best to suppress the enemy fire if we were willing to pick him up, so I told him we would give it a try. By suppressing, the company commander meant they would open up with everything they had, hoping to keep the "bad guys" heads down while we evacuated the wounded.

As we neared the area, the company commander threw smoke and we could see they were located in a small wooded area between two open rice fields. Since they were receiving fire from a heavy tree line located about 100 meters to their east, we decided to come in low-level from the west. I could see the other infantry company hunkered down on a dirt road directly below us, so I let down over them and began flying at about 50 feet for about three-quarters of a mile across an open rice paddy. As we reached the wooded area where the wounded man was located, I popped up over the trees and began searching for the smoke. It quickly became obvious that we couldn't land where the smoke had been thrown because the clearing was much too small. We were conscious that we were in a bind because we were hovering above the trees and the "bad guys" were shooting at us from no more than 100 meters across another open rice field to our east.

I quickly turned our tail towards the "bad guys" and began searching for some place to land. The crew chief was seated on the left side of the aircraft and called over the intercom, "There's a clearing about 50 meters off to our left rear that we might be able to get into." I told the company commander we couldn't land where he had thrown the smoke and asked if the clearing to our left rear was secure. He said he had troops deployed in that area, so we hovered backwards to keep our tail pointed towards the enemy.

That clearing also turned out to be too small, but there was nowhere else for us to land. Using our hoist wasn't an option because the "bad guys" had a clear shot at us from a short distance away, so we had to get down into that clearing somehow and quick. There were large trees on three sides of the clearing and an old, dead snag in front of it. Since we had no other choice, I put the nose of our helicopter as close to the dead tree as I could and began backing up to try to insert the tail rotor between two large trees that were behind us. The crew chief and medic were lying on the floor telling me which way to move the tail rotor to avoid obstacles. It was a painfully slow process because I would back up a foot or two and let down a little as we tried to fit the helicopter into the clearing. I was concentrating on keeping the main rotor blades away from several large limbs sticking out from the dead tree in front of us because hitting something that hard would have meant disaster. Finally, I felt our right skid hit something solid, but knew we weren't on the ground yet. I looked down into the tall grass on my side and saw a stump and a log from a tree that had fallen years before. The right skid was sitting crossways on the log and the left skid was hanging out in space, about three feet off the ground. I asked the crew chief and medic whether we could move to either side or to the rear and both said we couldn't move without hitting the trees.

Since we couldn't move in any direction, I asked the crew chief whether someone standing on the ground could lift the patient high enough to get him into the aircraft. The crew chief said he thought we were close enough, so I said, "Well, this is as far as we're going." At that point, I looked out to the left and saw two soldiers crawling along the ground about 30-40 meters away and they were dragging the wounded man behind them. I looked out the right side and saw an infantryman almost directly below my door and he was firing his weapon on full automatic towards the rear.

Our situation was not good because we were about three feet off the ground in a very unstable hover with a battle going on all around us. The crew chief watched the slow progress of the men dragging the wounded man, so he asked, "Do you want me to go help them?" I said, "Go ahead," so the crew chief jumped from the aircraft with a litter under his arm and ran to the wounded man. When he got there, he asked the soldiers to help place the wounded man on the litter. Because of the courage he demonstrated, both of the infantry soldiers got to their feet in order to help him. I believe our crew chief's courage that day was the major reason why the rescue was successful.

As they were carrying the patient towards our helicopter, I heard the company commander scream over his radio to his weapons platoon leader, "Get those goddamned M-60s (machine guns) going. I've got a Dust Off on the ground and they're going to blow him away." The weapons platoon leader responded, "We're firing everything we have and we're about to burn the barrels off our weapons, but we can't suppress them." I could hear bullets flying past us, but there was nothing we could do except wait. When the crew chief finally reached the aircraft with the wounded man, he and the other two soldiers lifted the litter over their heads and slid him into the patient compartment.

Just then, my copilot spoke up and said, "Hey Sir, look in front of us." About 50 meters to our left front, I saw two enemy soldiers who had apparently climbed out of a tunnel and were aiming a rocket launcher at us. We saw it fire, but the warhead hit one of the limbs sticking out from the dead tree in front of us. There was a bright flash and smoke from the explosion, but the only damage we incurred was a few nicks in our windshield. After missing us, the two enemy soldiers began running across open rice paddies towards a tree line about 100 meters to their south. Two of the 2/12th's infantrymen saw them and began shooting at them. Their bullets kicked up dirt all around the fleeing men, but neither one was hit. Just before they reached the tree line, one of the enemy soldiers threw the rocket launcher down before disappearing into the trees. Not long ago, I was talking with the fellow who was flying as my co-pilot that day and both of us admitted we were pulling for the "bad guys." They had guts to do what they did and we wondered whether they survived the war or not.

Heavy automatic weapons fire was still coming from behind us, so I told the crew to hang on tight because I planned to lean it over as soon as we cleared the tops of the trees. After takeoff, I stayed as close to the trees as possible and then ducked down to cross the same rice paddy we had flown over when coming in. Despite thousands of rounds being fired during that episode, we didn't take a hit other than from the rocket propelled grenade fragments.

We delivered the wounded soldier to the 12th Evacuation Hospital at Cu Chi and went to lunch. Just as darkness closed in, we received another call from the same unit. By now, both companies had been joined into a single task force and the senior company commander, Captain (later Major General) Joe Rigby, was in command. They had moved another mile or so further south and were in an area of heavy jungle. As usual, we switched to their radio frequency and heard Captain Rigby talking with a gun ship pilot who reported automatic weapons fire coming from a bunker about 150 meters to the east of the American position. He said the size and number of the tracers made him believe it was a twin .51 caliber machine gun firing. He also said he and his wingman had been shooting rockets and machine guns at the bunker, but were not able to knock it out.

I then called Captain Rigby and told him we were about 10 miles out. He said he was still receiving fire at his location and had arranged for the gun ships to provide cover for us. At that point, one of the gun ship pilots called and told me to approach low level from the West and that he would pick us up before landing, but cautioned me not to fly past Captain Rigby's strobe light on the ground because that would put us directly over the enemy bunker. We began our approach and saw the gunships turning to fall in behind us. When we reached the strobe light, we landed immediately and, as our eyes grew accustomed to the darkness, we could see we had landed on one side of a large clearing. There were heavy woods to our front, right, and rear, but there was a clearing to our left that sloped downhill for about 200 meters before reaching jungle again. The "bad guys" began shooting at us from the bottom of that grade, but they apparently couldn't get a good silhouette in the darkness and their tracers passed harmlessly overhead.

As I recall, we loaded four wounded before telling the gunships we were ready to come out. As an aside, I can't say enough about the gunship pilots we worked with in Vietnam. They were super people and their courage knew no bounds. They did everything humanly possible to protect us and I've seen them put themselves into really dangerous positions to ensure our safety.

In this situation, the gunship team leader told me to hold on the ground until he gave me a signal to take-off. I watched as they flew a short distance to the west and then turned to come back towards the enemy bunker. They began shooting rockets and machine gun bullets at the bunker and, as they passed over us, the gunship leader told me, "Go!" As we started out, the gunships reversed their course to fall in behind us. A heavily loaded Huey like ours doesn't climb very fast, so the gunships adopted a standard practice of firing rockets and machine gun bullets underneath us on take-off to make the "bad guys" keep their heads down while we gained altitude. I can't describe how good it felt to watch them tearing up the countryside underneath us while we were trying to gain altitude.

Just before midnight, we received a third call, but this time it involved a group of several tanks and armored personnel carriers (APC) that were being sent to reinforce the 2/12th units. One of the tanks hit a mine about two miles short of their location while traveling on a narrow dirt road crossing a rice paddy. The explosion blew one of the tank's treads off and set it on fire.

When we switched to the mechanized unit's radio frequency, we heard the 2/12th Battalion Commander (Call sign: Barracuda) talking with the mechanized commander. The conversation went much like this: "This is Barracuda, where do you plan to land the Dust Off?" The mechanized unit commander responded, "We're going to put him on the road directly in front of the burning tank and we've got an armored personnel carrier further to the front to provide protection." Barracuda replied, "Negative. That's not a good idea because you've torn that road up pretty badly by now and he won't be able to land because of the dust. Why don't you put him in the paddies alongside the road?" The mechanized force commander responded, "We haven't swept that area and don't know what's out there, so we'd rather put him on the road." I still remember Barracuda's response, "Don't let that Dust Off get blown out of the sky, guys. You had better suppress with everything you've got while he's on the ground."

I called the commander of the mechanized unit and he told me essentially the same thing we had heard by listening in on his previous radio traffic. I asked about the burning tank and was told they had the fire under control, so it would present no danger if we landed close to it. He also told me there was sufficient space between the tank and the armored personnel carrier ahead of it. At that point, I asked the commander to hold his suppressive fire until he was sure we were on the ground because we might have to make a go-around if we had problems landing in the dust. The commander agreed, so we started in. We were about 150 yards out and concentrating on landing when the burning tank suddenly exploded. The explosion blew the turret and main gun tube assembly off the tank and it came spiraling through the air towards us. The whole assembly was enshrouded in flames, so I made a quick right turn to avoid being hit and began climbing. Several more rounds of heavy ammunition exploded inside the tank chassis and then the fire began dying down again.

Let me digress for a moment to tell you about the problems we faced during the dry season over there. The top layer of soil in Vietnam would turn into the consistency of talcum powder and, as a helicopter neared the ground, its rotor system would create an enormous dust cloud that completely enveloped the aircraft. Once inside the dust cloud, pilots could easily suffer what's called a "white-out" condition because you can't see anything outside the aircraft. As a consequence, landings had to be planned and executed very carefully or else disaster would occur.

The way I was taught to handle situations like that and subsequently taught my pilots was to approach into the wind, when possible, at about 60 knots of airspeed. As I neared the ground, I began surveying the landing site and everything around it to ensure I knew where all of the obstacles were located. Just before reaching the ground, I would slow to about 15 knots of forward airspeed. When the dust cloud began to envelop the aircraft, I stopped looking straight ahead and focused my vision down through the chin bubble beneath my feet. During this entire time, the copilot stayed on the gauges to make an instrument takeoff if things didn't go well.

If you were lucky, the swirling winds from the rotors would cause a clear spot of perhaps 18-20 inches in diameter to form directly below the chin bubble just before touchdown. If no clear spot formed, you faced two choices. The first was to climb out on instruments and the second was to continue descending until the helicopter's skids hit the ground. If you elected to do the latter, you had a microsecond to decide whether you had hit level enough to safely let the aircraft settle onto the ground. Hundreds of crewmen were killed in situations like I'm describing after pilots lost visual contact and either rolled over on touchdown or struck an obstacle while in the dust cloud.

I knew we would have significant problems with this particular landing because several tracked vehicles had passed over the area where we'd be landing. Contributing to our dilemma was the fact that we would have to land crossways on a narrow road that was elevated about six feet above the surrounding rice paddies. I knew we had to execute a good approach to avoid running into the embankment on the near side of the road or tumbling off the far side. In other words, we had to hit the road at exact dead center and doing it at night in a dust cloud made it even more difficult. I told Steve to get on the instruments and be prepared to take us out if I showed signs of losing control.

As I started in, I began looking for obstacles in the surrounding area and couldn't see anything except for the armored vehicles that would be on either side of us. I switched on the landing light and searchlight before the dust cloud began to envelop us and continued straight ahead. Unfortunately, I didn't get a clear spot under the chin bubble, so after what seemed like an eternity, I felt the skids hit and the aircraft rocked forward.

We hit fairly hard and, for a moment, I thought we had landed past the centerline of the road and were hanging off the far side. I decided to let the pitch lever down a little and we didn't rock forward any further, so I felt certain we were on the road. At that point, I let the pitch lever all the way down. When the dust cloud cleared enough for the mechanized unit commander to see that we were on the ground, he ordered every weapon to open up. For those of you who haven't been close-by when a tank begins firing, it is an awesome feeling. The tremendous blast of their main guns caused our helicopter to shake like a leaf in the wind and .50 caliber tracers filled the night sky all around us. As I recall, we picked up one wounded and one dead American and headed back to Cu Chi, hoping we were finished for the night.

At about 4:30 in the morning, my alert phone rang and it was the 2/12th again. As soon as we lifted off from Cu Chi, we knew we were in trouble because we could see flares filling the night sky in the distance and could see flashes of heavy artillery going in. We switched to the ground unit's frequency and began listening to a constant flow of talk. We quickly discovered the 2/12th task force was in dire straits because they were concerned about being enveloped by a larger enemy force and were receiving both mortar and heavy automatic weapons fire. We also learned an Air Force C-130 was dropping flares from high altitude and an Army helicopter was dropping flares from a lower altitude. Two helicopter gunships were providing some firepower and we could hear the battalion commander trying to coordinate everyone's efforts from his "Command and Control" helicopter flying over the battlefield. As we neared the battle site, we heard the gunship team lead report they were returning to Cu Chi to refuel and rearm.

I made our first call and told the battalion commander we were about 10 miles out. He gave me an update on the tactical situation and told me he had several wounded, but did not have an actual count. He also cautioned me that they were firing artillery from two different fire bases, one to the north and another to the south, so the rounds were impacting in a "V" shaped pattern on the east side of his troops' location. That meant we would be limited to approaching from the West and departing the same way.

I asked the battalion commander to stop the flares long enough for us to land under the cover of darkness, but he refused my request saying he was afraid his troops would be overrun if they "turned out the lights" or stopped the flares. By that time, I was a brash, young major on my second tour in Vietnam, so I told him it wouldn't do any good for me to get shot down while landing or taking-off, but I would try to work a deal with him. If he would shut down the flares while I was landing, I would turn on my rotating beacon for a few seconds after I was on the ground to signal that we were down. At that point, he could start the flares up again and I would call him when we were loaded and ready to come out.

The battalion commander finally agreed to my plan. In the meantime, I had been talking with pilots of the both aircraft dropping flares and they warned us to be careful because they had observed heavy firing in the landing zone. A minute or so later, the helicopter pilot reported his last flare was in the air and then the C-130 pilot told me their last one was in the air. When I saw both flares beginning to sputter and burn out, I turned off all of the lights on our helicopter and started in blacked-out. It was a pitch-black night and the only thing we could see on the ground was a single strobe light marking the landing site and flashes of artillery rounds exploding east of the landing zone. Just before reaching the strobe light, I turned on the searchlight and saw that we would be landing is a small clearing perhaps 100-150 meters across and I could see what appeared to be an old logging road that bisected the clearing from West to East.

I then saw the soldier holding the strobe light and he was lying in what appeared to be a shallow ditch alongside the road and was clutching the strobe to his chest. We saw wounded soldiers scattered on both sides of the road rather than being clumped together as we had hoped in order to ease the loading. I picked a spot about center of mass of where the wounded were located and began to land. We had been told the "bad guys" were shooting mostly from the east and southeast, so I kicked the tail of our helicopter around to point in that direction and landed next to the road.

To digress for a moment, I attended a promotion ceremony at the Pentagon several years later when Steve Peth, who was my copilot that night, was being promoted to Lieutenant Colonel. One of the attendees at the ceremony was a Major General by the name of Joe Rigby. While talking with him, we were shocked to find that he had been the task force commander on the ground that night. You can imagine how surprised we were and we spent a long time telling our different perspectives. He said he was lying in the ditch immediately behind the soldier holding the strobe light and said enemy fire was passing right over his head, but he felt obligated to thank us for coming in, so he stood up just as I kicked the tail of our helicopter around toward the "bad guys." He said my tail rotor came within inches of his face and he could still remember the buzzing sound it made as it went past his head.

After we were on the ground, I shut off the searchlight and turned on our rotating beacon for a couple of seconds. Then, flares began filling the sky above us and the landing zone was soon lit up like mid-day. At that point, we could see wounded scattered everywhere and that really slowed the loading. In the brilliant light of the flares, it didn't take long for the "bad guys" to get our range and bullets began striking the rear of our helicopter. After what seemed to be a lifetime, the medic told me they had one more wounded left to load, so I called the battalion commander and asked him to shut down the flares while we came out. This time, he refused my request saying the unit immediately behind us was under heavy attack.

Under most circumstances, we considered it to be a cardinal sin to take-off over the same route we used to come in, but we didn't have a other choice in this case. Artillery was falling behind us and the "bad guys" were shooting from our left, right, and back of us, so the only alternative was to take-off to the west over the same route we came in over. Unfortunately, the sky above us was filled with flares, so it would essentially be the same thing as a daylight take-off.

After making sure all of our crew was on board, I pulled pitch and we started out. Just before reaching heavy jungle on the opposite side of the clearing, we began transitioning from the light of the flares into semi-darkness. At that moment, sheets of tracers began coming up from the jungle below us and began striking the bottom of our helicopter. I saw a bright red flash as a tracer round came up by the left side of my seat. It hit the collective lever and nicked my left thumb before exiting through the top of the aircraft.

Several more bullets hit us and then I heard a blood-curdling scream right behind me. The medic told me one of the patients had been hit in the back. I started to press the intercom button to ask how he was doing when something hit me hard. My head snapped back and hit the back of my seat and that must have knocked me a little cuckoo. Later, we found an AK-47 round had come through the lower corner of the windshield where it fits into the frame and hit my flight helmet just above my nose. The bullet penetrated the outer shell of the helmet and followed its curvature around to the side before exiting behind my left ear and lodged in one of the cross-members supporting the roof of the aircraft. Later on, the maintenance guys dug the bullet out and mounted it on a plaque for me. When the bullet came through the windshield frame, it carried a bunch of metal and Plexiglass shards with it that went into my left eye, cut my nose, and chipped a little place on my left cheek.

That whole experience was the strangest thing. I remember seeing a bright flash right in front of my eyes and then it felt like someone hit me with a baseball bat, but I didn't know what happened. The impact caused me to throw the cyclic. Fortunately, we had a standing operating procedure that required both pilots to be on the controls during takeoffs or landings in tactical areas for that kind of eventuality and we were following it that night, but I threw the stick so hard until I threw it out of the Steve's hands.

I remember looking back down at the artificial horizon on the instrument panel in front of me and saw we were in a descending right turn at about 150 feet off the ground, so I grabbed the stick to level the aircraft and pulled in power to start climbing again. I then squeezed the mike button and told Steve I'd been hit. His response demonstrated the worth of all that hard training at Fort Rucker because he replied calmly, "Roger, Sir. I have the aircraft."

After telling him I'd been hit, I sensed movement behind me just before the crew chief threw his arm around my neck and pinned me against the back of my seat because he was concerned that I might fall into the controls. I knew he was reaching for the lever on the right side of my seat that is used to tip the seat backwards into the patient compartment, so I remember stepping on the floor mounted intercom button and yelling at him, "Turn me loose, I'm okay." He still had my head bent back, so I yelled once again, "Turn me loose" and he did.

By that time, I had recovered most of my senses, so I called the battalion commander and told him we had taken heavy fire about 200 meters to the west of where we had been on the ground and he acknowledged it by saying he had seen the tracers and planned to shift artillery into that area as soon as we were clear. While I was talking with him, a fire warning light began flashing on our console, so I called the battalion commander again and told him we had taken several hits while on the ground and during takeoff and that now we had a fire warning light. I then asked him to follow us in case we had to put it down before reaching Cu Chi. He said he couldn't do it because both of his units were under heavy attack, so we had to make it to Cu Chi on our own.

I still didn't know what was wrong with me. All I knew was that my left thumb hurt like heck and I knew I had been hit somewhere else, but wasn't sure where. A short time later, I began to feel a little pain above my left eye and along my nose and felt something running down my left cheek. For some reason, I closed my left eye and could still see the instrument panel clearly, but when I switched and closed my right eye, I discovered I could only see a dull glow of light with my left eye, so I surmised something serious had happened. In retrospect, I may have become a little woozy on the way back to Cu Chi, because Steve told me later I kept saying, "Watch out for those wires at the west end of the hospital helipad. Watch out for those wires." I don't remember saying anything like that, but I do remember Steve telling me, "Sir, I know where those damned wires are!"

When we got to the hospital, I took my helmet off, laid it on the center console, and sat there. When all eight of the casualties we picked up were unloaded, one of the crewmen and a hospital corpsman came around to my side and said, "Okay, let's get you out of there." I remember climbing out and walking to the receiving room. When we got there, it was packed with wounded and hospital staff, so the corpsman told me to have a seat along the wall.

I knew several of the staff in the 12th Evacuation Hospital and recognized some of those working in the receiving room. One of the nurses stopped by to check on me and said, "Hey, Major Moore, I didn't know that was you!" A doctor came by later and said, "You brought us some bad ones, so we're really busy right now, but we'll get to you in a little while."

Several minutes later, I was helped to an examination table and a perky nurse second lieutenant appeared down by my feet and said, "Hey, Major, these look like new boot laces you've got on. Are they new?" I remember wondering what kind of stupid question she was asking until I saw her whip out a pair of scissors from a carrier on her belt and then she began cutting my bootlaces. After pulling my boots and socks off, she said, "And these look like brand new fatigue trousers too" as she began to cut up my pants leg. As she got close to my crotch, I begged for her to be careful, but she laughed and kept on cutting. Very soon, I was lying buck-naked on the exam table and surrounded by people, many of whom I knew.

About that time, my executive officer, Captain George Hurtado, walked in and said, "Hey, Major, have you seen your helmet?" I answered, "No, what's wrong with it?" He continued, "Well, it's got a hole in the front and one in the back and, when I saw it, I thought the bullet had gone straight through your head." I didn't have the foggiest idea what he meant until I saw my helmet several days later.

A few moments later, the Chief Nurse, a sweetheart of a person named LTC Mary Francis McLean, came by and asked how I was doing. I told her I was okay and then asked for a sheet to cover up with. Mary Francis simply laughed at my request and said, "Doug, we've seen lots of helicopter pilots without any clothes on and all of you guys look exactly the same." She then turned on her heel and went to check the other guys who were more badly wounded than me.

A few minutes later, a physician came by and began poking me and prodding me over every inch of my body. From somewhere deep within the recesses of my mind, I remembered that was what he was supposed to do, to make sure no entry or exit holes were overlooked. Finally, he said, "Your thumb may need some stitches, but they can wait. The first thing I need to do is clean some of that crap out of your left eye so I can take a good look at it and then we'll get some x-rays."

He picked up a large container of liquid and said, "Now, this may sting a little bit." Whatever he poured into my eye burned like liquid fire, so I instinctively tried to reach a hand to my face, but couldn't do it because I discovered a pretty nurse captain was holding both of my hands in a firm grip. When the doctor finished, she leaned over and said very quietly, "Don't worry, Major Moore. You're going to be all right." For whatever reason, that was exactly the reassurance I needed at that moment. From that moment on, I knew I was in good hands and stopped worrying about whether I would lose vision in my left eye and have to stop flying. I never learned who that beautiful nurse was, but I will be forever indebted to her for her kindness that night. The nurses in Vietnam were solid gold in my estimation and never received the recognition they deserved.

After the x-rays were done, both my eyes were patched and I was flown by helicopter to the 24th Evacuation Hospital at Long Binh to be evaluated by a neurologist and ophthalmologist. There was some concern that I might have lost consciousness after being hit and, if I had, that would have meant an end to my flying days. The care I received at the 24th Evacuation Hospital was great too, but my stay there was one of the worst experiences of my life. After checking me over briefly in the receiving room, I was taken to a ward where I fell asleep. Sometime later, I remember being awakened by someone screaming in pain and another patient kept calling for his mother, over and over again. When someone came to check on me, I asked about the noise. The hospital corpsman told me I was in the neurosurgical ward and several of the patients were suffering from gunshot wounds to their heads. Listening to all of that agony had to be the worst three days of my life.

With patches on both my eyes, I didn't have a clue whether it was day or night and the time passed so slowly. Someone would stop by occasionally to check my vital signs and a doctor would stop by occasionally to look at my eye and to ask how I was doing. I believe it was three days later when two doctors removed the bandages and performed several neurological checks. They seemed satisfied with the results and one asked if I wanted to go to Japan for a month to recuperate.

I told them I had been in Japan prior to coming to Vietnam and wasn't interested in going because it would mean giving up my command and being assigned to a different unit when I returned. Instead, I told them I wanted to get back to my unit as soon as possible. Later that day, I was taken by ground ambulance to the nearby 93d Evacuation Hospital where an ophthalmologist removed several metal and Plexiglass fragments from my left eye.

That afternoon, I was moved from the neurosurgical ward to a medical ward and got my first good night's sleep. The following morning, I was discharged from the hospital and my boss picked me up. Since the flight surgeon had grounded me for at least two weeks, he wanted me to stay with him at Long Binh, but I declined his offer and called the 159th to come pick me up.

One of my more interesting experiences in Vietnam occurred shortly after the North Vietnamese bounced an AK- 47 round off my hard head. I returned to my unit on or about 16 December and, a couple of days later, LTC (Dr.) George Helzel, Commander of the 25th Medical Battalion, called me and said the Chief of Staff of the 25th Infantry Division wanted to see both of us right away. When I asked why, LTC Helzel said, "I don't know, but he wants to see us now!"

When we got to the Chief's office, he shooed everyone else out and told us to pull chairs close to his desk. When everyone else was gone, he turned to us and said, "What I'll be discussing with you is at the Secret or Top Secret level, so keep it close-hold. No one else knows anything about this except for the G-3 and the Division Commander."

After that unexpected warning, the Chief of Staff continued, "We have information concerning a very sensitive mission that may be coming our way and I need a pilot who knows the area around Tay Ninh like he knows the back of his hand." I responded, "Sir, you're looking at him. I flew in this area for a year during my previous tour and I've been here for nearly six months this time." The Chief looked at me and said, "But you just got out of the hospital, didn't you?" I said, "Yes, sir, but I can get back on flying status again in a heartbeat."

The Chief of Staff continued, "We understand the North Vietnamese plan to release some American Prisoners of War (POW) as a goodwill gesture on Christmas Day and we need a Dust Off to pick them up. Can you do it?" I said, "Yes Sir." He then said, "Okay, pick your best crew to go with you because I don't want any problems."

The Chief of Staff was one of those officers you didn't mess with, so I replied, "Okay, sir, I'll pick my best people." The Chief closed with, "Be at Tay Ninh tomorrow at 1:30 PM for a meeting at the Third Brigade headquarters. Now, get out of here!"

When we walked out, LTC Helzel turned to me and said, "I thought the flight surgeon grounded you for at least two weeks?" I replied, "I'm on my way to see him right now and, if I need any help, will you support me?" LTC Helzel looked at me and said, "Well, okay." I knew the flight surgeon fairly well and didn't believe he would give me any grief, but it didn't hurt to have another doctor in my corner as insurance.

I told the flight surgeon I needed an "Up Slip" because the Chief of Staff wanted me to fly a mission for him, so he asked me two questions, "Are you having any dizzy spells? Can you see all right?" I told him I was fine, so he said, "I'll put an "Up Slip" in your records." That's how easy it was to get back on flying status after being wounded and I never got the two weeks off that I had been promised.

I picked a W-1 warrant officer by the name of Jim Daily to be my copilot and the two of us selected the crew chief and medic we wanted to fly with us. The crew chief was Carmen Ciampa, but I cannot remember who the medic was. I gave them a brief outline of what I had been told and asked them to keep it close-hold. The next day, we were anxious to learn what the mission might entail, so we arrived at Tay Ninh about 30 minutes early. Jim and I went to the Third Brigade headquarters to ask where the briefing would be held and were directed to a nearby building, so we told the crew chief and medic to stay with the aircraft and headed for the meeting area. When we arrived, we were surprised to see several armed guards around the building.

There I was, a young major with a W-1 trailing me, and we walked into a room filled with high-ranking people. There were Army, Air Force, and Navy officers; people in civilian clothing (either State Department or CIA); and two brigadier generals already there. Jim and I took a seat in the back of the room and, after a short wait, the Chief of Staff and other VIPs entered. An Army major began the briefing by telling us a clandestine message had been received from the North Vietnamese indicating they planned to release several American POWs on Christmas Day. He said the release would occur at or across the Cambodian Border west of Tay Ninh and the purpose of the meeting was to discuss planning that had been underway for several days.

The briefing continued in excruciatingly hot weather and each phase of the plan was discussed in minute detail. For instance, an infantry battalion would be on standby at Tay Ninh airfield with enough helicopters to lift the entire unit at one time. All nearby artillery, including a long range, 175mm howitzer unit, would be prepared to fire on targets in and around the release site. The Air Force would have two squadrons of fighter/ bombers airborne to respond if the need arose. Finally, they told us a 20 mile radius "No Go" zone would be established around the release point into which no ground units or aircraft could penetrate other than the pick-up aircraft.

There was only minimal acknowledgement of our role, so the Chief of Staff finally stood up from his front row seat and came striding down the aisle. As he passed where Jim and I were sitting, he said loudly, "You guys know what to do, don't you?" I said, "Yes, Sir." So the Chief continued, "Well, come on then, you don't have to stay and listen to the rest of this crap!"

We walked out behind him, leaving everyone else staring at us and wondering who in the hell we were. When we got outside, the Chief of

Staff turned to me and said, "You guys ready?" And I said, "Yes, Sir, we're ready." He then said, "Okay, you'll be given detailed instructions when the time comes. All I want you to do now is make sure your aircraft is ready and you should study the possible pick-up sites on your map."

On Christmas Day, we returned to Tay Ninh. We were supposed to be there at 10:00 in the morning, but arrived about an hour early. After parking our aircraft in its revetment, several staff officers from the 25th Infantry Division came by to inspect it and found it to be in good order. A CIA or State Department representative stopped by and told us to keep our weapons slung on the backs of our seats unless we had to use them. He also told us not to take any cameras or recording devices and warned us against making any undue facial expressions or other gestures that might jeopardize the mission.

The POW release was scheduled to occur at noon, but nothing happened. We continued waiting until about 4:00 when a captain ran from the operations center and said, "Okay, guys, everyone go home. Remember the Christmas truce ends at midnight, so watch yourselves!"

I wasn't satisfied with his brief information, so I walked over to the operations center and asked what happened. Their response was, "We don't know. It just didn't happen." At that point I asked, "Well, what was supposed to happen?" Their answer was, "We don't know." We were completely puzzled by the day's events, so my crew and I climbed into our helicopter and returned to Cu Chi.

There was no more information about the POW release until shortly after noon on the 28th of December. I had just returned from flying another mission when our detachment clerk told me the Chief of Staff wanted to see me right away. I hurried to his office and the Chief told me, "Everything is on for New Year's Day. Be at Tay Ninh at 09:30."

On January 1, 1969, we returned to Tay Ninh and an Army lieutenant colonel was waiting when we got out of the aircraft. He asked us to gather around him before saying quietly, "We think it will be a "go" today. Just before you launch, you'll be given a set of map coordinates. Now, here are two code words for you to remember. The first is to be used to call in the Air Force in case it's a trap and they begin shooting at you, but if you successfully pick the POWs up, here's another code word for you to use. Call us as soon as you are out of the pick-up site and transmit the code word followed by a number indicating how many POWs you have on board. Are there any questions?" At that point, I asked, "How will the landing zone be marked?" His response was, "I don't know. You'll be given a set of map coordinates and that's all I know."

We stayed with our helicopter for nearly two hours in terribly hot weather and were beginning to believe it was going to be a repeat of

Christmas Day. Suddenly, an officer ran from the operations center and gave me a handwritten set of map coordinates. We quickly checked them on our map and found the pick-up site was not across the Cambodian border as we had been told to plan for. Instead, it was a few miles inside South Vietnam in an area of heavy jungle that was commonly called the "Saw Tooth Woods." I had been on several operations in that area previously and always drew heavy automatic weapons fire.

As the crew untied the rotor blades, Jim and I made one last check of our weapons to ensure they were as inconspicuous as possible. The take-off we made that day was one of the strangest I've ever experienced because the skies around Tay Ninh were normally filled with all sorts of airplanes and helicopters, but, on that particular day, we couldn't see another aircraft in the air anywhere.

Jim navigated while I flew and as we approached the "Saw Tooth Woods," we began noticing small clearings near where the coordinates were leading us. As we neared the coordinates, I saw a large North Vietnamese flag flying in a small clearing, so I told the crew, "That's probably it. Let's land by the flag and see what happens." At that point, I called the operations center at Tay Ninh and told them we were landing.

We landed a few yards from the flag and kept the engine running. A few minutes later, we saw eight North Vietnamese Army (NVA) soldiers dressed in bluish-gray uniforms and carrying AK-47 rifles coming out of the woods to our right front. When they were about 10 meters away, they formed a semicircle in front of our helicopter facing us. We sat there for several more minutes before seeing another group of NVA soldiers coming from the same woods. Within that group, we could see what appeared to be three Americans dressed in lighter colored clothing.

Even from that distance, we could tell one of the Americans was black and he appeared to be in serious trouble because he kept stumbling along as if he could barely walk. I told our medic to get out of the aircraft and wait to see what kind of reaction he got from the NVA soldiers standing in front of us. If they didn't object to him getting out, then he was to go help that soldier. The medic jumped out and no one seemed to pay him any attention, so he hustled across the clearing to reach the approaching group. Once there, he pulled the POW's arm over his shoulder and helped him to our aircraft.

While this was going on, a large group of people dressed in civilian clothing began coming out of the same wooded area. We assumed they were North Vietnamese media because they had cameras and began taking pictures as the POWs were being loaded. One of the photographers walked around to the front of our helicopter and pressed his face and camera against our windshield on Jim Daily's side. Although we weren't supposed to make any facial expressions or do anything overt, I discretely stepped on the intercom button on my side of the floorboard and whispered, "Smile Jim. Your picture is going to be on the front page of the *Hanoi Daily* tomorrow." Jim burst out laughing, so I said, "Don't laugh, Jim. Don't laugh!"

After everyone was loaded, we began our take-off and couldn't believe it had gone so easily. Once we gained enough altitude, I called the operations center at Tay Ninh and gave them the code word meaning we had picked-up the POWs and gave them the number three, meaning we had three POWs on board. Then we headed for Long Binh, about a 45-minute flight away.

Just before Christmas, our unit received Red Cross Christmas bags containing shaving cream, lotion, razors, and that sort of thing, so our medic and crew chief saved some for the POWs. They also brought along sack lunches they had scrounged from our mess hall containing sandwiches, cookies, and drinks. Once airborne, they tried to engage the POWs in small talk and attempted to get them to eat, but the POWs ate very little and their only responses were a quiet "thank you" when the crew did something for them. All appeared to be in shock and the black soldier who was later identified as Specialist Fourth Class James Brigham seemed to be the worst.

When we landed at the 24th Evacuation Hospital, a large crowd was waiting for us. Photographers were running all over the place, so I told our medic, "Grab the black guy and help guide him to the receiving room." As they walked from underneath the rotor blades, several general officers surged forward to greet the POWs and our medic released Brigham's arm in order to salute. Sp4 Brigham continued walking straight ahead and collided with one of the general officers as if he didn't see him.

That was our last involvement. There was no debriefing afterwards and no one from the 25th Infantry Division would share any more information with us. It was almost as if the release never happened, so we went back to the war.

Several years passed before I was able to gain any kind of insight into the POW release. While attending the Army War College in 1976-77, I needed to write a lengthy paper on some military topic, so I decided to pursue it again. Fortunately, one of the crown jewels of the Army is something called the Military History Research Collection (MHRC) co-located with the Army War College at Carlisle Barracks, Pennsylvania. I knew they had records on everything from the Revolutionary War to present day, so I went to their research department and asked for help. Several weeks later, a wonderful research assistant called to tell me she had several items that might interest me. I hurried to her office and was handed a large stack of State Department, CIA, DOD, and Army documents. Most had once been highly classified, but she was able to get them downgraded for my research.

I found the documents to be fascinating and couldn't believe how many other agencies had been involved in the POW release. I learned how the initial contacts between the two governments had been made and how important meetings had been arranged. One of the operation plans I received described the massive support that had been standing by for the release, of which we were only a tiny part. More importantly, I learned how a courageous Army Lieutenant Colonel by the name of Jack Gibney had met twice in the field with the North Vietnamese to negotiate the terms of the release. The documents gave me far more information than I needed to complete my War College paper, but I knew I had to talk with LTC Gibney to get his personal perspective of the operation. My Faculty Advisor agreed and told me I should get the story published in one of the Army's professional journals.

After a couple of years of trying, I finally learned LTC Gibney had been promoted to colonel and was assigned to the Pentagon. At the time, I was stationed completely across the country at Fort Lewis, Washington, but a trip to the Pentagon came up unexpectedly, so I called him and asked for a meeting. Once there, I gave Jack a copy of the paper I had written and asked him to review it for accuracy. I also told him what my Faculty Advisor had recommended and asked whether he had any objections to an article. A couple of weeks later, Jack sent me several pages of hand written notes that I used to write an article entitled "Face Off in the Jungle and Three Came Home" that was published in *Army* magazine.

The formerly classified documents also described how Sp4 Brigham had been captured after his convoy was ambushed while passing through a large rubber plantation on Highway 1, about 10 miles south of Tay Ninh. By coincidence, another 159th crew and I responded to that ambush and both of us flew several missions under extremely heavy fire that afternoon. During the ambush, Sp4 James Brigham received a head wound and was taken prisoner when his section of the convoy was overrun. A North Vietnamese doctor operated on him while he was in captivity, but a large brain abscess developed and probably caused the stumbling gait and other conditions we noticed when we picked him up. Sp4 Brigham was immediately flown to Walter Reed Army Medical Center for surgery, but died shortly thereafter.

The North Vietnamese tried to capitalize on the news of Sp4 Brigham's death by flooding the newspapers and radio programs of the Communist world with propaganda saying the Americans had killed him because he planned to tell the world how well he had been treated as a black man in captivity.

I look back on my experience in 1968-69 with great pride because of the tremendous officers and enlisted men in the 159th. There was never a better group of men and they deserve all the credit anyone can give them. They earned it and should be proud of their service.

My Talk to a Vietnam Veterans Group

Debby Maynard

September 22, 2017 – Dover, Delaware, USA

What an honor it is to be here today and especially for the opportunity to talk about what women did in Vietnam. I've found that most Americans are surprised when they learn that women served in Vietnam, or else they make comments like "Oh, you were in the rear where there was no action, right?" They seem shocked when I tell them 7,484 American women served in Vietnam and that 68 of them lost their lives there.

I think most of you guys would agree that, if it's possible to have a good job in combat, *you* had one of them. Flying as part of a Dust Off crew and saving the lives and limbs of thousands of American soldiers must give you enormous pride in what you did.

I also had a good job because I operated recreation centers for the enlisted soldiers where they could relax and enjoy time away from their officers and NCOs during breaks from combat. In the encounters I had with those incredible men, I learned more about the human spirit than I ever learned in all of my sociology and psychology classes and rarely a day goes by without my being reminded of their bravery, fortitude, and sacrifice.

In 1968, as I was preparing for graduation from San Francisco State, I wanted to do a little traveling before entering a teaching career like my parents. As the eldest of four daughters, I also felt very close to my father, who was a B-29 commander during WWII, flying thirteen bombing missions over Japan. By the way, my Dad is 99 years old and still very active. I'm so proud of him.

Since I had no brothers, I also felt a need to support our young men who were being drafted and sent "a world away" to a place many of them probably couldn't find on a map!

After learning the Department of the Army had a program that had recently lowered their minimum age from 23 to age 21 for young, single, college graduate women or girls, I went for an interview for a job with something called Army Special Services. And yes, we were called "girls" in those days. The recruiter talked about exciting positions in Europe and elsewhere, but after putting my name on the dotted line, I went for a physical at Oakland Army Terminal, where a nurse told me I was headed for Vietnam!

After what seemed to be several days on an airplane out of Travis AFB, we finally landed at Saigon and the first thing that hit me was the oppressive heat and awful smell. Another girl and I in-processed together. Prior to our arrival, we had no formal training, so we spent three days getting ID cards, learning about the local culture, and then learning a barrage of military terms and slang that we would need in our new positions. As some of you know, the military speaks an entirely different language and we had to learn what PCS, DEROS, XO, CO, EM, SP4, PSP, and bunkers meant. Even harder was to learn military time – "it's not 2 pm, Miss, it's 1400 hours"!

We were then told that we would learn our REAL MISSION through "on-the-job" training provided by our individual Club Directors, so I was anxious to get on with it and learned that I'd be going to Soc Trang, a tiny Army airfield located deep in the Mekong Delta. Early the next morning, my Area Supervisor and I boarded an Air Force C-130, the only passengers on board, as the entire cargo space was filled with wooden crates. After a few landings and take-offs, we slammed down on the short runway at Soc Trang and my Area Supervisor told me the troops would probably be very excited to meet "the new girl." As we began taxiing to the parking area, we looked out the window and saw ¾ ton trucks and deuce-and-a-halfs racing towards our aircraft, so Riki said "Look, Debby, they're coming to see you!" Well, that flattery lasted about 30 seconds, because we quickly learned the airfield had been without BEER for two weeks and the cargo we were carrying was in fact pallets of beer!

I then met Louise, my new boss and club director and learned she wanted me oriented quickly because she wanted to go on R&R. It was then that she told me we were the only two girls on a post with 400 men and that we lived in the same building with the junior Dust Off pilots. "What...?" I thought. "Living with guys?"

As all of you know, Dust Off pilots, like my husband and their crews, are those who bravely fly into combat to rescue the wounded and dead. As it turned out, the guys in the 82nd Med were great and adopted us like sisters. They were very protective of us and always ensured we got to the bunkers when we got mortared or rocketed, but they also teased us unmercifully.

To separate our living space from the men, they built a wall about eight feet tall around the tiny room that Louise and I shared, but there was open space above the wall up to the ceiling, so we could hear them talking and I'm sure they heard us. And yes, ladies, guys do gossip, just like women. More importantly, we'd hear them all hours of the night racing down the hall to their choppers which were parked about twenty feet from the entrance to our room. We'd hear them roar off and were always relieved to hear them return, only sometimes to hear some middle-of-the-night gruesome details about their missions.

As I mentioned earlier, we were there to provide a "home-away-from-home" for the enlisted men where they could relax between combat operations. Every item in each facility was there for their enjoyment and was free. There was coffee, punch, popcorn, games, cards, ping-pong, pool tables, and musical instruments. We also planned a monthly calendar of events to challenge and encourage the soldiers' intellectual, competitive, and social interests. Popular were our movie nights, Bingo, pool tournaments, and unit parties.

As I mentioned earlier, our clubs were a safe haven for the enlisted men. Officers and NCOs couldn't use our facilities except when we planned unit parties with the sole purpose of letting the young soldiers "poke fun" at their officer and NCO superiors. Were we successful with our efforts? Let me give you one example. We had to turn in monthly reports outlining the number of hours that soldiers spent in our clubs and I distinctly remember one report I turned in while at Cu Chi that showed we had 110,000 hours of "Soldier Visit Time" for that month.

One of my saddest memories was one morning when I was having breakfast with a Dust Off pilot and reminded him that he was invited to come to his "Unit party" that night. His reply was, "Deb, I just don't have the time for that kind of stuff, but I'll think about it. As it turned out, he'd didn't have the time. He was killed later that morning! That was one of the harsh realities we all had to face in Vietnam and there were many others. I remember one of the guys in our hootch who passed out cookies that his Mom had sent, along with a photo of his beloved yellow lab, Sandy. Denny was so worried that his elderly dog would die before he returned home. As it turned out, Denny was killed a few weeks later.

In addition to running our clubs, we were asked to learn about the missions of different units on our basecamps. We would often visit their work sites where we would listen and empathize with their feelings about daily encounters with fellow soldiers, their superiors, local nationals, and, most importantly, the enemy!

Perhaps my greatest understanding about what was happening and how it affected our troops came from conversations I had with soldiers in the privacy of our Recreation Centers. When the men came in from the field for a few days, they would often seek us out for essentially a "Big Sister" discussion. One heartbreaking event occurred when a group of GIs came in and one was drawn to a new litter of puppies that our mascot dog, Deros, had delivered. He quickly asked if he could "have dibs" on the caramel colored one when they came back in on their next "stand-down". I promised him I would save the puppy and he seemed so excited. About six weeks later, I noticed one of the guys from his unit and said, "Hey, I've got your buddy's puppy and he's ready to go." The soldier glared at me and said, "He won't be needin' it. He got "blowed away" last week!" He then uttered an expletive and stormed out of the club.

We also heard sad stories, ranging from "Dear John" letters, to stateside family deaths, to economic woes, and encounters with local "friendlies" who turned out to be the enemy. Often these tragedies caused these young men to become hypersensitive, untrusting, and doubtful about their mission. We tried hard to have them see the more positive side of our involvement, but, sometimes, there was nothing to do except shed tears with them.

I remember one afternoon when a sandy-haired GI asked me for some stationery to write a letter home, and he seemed quite upset. I helped him with some spelling and then he proceeded to tell me what was bothering him. His unit was entering a local "friendly" village when a beautiful little Vietnamese girl came out to greet them while holding a bouquet of flowers in front of her. When his squad leader bent down to accept the flowers, the Viet Cong detonated a C-4 plastic explosive, hidden on the little girl's chest. Several of the soldiers, including his squad leader, were killed or wounded. After witnessing that carnage, this young soldier said he was ready to "take out" every Vietnamese he saw! I talked with him for a long time and finally got him to agree to see his unit chaplain. Even now, some forty-eight years later, I still ache for those men and the choices they had to make.

One of my favorite experiences in Vietnam was hosting orphan's parties at our club. Several of our units would ask their families in the States to send toys, clothing, and treats to support this effort. The children would sing and dance for our soldiers and our guys would simply "melt" at the sight of their smiles, temporarily forgetting the nasty side of the war.

The memory of one little girl I saw at my first orphans' party will never leave me. I still refer to her as "my baby." She was about two years old and was holding a balloon we'd given out to the children. I noticed she had the balloon wedged between her lower arm and waist and it was then that I noticed she had no hands. When I asked the nun from the orphanage what had happened to her, she said that the Viet Cong had come through her village shaking down the villagers for rice. Her family had none to give them, so they took their youngest child and cut her hands off. At that moment, I wanted the severest form of punishment exacted upon the people who had done that to her! I still have her picture in my bedroom and look at it every day. My fondest hope is to someday know what happened to her.

Along this same line, many local Vietnamese worked on our basecamps where they cleaned and did laundry in our hootches and recreation centers. One morning, my Mama San was late for work and seemed so sad. I asked what was wrong and she pulled out a tiny photo of her 12-year old son. We had heard there'd been trouble in the "vil" or village the night before. It turned out that Mama San's little boy was one of ten kids who drove village workers to our basecamp on little motorized carts called "cyclos". The VC came through the village rounding up these young drivers, cut their heads off, and kicked their heads down the middle of the village like soccer balls. I could not believe Mama San's courage and dedication, coming to work, hours after that horrible crime, but she didn't want us to believe she was a Viet Cong sympathizer!

One of the saddest things I saw in Vietnam involved a program that was commonly called "McNamara's 100,000." Some of you may recall in the mid-sixties, the Secretary of Defense began a program to enlist young men who scored as Category 4 or "CAT 4's" on the Armed Forces Qualification Test, which meant their IQ was 65 or less. Many could barely read or write. We often helped them by reading letters they received and helped them write letters home.

One soldier I remember came in late one evening and wanted to show me a picture of his girlfriend that he had painted on velvet at one of the PX vendors. He told me he was leaving for home soon and excitedly told me that he and Juanita would be married. I told him he looked way too young to be married, but he replied "Oh, Mam, I've been married before." He then went on to tell me that his former wife "went and got herself pregnant at the age of 15" and then had problems dealing with the baby crying all of the time, so she put rat poison in the infant's formula. She was apparently sent to a state detention facility and he was told he could go to jail or to Vietnam, so he decided that Vietnam was the best alternative because he could "shoot real good."

He was very proud to say he had a new girlfriend who already had a son and he couldn't wait to get home, where his first stop would be at "Taco World." When I asked was he anxious to have Mexican food, he responded "Oh, no Mam, that's where Juanita works." He then told me that he planned to go back to college where he wanted to become an orthopetician. When I asked what an orthopetician was, he said "Oh Mam, you know, one of them baby doctors, so if Juanita tries to do something stupid, I can catch it in time." Unfortunately, we met lots of men like him and it was shocking to say the least.

After all these sad tales, let me share something humorous, that we heard from one of the soldiers who visited our recreation center, and was later validated in our 25th Division newspaper. A group of infantrymen were out in the jungle north of Cu Chi and digging in for the night when one of them spotted a Viet Cong sniper hidden in a nearby tree. Knowing he would be shot if he made a fast move, he began softly singing a parody of the Beatles song "Hey Jude" to his buddies that went something like this "Hey Dude, look over there. There's a bad guy in the bush." One of his buddies picked up on it and sang back in the same manner asking where he was located. Once the location was established, another soldier shot him out of the tree. I can't imagine how they maintained their cool at time like that, but it is so typical of the fortitude of the American soldier.

Did we have any impact on the men we worked with in Vietnam? Let me share something that may say we did. About three years after I returned from Vietnam, I was sitting in the San Francisco airport waiting for a flight when I noticed three soldiers in uniform sitting at another gate about 50 feet away; one of them seemed to be pointing at me. Finally, he got up and walked over and said "Mam, you're gonna think this is crazy, but were you ever in Vietnam?" When I said yes I was, he turned back towards his buddies and yelled, "See, I told you. You owe me a case of beer!"

He then told me that he was on a helicopter coming in from a combat operation where his unit had lost several men. He said he told himself that when he got out of the field, he planned to grab the first "Round Eye" he saw and hug her tight. They apparently landed at the Hotel 3 heliport where I was waiting for a ride back to Cu Chi and saw me. I then asked whether he came over to say hello and he said, "No Mam, I didn't, but I knew I'd always remember you." I then asked whether I could give him a "big hug" and he said, "oh, yes mam, you sure can!" Several people sitting around us there in the terminal overheard our conversation and stood up and began clapping for him.

He then said, "And Mam, can I ask you one more question? Did you have red suitcases?" When I told him I had gotten them as graduation presents from college, he shouted back to his friends "Red suitcases! You owe me another case of beer!"

I was fortunate to be asked to speak at the Vietnam Memorial in DC on Veterans Day last year about the women who served in Vietnam. I've been to the Wall many times and always touch the names of the seven men I knew personally who lost their lives in Vietnam, but, each time I'm there, I stare at the wall and wonder how many more names of the thousands of soldiers I talked with at our recreation centers or at their units or firebases are inscribed there. I will never know, but I'm so happy that I might have been a small part of their lives during our time in Vietnam.

In closing, not a day goes by when I don't think about my experiences in Vietnam, the good times, the challenges, and the sad times. I learned more about myself than I ever would have if I had gone directly into teaching. I value my time with those wonderful young soldiers and the Vietnamese Nationals I came into contact with. I also learned about our

"World Family" and their cultures and understand that we Americans don't always have the correct answer. Mostly, I think about the friendships we developed, however short, and I will always remember those I knew who served.

Finally, I want to thank all of you who served and I honor you for your service and sacrifice to our beautiful nation.

My "Malta Story"

Graham Scott

November 1977, Sergeant Ron Cameron, the Sgt in charge of the Administration of our section, Air Traffic Control, RAF Kinloss presented me with an ultimatum. "RAF Personnel Management Centre (PMC) is offering you an overseas tour, Malta, but it is only for 15 months," (up until this time, tours in Malta were for 3 years; the reason this tour was to be so short was because the British Armed Forces were due to withdraw from Malta by the end of March 1979). SATCO advises that if you do not take it, your next tour will be an Area Radar Unit!"

That settled it! I was not prepared to enter that deep hole that took years for Assistant Air Traffic Controllers (AATC) to climb out of. So the answer was an immediate yes. Within days I was on two weeks embarkation leave after which I returned to administratively clear from the station and depart. I spent the night before the flight to Malta at the passenger transit hotel, Gateway House at RAF Brize Norton. The flight out was on the weekly trooper, a VC 10 of No 10 Squadron – if you are one of those people who must seat facing the direction of travel on a train, then I suspect you would not like travelling on RAF transport aircraft, as the passenger seating all faced the rear of the aircraft, an additional safety measure I believe.

One of my fellow passengers was Sergeant Ray James who was stationed at RAF Luqa, commanded by Group Captain CA Vasey RAF, and until recently worked in Air Traffic Control (ATC); he made himself known to me and told me that I was to be working in ATC. Ray, who was a recent graduate of the Open University, was moving over to Station Operations. I was accommodated in a four-man room, on the ground floor of a four-storey barrack block, the third of four on the domestic site, which was separate from the operational site. Each floor had its own veranda. The Airmen's and Sgts' Mess was across the parade ground from the blocks as was the RAF Police Club and above it on the first floor, 'The Gladiator Club,' the Junior ranks club. ATC was on the other side of the airfield and we would walk to work using a shortcut which utilised the underpass which ran underneath Runway 32/14, or the "civil" runway, only available to RAF aircraft in an emergency. I discovered I had been entered in the section Christmas draw before I had even arrived and won a bottle of scotch! Welcome to Air Traffic Luqa! Now, the food in the Kinloss Airmen's Mess was judged to be amongst the best in the Royal Air Force, the catering staff having won the Joliffe Trophy; the food in the Luqa Airmen's Mess I judged to be amongst the worst in the Royal Air Force. Thank goodness for the *'Cross-Keys'* or *'Easy-Shop'* as it was also known. This was a little café on a street corner in Luqa village run by Guido, his wife and two daughters. Guido's wife was like a mother to all of us single lads who frequented the place.

When I arrived, No 203 Squadron which operated Nimrods had only days to go before they were disbanded. By the New Year, the only RAF flying unit based in Malta was No 13 (Army Cooperation) Squadron who operated the Canberra PR7 in the photo-reconnaissance role. They were also situated on the other side of the airfield. RAF Luqa was also the site of the civil air terminal and base of the national airline Air Malta which operated Boeing B720Bs, while the cabin crew were Maltese, the aircrews were Pakistani. Pakistan International Airlines was a major stakeholder in Air Malta. Other airlines which operated to Malta International Airport on a regular basis were British Airways, Britannia Airways, Monarch Airlines, Alitalia Airlines, and Libyan Arab Airlines.

As well as working with fellow Brits, like all the other sections at RAF Luqa we had a contingent of local RAF Malta servicemen working with us. Apparently, they had different working conditions from us but there was no sign of it in our section. We also worked alongside Maltese civilians as the RAF was training them to take over the running of Malta International Airport when the British Armed Forces withdrew.

My duties as an AATC were almost the same as those that I had at Kinloss but with one important difference I now had to work alongside the Approach Controllers in the darkened approach room. However, the novelty soon wore off, since as part of my duties involved contacting on the hour, every hour, our only military diversion airfield, the joint Italian Air Force/U.S. Navy airfield at Sigonella Sicily, to get an update on their weather. So imagine a Scot speaking to an Italian colleague asking for the weather. It normally resulted in me having to repeat myself several times, each time getting increasingly louder while all my Italian friend would say would be various Numbers ranging from 5 to 2, with strength before the number but I got there in the end. On one occasion, when I looked up, there was a line of grinning controller's faces.

Armament Practice Camp

To the north of the airfield, almost aligned with Luqa's runway 14 was the disused runway of the former RAF Ta Qali. To the south of the airfield, almost aligned with Luqa's runway 32 was the active runway of our satellite airfield at the former Royal Naval Air Station at Hal Far. Active because helicopters which included the French built Super Frelon of the Libyan Armed Forces operated from there. It was always a concern of our SATCO,

The ill-fated WT530.

Air Traffic Control Tower, Malta

Squadron Leader Graham Woods, soon to be promoted to Wing Commander, that a pilot would sight the runway at Hal Far or Ta Qali and having received landing clearance for Luqa, land at Hal Far or Ta Qali. It did happen! The aircraft concerned was a helicopter which landed at Ta Qali. Another concern Sqn Ldr Woods had about runway 32/14, 11,627 foot/3,544 metre long, was the potential of a disastrous runway incursion. At that time there was no parallel taxiway, therefore to use runway 32, aircraft departing from the civil terminal had to backtrack the runway. In fog or other conditions of bad visibility the potential for an unauthorised runway incursion and collision was very real. As a result of the SATCO's concern, a small observation post was built on the western side of runway 32/14 and manned by a Maltese civilian whose sole responsibility was to inform the Visual Control Room, on top of the ATC tower of any unauthorised incursion.

If Royal Air Force aircraft had been allowed to use this runway, it would have caused a lot less work and inconvenience, but why make life simple? RAF aircraft could use runway 14/32 only in cases where the pilot declares an emergency, otherwise as soon as the wheels touch the tarmac, the UK Government became liable for a share of the runway construction costs.

Malta was also the Armament Practice Camp (APC) for RAF air defence fighters. During my time on Malta, we were visited by five of the UK based squadrons, nine Phantoms or Lightnings brought out to Malta by nine Victor K2 tankers. Three of the Victors landed at Luqa and since a Victor had three points from which fuel flowed, I always assumed that these three had brought the fighters all the way from the UK.

What I did not realise was the flow rate of the central hose was faster than the flow rate of the two hoses from the wing pods, therefore two fighters could only be refuelled at once and not three. The centre hose was used to refuel larger aircraft. Since the fuel a tanker passes to a receiving aircraft comes from its own tanks, on deployments such as this, the tanker itself has to have its tanks topped up in order to be able to continue to refuel any receiving aircraft. What happened when the fighters came out to Malta was that three tankers would pass all their spare fuel to the other six tankers before turning back to Marham. Three Victors would then pass on their spare fuel to the other three tankers, before landing at their destination, normally Nice. All this time they and the last three Victors would be refuelling the fighters, with the last three tankers continuing with them to Malta.

Guard Duty

The Squadrons stayed for about a month firing coloured tipped 20 mm cannon shells at a banner towed by a Canberra on a very long wire, flying a figure of eight pattern. This did not stop the Canberra crews from reminding the fighter crews that they were pulling the target, not pushing it. There was one incident where the tug aircraft was damaged in the range. It is unclear whether it was by the tow cable or 20 mm rounds but there were no injuries, just an extremely annoyed pilot. The fighter squadrons were located on no. 3 Aircraft Park. An area I and a companion had to patrol one night as members of the station guard force. Two hours on, wandering up and down the flight line, armed with the Self Loading Rife with a magazine containing five 7.62mm rounds. A superb infantry weapon, but not one suited to airfield security. The 9 mm Sterling Sub Machine gun or perhaps even a shotgun was better suited. We had four hours off, and if you timed it right you would only need to go out once during the whole duty. The first Squadron to come out was No.29 in January to be followed by nos. 43 & 111 Squadrons, nos. 5 & 11 were the last fighter squadrons to deploy to Malta in the summer of 1978.

We also patrolled No. 4 Aircraft Park, whenever there was visiting aircraft night stopping. These would be C-130 Hercules or Buccaneers, Jaguars, and Harriers over from Decimomannu Sardina, for the weekend. "Deci" was an Italian Air Force station where RAF offensive support or "mud mover" types went for their APC.

I was only involved in one station exercise during the time I was in Malta and it was a one-day exercise designed to test security. Higher authority thought that with complete withdrawal imminent the hardliners amongst the Maltese people might take advantage of the situation. A real threat as the theft of our bird control unit Landover demonstrated. It started on a Sunday morning with the orderly sergeant rounding up as many airmen and senior non commissioned officers as he could find on the domestic site. A party of us under the command of two SNCOs were dispatched to guard a bulk fuel installation (BFI) that was sited off base. We were all armed with the weapon we were qualified on but without magazines, without ammunition. Clearly, armed British servicemen, off the sovereign base area, were a sensitive subject and the Maltese were not to be upset. This was at a time when airmen, other than members of the RAF Regiment were not tactically aware. I would learn, on the general service training 1 course I attended some years later, that being a sentry did not mean standing in a box for all the world to see. The chief technician in charge of our party shouted up to me, "*Watch your back!*" When I turned my head I saw a few feet away a young Maltese man armed with a shotgun, which I knew did have ammunition. He was no doubt hunting the Blue Rock Thrush, the Maltese national bird. He asked abruptly "What are you doing here?" I thought the answer was obvious so declined from replying. He, then continued on his way. Apart from a visit from two Royal Marine Officers, that was the only activity during our shift. We were later relieved and taken back to the operational site of RAF Luqa, where having no further need of us, at that moment in time, we were released from duty. Later that evening, I and some friends went to the station cinema which was also on the domestic site. When we came out we learned that the RAF police had been looking for us, there was a need for our services after all.

The Kiev Gives Up Her Secrets

No. 13 Squadron in the meantime had been continuing to fly operations. They often went to Villafranca in Northern Italy on NATO business, as well as to RAF Wyton, their new home from October 1978. They deployed to Masroor, Pakistan for an exercise during this time taking one of our Warrant Officers with them as ATC liaison officer. We could see them, well see the flash anyway, during night flying as they took photos of the range safety/air sea rescue launches of No. 1151 Marine Craft Unit (MCU) stationed at Marsaxlokk in the south of the Island. However, I knew very little about their day-to-day operations and I am indebted to Paul McDonald for this account of an intelligence gathering coup from his book, "Winged Warrior". This occurred on a very windy Wednesday in March 1978, I remember this particular day because the VC 10 trooper was diverted to Sigonella. Paul, then a Flying Officer on his second tour, relates that 13 Squadron had stacked for the day and he hoped that he and his navigator, Fred Stokes, would soon be released from duty too. No such luck. They were called to station operations to be briefed for a sortie.

The Soviet Aircraft Carrier Kiev, the first of an entirely new class of warship and her attendant missile cruisers and missile destroyers were known to be at sea and nearby. Their task would be to locate her and when her stern was out of the water, to photograph it. Easy, no? They returned to the Squadron and prepared for the mission. With gale force winds, there was some doubt as to whether the flight could take place. "Rudder locks" was in force; this meant that the Aircraft's rudder was clamped to the fin ensuring that the strong forces on the rudder caused by high winds would not impose a strain on the pilot's legs when he placed his feet on the rudder pedals. Ground crew would remove the locks prior to the aircraft lining up on the runway.

The aircraft assigned to them was WT530, take-off was normal, and they headed for the designated search area. After searching for some hours, no sign of the Kiev task group could be found, and approaching the limit of their remaining fuel they decided to make one last sweep before returning to Luqa.

20 miles to the east north east of the island, on the extended centre line to runway 24, they found the Kiev task group! With every gun and missile launcher of the task group tracking them, they set themselves up for the photo run, took the photo and headed home. If I remember correctly they recovered to our satellite airfield at Hal Far, the tower there being manned by extra staff brought in. The photo they took astounded the photographic interpreters; it was not the Kiev's stern that was out of the water, but the bow. The photographic interpreters knew that given this a naval architect could work out important information regarding the new Soviet carrier, information such as maximum speed, and displacement. The Air Commander Malta, Air Commodore H. D. Hall wasted no time in presenting the photograph to his immediate superior, the Admiral commanding British Forces Malta, Rear Admiral Sir O. N. A. Cecil KBE, CB, NATO Commander of the South East Mediterranean and Flag Officer, Malta.

13 Squadron were our next-door neighbours on the far side of the airfield at Luqa, their squadron headquarters was just across a road that lead to the aircraft dispersals that were in front of the tower and stretched along the southern taxiway. Our watch supervisor, Flight Lieutenant Paul Miller developed a close working relationship with the Squadron; he worked as the Squadron Ops Officer during their last exercise in Malta, just weeks before their return to the UK.

The Squadron left Malta in October 1978; a parade was held to mark the end of the RAF presence on the Island. The reviewing Officer was the Air Officer Commanding-in-Chief (AOC-in-C) Strike Command, Air Chief Marshall Sir David G. Evans. A short flying display followed.

The squadron's departure also meant that we in Air Traffic Control would lose many of our controllers. Three of the Flight Sergeant Aerodrome Controllers were posted home, as were many of the Radar Controllers, most to RAF Shawbury as instructors. This only added to the problems the SATCO and superior officers above him were having training new Maltese controllers. Eventually, an arrangement was made whereby the RAF would train new controllers if Malta could find some and owing to the validation of the Maltese ones, they, the validated Maltese controllers would only do the training provided two more RAF controllers were sent out from the UK – one of these controllers was Flight Lieutenant Jo Turner, who was detached from RAF Coltishall.

A Tragic Return

It was a little under two months before an aircraft of 13 Squadron returned to Malta. Canberra PR7 WT530 stayed the night before continuing its journey to Cyprus. Business in Cyprus complete, it started its return journey to the UK staging through Luqa on the 6th December 1978 and night stopping. Then came the 7th of December.

Jo Morris Turner, as she is now, is on record as saying that she will never forget the crash of ill-fated WT530. I think those who witnessed this event will never forget it either. I was on duty that afternoon in the visual control room (VCR), on top of the ATC tower. I remember watching the Canberra rolling down the runway after having received its take off clearance. The aircraft had rotated and was beginning to get air under its wheel when two large objects appeared over the aircraft. Then parachutes started to unfurl, the aircraft disappeared from view and there was an explosion and huge fireball.

The Aerodrome Controller had hit the crash alarm and passed the necessary information to the crash/rescue crew, including aircraft type, POB (number of people on board), and position on the Airfield. The last 800 feet of runway 24, total length 7,799 feet/2,377 metres, is downhill and therefore the threshold of runway 06 could not be seen by those of us who were in the VCR. Since that was not the runway in use the runway control caravan was not in its customary position, therefore, the Aerodrome Controller had no way of knowing that the aircraft in fact had gone through the boundary fence, two stone walls and across two fields, (Maltese fields are not very big).

The pilot and navigator had abandoned the aircraft without making any emergency call. Clearly something catastrophic had happened. The third person on board, who would have been sitting on a fold-away seat next to the pilot, having no way to escape, was killed. The SATCO and Flt Lt Turner had been outside the tower when the crew ejected. Squadron Leader Woods was soon in the VCR. he told me that he wanted to know how long it took for the fire to be put out. The crash/rescue crews had to exit the airfield via the nearest crash gate, and then find their way to the crash site. Jo Turner was meanwhile, making three cups of hot sweet tea which she subsequently brought up to the VCR. The perspex on my desk was to be covered in chinograph scribbling as I recorded the developing incident. "Write down everything" said the civilian ground controller, "They will try to pin this on us if they can." "They" were the board of enquiry, which was convened to investigate the loss of WT530. In fairness to the Ground Controller, another civilian controller colleague many years later spoke of having an "impression", after being called as a witness to a Board of Inquiry investigating the crash of a Phantom into the North Sea which was under the control of a Fighter Controller. Appearing before a board of enquiry is not an experience I wish to repeat. The findings of the board were that the aircraft was lost because of a double engine failure, caused by fuel contamination.

The crew after receiving treatment for their injuries in the station medical centre were medically evacuated to the UK on the weekly VC 10 flight. The deceased passenger, Flying Officer Robert Marshal, who came from Kent, now lies in St James Cemetery, Dover.

My time on Malta was drawing to a close, I left the island the following month again on a VC 10. My colleagues who stayed right to the end, 31st March 1979 returned to the UK on board a Royal Navy County Class destroyer, HMS London. I enjoyed three weeks disembarkation leave (two weeks plus one day for every month after the first six months), before reporting to my new unit, RAF Wattisham in Suffolk.

The Return

The economic impact of the British Armed Forces withdrawal should not be underestimated; it was a very worrying time for people on the islands. Tourism was and still is a key industry, along with the oil industry. Despite the frequent RAF Association European Area Autumn Conferences held on the island, organised by the Malta GC Branch, I was never tempted to go back. That was until 2015. The catalyst was an opportunity to spend a long weekend in Malta, mixing sight-seeing, an airshow, and museums. It proved to be an enjoyable weekend, a trip down memory lane.

I Learned Leadership – From That!

Graham Scott

I served with good junior and senior NCOs, but I also served under a very small minority of bad junior and senior NCOs and it is the bad ones that I tend to remember the most. These NCOs had not undergone any form of training for their new role; most of them didn't need it. Clearly, the Royal Air Force decided that a change was needed and all NCOS had to be aware of what was expected of them.

Mention the town of Hereford in Military circles and minds will turn to Stirling Lines, the Special Air Service (SAS); however, 33 years ago Hereford was also the location of a Royal Air Force station which was part of No 22 Training Group. Hereford was not only home to the WRAF recruit training school, but trained Personnel and Administration clerks, suppliers, and all categories of catering staff.

My acquaintance with Royal Air Force Hereford came about in early 1985 when, selected for promotion to Corporal, I reported one Sunday afternoon to the General Service Training School to undertake the General Service 1 course, which would give me the knowledge and skills to undertake my duties as a new junior NCO. Some GST1 graduates would be returning to their units, I on the other hand would proceed on posting to a new unit upon completion of the course.

That Monday morning the course was marched down to stores where we were issued with another set of disruptive pattern materiel (DPM), smock, trousers, shirt, and heavy duty jersey — all in army green — and a set of puttees that you wrapped around your ankles, so that you could stuff the bottom of your trousers into them.

The course consisted of classroom lectures and exercises and there were also more demanding practical exercises, and the first one occurred that evening.

Monday evenings at RAF Hereford were "domestic", more commonly called "bull" nights in the British Armed Forces. One member of the syndicate was appointed "i/c the block" and had to supervise the bull night ensuring all areas were covered and this he did by allocating tasks to the other syndicate members, who in addition to their individual bed spaces had other communal areas to look after, such as the showers, bathrooms sinks, laundry room etc. No strangers to bull nights, we regarded them as a necessary evil. There were several syndicates living in the block, several "i/c the block" and it is fair to say everything was covered; it was the easiest bull night ever.

One of the paper exercises in the classroom was being the Orderly Corporal and consisted of making logbook/key registry entries in response to incidents or occurrences that we came across in a written scenario we were required to read.

We also watched the film "Twelve O'Clock High" starring Gregory Peck. Unfortunately we did not get to see it all, just enough to identify the three key concerns of leadership that we had covered in lectures. In no particular order the concerns are the individual, the mission, and the group. I say in no particular order because which has the priority depends very much on the situation. A casualty, caused by terrorist action, would have the highest priority in peacetime and be evacuated for medical attention as quickly as possible. This would not necessarily be the case in war.

The ceremonial aspect of service life was also included in the curriculum and I got my first opportunity of commanding a group of airmen and taking them through a sequence of drill movements on the Parade Square.

We were facing each other: my left was their right, and their right was my left – very important when it comes to issuing the executive command when the flight are on their left, my right, foot. There were no comments from our syndicate commander, a Sergeant from Northern Ireland, so that may have been good, or that may have been bad.

The course ended after an exercise designed to teach us the military skills that we would need. It took place in a military training area that was frequented by that other unit located at Hereford, but they had better things to do than play with us.

The day before we deployed we spent weapon training on our person weapon, the self-loading rifle (SLR). Our instructor, another trainee who came from another syndicate, was well placed to remind us on what we should know when it came to handling a SLR, being a rockape. Why exactly members of the Royal Air Force Regiment are named after primates who live in Gibraltar I do not know.

We lived in tents but, being February, the tents themselves were under cover in one of the unused buildings on site. Quite a change from spending a freezing night in a tent in the middle of a disused Lincolnshire airfield in the middle of December a little over 10 years previously. I am also sure that the trenches outside the building were already dug when we took up residence. This is where our first lesson took place and that was Sectors of Fire. Something a Junior NCO would be responsible for allocating. Simply put, all it involved was giving each man an area of no man's land to monitor and if he saw anything he was expected to take the appropriate action, that being to report it, and engage it if it was identified as being hostile. Each allocated sector should overlap, therefore ensuring that the unit's front was fully covered.

Shortly afterwards, I learned what it was to be a modern day sentry. First off, I was lying down at my post, not standing up for the world to see. All this was new to me, as I had never been a member of any of my previous unit's guard forces, mobile or otherwise, but others had, including our "leader" at this time. I was watching my sector of fire when a returning patrol came into view, our leader also saw the patrol approaching and ran up to me with the instruction "Make sure you challenge them!" Why challenge a patrol that are carrying the same weapons and wearing the same uniform, it is obvious they are on our side, right? Well no, and he was the boss, so I duly shouted the challenge "Air Force, Halt, who goes there?" Imagine my surprise when every single one of the approaching patrol hit the "dirt". What have I done? Our leader ran up and invited the leader of the patrol to come forward. After establishing his credentials, the patrol leader was invited to call forward one by one the members of his patrol so that their credentials could be verified and they were allowed to pass.

Patrolling was another activity we were involved in and this is where I learned the art of giving fire control orders, and also regretted not having the use of a light machine gun that was originally manufactured in the Czech town of Bren. We were walking line abreast on the left flank of an abandoned building on higher ground when we came under fire; we immediately hit the dirt. In this position I could see the rising ground ahead offered us some cover, so I started crawling towards it followed by my syndicate colleagues. We must have been being doing something right because I heard our syndicate commander who was strolling on the ground above us and watching what was going on mutter "good". On reaching the bank, I took stock of the situation, figured that the direction the fire most probably originated from was the abandoned building and saw a solitary figure by the window and decided he was responsible, he was hostile and I not only had to return fire, but I had to get the group to return fire in the desired direction, assuming that they not necessarily knew where to direct their fire.

This is where I wished for a Bren gun because all I had to say was "watch my tracer" and start firing round after round in the gunman's direction with every fifth round, tracer ammunition, showing the way. It was not to be. Therefore, I had to give an alternative command, not as snappy as you see on films, but what would you expect from an assistant air traffic controller? The command gave the location of the target, range to the target, and to tell the truth I hadn't a clue how far he was. All weapons had blank firing attachments (BFAs) fitted to the weapons muzzle so unless you shot someone at point blank range they were not going to get hurt. I fired one round and was surprised to discover that I could not fire another round, so I immediately applied the immediate action drills. Safety-catch on, bringing the weapon down my body, from the prone position. I was now on my back and inspecting the barrel of the weapon and there I found the cause of my problem. The gas port was fully open. SLRs do not function as designed with their gas ports open, I had left it open from our weapon training the day before. I fully closed it, cocked the weapon, switched the safety to off and recommenced firing.

We killed/scared off the lone gunman and returned single file to "camp". The sentry failed to challenge us and our syndicate commander passed a suitable derogatory remark in the sentry's direction as we passed.

That night our syndicate was manning the trench outside the building housing our tents when it began to rain, and it was heavy and prolonged rain. So heavy and so prolonged, the bottom of our trench began to resemble conditions not unlike those encountered during the Great War, very muddy, very wet. However, unlike the Great War, (remember the three concerns of leadership), there was a benevolent voice at the other end of the field telephone who told our leader at that time to get us inside. Our leader on being ordered to abandon his position wanted to make sure that the person giving the order was genuine and started the authentication process. This is where a two-letter challenge is given in the phonetic alphabet, to the person giving the order/ instruction based on the actual time. The response should also be given in the phonetic alphabet, also two letters, based on the actual time. Both the challenger and the challenged needed to have the same challenge/response two-letter 24 hour tables (which was classified information when I worked in RAF Wattisham Wing Operations, but were not for the purposes of this exercise). The response he got was not quite what he was expecting, and not what anyone was expecting. He was told to "stop fucking around and get everyone inside". The poor chap was not impressed, as he was only doing what we had been instructed we should do. These days he could probably sue the Ministry of Defence for hurt feelings. So we abandoned the trench and went inside where a hot drink was waiting for us.

During a lull in the action the following day, I was surprised to see a United States Air Force Europe (USAFE) Republic A-10A Thunderbolt II fly over the site. Whether this was planned or not I do not know, but clearly the pilot saw us and frankly at that low height and slow speed – a fast jet, an A-10 is not – he could hardly miss us. What followed was perhaps the pilot showing off or a simulated attack. It started with the aircraft standing on one wingtip making extremely tight turns, pirouetting like a ballerina. After completing 360 degrees the aircraft did a flypast, or strafing run, before pirouetting 360 degrees in the opposite direction and coming back doing another flypast or strafing run. This he did a few times before continuing on his way. It did not occur to me, standing there impressed by the performance and contemplating just what it was that this aircraft, a 30 mm cannon with wings, brought to the battlefield that perhaps I should be running around shouting "Air Raid Red, Air Raid Red, Take Cover!". It did not occur to anyone else on the course either, and the directing staff did not comment on it, and who is to say that some Chief Tech, some Flight Sergeant would not have yelled "What do you think you are fucking playing at?". It was said that the Soviet armoured fighting vehicle crews feared this aircraft. However, it should be borne in mind that no matter the fearsome reputation that any warplane has, it is only as good as the man or woman in the cockpit.

That night we were back in the trenches where the lesson for the night was crowd control, with a bit on how to deal with insubordination or more accurately, how to deal with a stroppy WRAF. Our syndicate were all male, the crowd in question were all female, all apparently members of the RAF Hereford Sergeant's Mess. Suffice to say that crowd control turned into fraternising with the enemy. Some good *craic*, as the Irish say, developed and the reference in the book where it said that the troops must avoid dialogue with the crowd went completely out the window despite our leader's brave attempts to keep everything professional and on a formal basis; but matters got "heated" when a protester objected to being manhandled – the theatricals had to be seen to be believed, and he had to call on reinforcement from another syndicate in the shape of a WRAF. The WRAF was ordered to do a body search on the "troublemaker". Obviously well briefed by the directing staff, she refused and a "relationship" soon developed between the protester and the WRAF. The pair of them were very comical, but our leader was not laughing. After repeated refusals to search this woman, our leader asked for her name and number amongst other things with a view of taking disciplinary action.

Four years previously, the Greenham Common "peace camp" was set up in response to the U.S. deployment of cruise missiles to the airbase. Actually, the peace camp consisted of several peace camps set up along the perimeter of the base. RAF personnel were deployed to Greenham Common to assist the U.S Air Force with security. Although I was never deployed, several of the airmen from my new unit were. Although the women did succeed in cutting down the fence, in several places in 1987 none got anywhere near the missiles, luckily for them.

The missiles left the base in 1991 and that was more to do with the collapse of the Warsaw pact than it was the Greenham Women. However, they stayed, not for long, but the excuse they gave was that they were protesting against Trident.

I have no doubt that RAF Airmen assigned to Greenham Common, specifically to stop these women getting anywhere near the missiles, saved lives – their lives.

The following day was endex! We were to march out of camp to rendezvous with a helicopter that would take us back to camp. Or so the directing staff told us, and had been telling previous courses to ours. We knew it to be untrue of course and our response was "Yeah, right". I have no idea just how far we had to "yomp" to meet the transport that took us back to camp; it certainly was not the 85 miles the Royal Marines had to march from Port San Carlos to Stanley, clearing Two Sisters and Mount Harriet on the way, less than three years previously, carrying practically everything they needed on their backs which was a great deal heavier than what I had on my back. I appreciated just what they had achieved and I also appreciated the need to be fit for battle.

However, it needs to be said that running 1½ miles in fifteen minutes, in sports kit is NOT a battle fitness test (BFT).

We were absolutely filthy, our weapons were absolutely filthy and the priority when we got back to RAF Hereford was to clean our weapons — which did not take as long as one might think — return them to the armoury, then we could hit the showers, hoping that those who had gone before had not used up all the hot water. We also had to clean the DPMs before returning them to stores.

We returned them the next day, the final day. What remained of the course was the course critique, an informal chat with the syndicate commander where he told you that you had passed, I never heard of anyone failing these courses. Officers commissions were signed by the reigning Monarch, Warrant Officers warrants were signed by the Secretary of State for defence, and GST1 and 2 graduates had their certificates of course completion signed by the Officer Commanding Training Wing. Nice touch.

Gas, Gas, Gas!

Chris O'Brien

I was a Lance Corporal of 19 years of age in the desert on Operation Granby in 1990/91 during the first Gulf Conflict. I was a vehicle mechanic in the REME attached to an Armoured Engineer squadron, Chieftain and Centurion tank based specialist armoured engineers.

The air war had started and we were sat south of the Iraqi border waiting for the order to go over the border and into Iraq. On the horizon there were constant flashes of artillery shells landing, MLRS strikes or aircraft dropping ordinance. During one evening we were in a static location and carrying out our usual daily routine, staging on in the truest military style day and night, making sure everything was working and not clogged up with sand, nose bags eaten, weapons loaded and grenades to hand.

Out in the distant desert came the shout "Gas, Gas, Gas!" and the alarm was raised via the use of the fantastic bit of chemical warfare detector – NAIAD.

Breath held, eyes closed, back to wind, crouching down. Your training kicks in. This is the real shit! A gas attack, we've been located and gassed! Saddam did it to his own people so why not us infidels?

Fumbling for my respirator, I opened the top pouch, I couldn't breathe, couldn't open my eyes. I took out and forced the rubber respirator over my head and onto my face.

One long breath out, forcing any air in the respirator (ressy) out of the mask and then a breath in through the canister, a struggle with the first breath-in restricted, as the air is dragged through the chemical filters.

I opened my eyes to a familiar scene we had practised hundreds of times in training, my mates all bent over and putting their own masks on. There was debris everywhere from dropped equipment and guns, plates, clothing, but no explosions ... no clouds of toxic gas ... just the alarm still going off in the background and the sound of your own Darth Vader-style breathing.

I buddied up with my Staff Sergeant Commander – Frank – and suited up with the cumbersome NBC suit, rubber gloves like black heavy duty marigolds, rubber over boots with 30ft of lace on each boot and checked the fitting and seal for each other and dabbed with detector paper, no chemical splashed on us so far.

We spoke about the action to be taken and agreed until we received further orders to get under cover and into our vehicles with radios on permanently to listen out for the next move and order. Here we go, now the war for us is here and we need to work together and fight.

Myself and Frank climbed into the back of our 432 tracked vehicle and closed the door. The steel door latches came on. The radios – we had three communication systems in our vehicle – were on, and there was no chatter, no orders, no messages. I checked the system which was definitely on and working. Now we waited.

We looked at each other through the respirator lenses (like looking through the bottom of a milk bottle) and chatted in muffled voices. We waited and waited. Hotter and hotter we were getting. Nothing said or heard. The only thing for it was to try and sleep.

It's funny but I have always been able to sleep in any circumstances and wherever I have been, (I woke up on a wall several times and on top of a bus shelter, but that's for another time). And sleep I did, like Darth Vader having an asthma attack, deep and sound.

I was woken some time later with my ressy digging into my face, as there was a bang on the rear door – what was happening? Had we missed something? I couldn't rub my eyes or scratch my nose still with my mask on. I opened the doors heavy steel latches from the inside slowly. Dawn light came in and my eyes became accustomed to the light through my thick glass lenses.

In front of me were two of my closest buddies, Scouse and Bob. They took one look ... that's all it took ... and they were on the floor laughing in floods of tears and howls.

"What are you doing still in your ressy?" They howled laughing.

I resisted the urge to react violently, slowly removing my hood, lifted my mask off my face to breath in fresh air and took my respirator off.

"How long have you been de-masked?" I asked once I could be heard over the laughing.

"About 7½ hours!" They came around and told everyone, well almost. "That's a record!" (hahahahaha).

Scouse giggled: "It was a false alarm and no attack, we were only masked up for about 15 minutes (hahaha), ooohhh, I can't breathe," he mocked.

I shut the door.

There was a red line that ran around Frank and my faces for three days, like a line on the London Underground map, before we couldn't see it any longer.

To this day my two best mates still remind me at every occasion (weddings, reunions etc) of the day that door opened and they saw us still masked up in our almost eight-hour record in a respirator for absolutely no reason.

We did go into battle in Iraq against the Republican Guard but we were _never_ gassed and we all came home safely.

The Royal British Legion - Paris Branch: Its History

Janet Warby

The first history of the British Legion in Paris was printed in a little red-covered booklet in 1925.

It first recounts how, in England, the four competing ex-servicemen's organisations, The Comrades of the Great War, the National Association of Ex-Servicemen, The National Association of Discharged Soldiers and Sailors, and the Ex-Officers' Association were fused together, thanks to the great influence of Earl Haig, into the British Legion at Whitsuntide, 1921. H.R.H. The Prince of Wales graciously consented to be Patron, and Earl Haig was elected chairman.

The history continues:

On May 4th 1921, a party of gentlemen, mostly belonging to the Veterans' Association then formed in Paris, met to consider the formation of the Paris Branch of the British Legion. They decided then and there to start the Branch and it was in the following month of June that it fairly began to work.

The British Ambassador, Lord Hardinge of Penshurst, and Field Marshal Foch consented to become Honorary Presidents of the Branch and Rear-Admiral Sir Edward Heaton-Ellis was elected Chairman.

Mr. George Norbury was a member continuously from those very first days until his death in 1988. He recalled being summoned to tea at the Racing Club de France by Admiral Heaton-Ellis, and subsequently taking part in a meeting at the Methodist Church Hall, near St. Lazare, when the Branch was set up.

There was soon an active social life going on, with an annual dinner at the Salle Lutetia, and eventually the Branch acquired premises in the old camp of the R.C.M.P., on Boulevard Lannes. There was a paid Secretary, (not so now) Mr. Arden, sent from London H.Q., and the Branch was very busy looking after the numerous ex-servicemen and their dependents who fell on hard times in France. The story of one such is recounted in the 1925 history:

An ex-Duffadar of the Bombay cavalry. This man lost his right arm in action on the Belgian front. During the war he had married a French woman (like many did) by whom he had two children and with his war gratuity he bought a small business in Amiens. He made bad debts and eventually sold the business and came to Paris in search of work, where his small savings were soon exhausted. He very properly came to the Legion and it succeeded in finding work for him and fighting over his pension with the Indian Government until at last a satisfactory settlement was reached.

On 24th July, 1924, the British Commonwealth War Memorial plaque in Notre Dame was unveiled by H.R.H. Prince Edward of Wales, accompanied by his brother Prince Henry, in the presence of the President of the French Republic, Monsieur Gaston Doumergue and Marshal Foch. From that year onwards there has been an Annual Service of Remembrance in Notre Dame at 15h00 on the 11th November. The British Legion organises this Service of Remembrance to remember those who paid the ultimate sacrifice. Only the Second World War interrupted this event.

In 1921 the French Government had laid to rest the Soldat Inconnu at the Arc de Triomphe, but is was not until 1923 that there was a rekindling of the flame as a national ceremony on 11th November. It was the following year, on 4th August 1924, that the British Legion initiated its own ceremony of rekindling the flame, a tradition which continues to the present day, interrupted only by the Second World War. This was by special invitation of the City of Paris Officials, a tradition we maintain to this day.

In 1928, the Legion acquired a lease at 8 rue Boudreau, and George Norbury was once again on the spot. "You have never seen such a filthy looking hole in all your life," he told one member when asked how we came to be in Boudreau. "It was like the Black Hole of Calcutta. But a number of members, including especially a group of executives from the British banks, rolled up their sleeves and cleaned it up until it was habitable".

For several years before the outbreak of the 1939 war the Chairman of the Branch was Lt. Colonel Fred W. Abbott, and a bound copy of minutes records the doings of the Legion from 26th January, 1938 until May, 1940. It optimistically concluded:

"The next General Committee Meeting will be on Thursday, 13th June 1940".

In the event, the next Provisional Committee Meeting, to discuss the re-formation of the Branch, took place, as the very first, in the Methodist Church Hall, on 14th December, 1945. Mr. C.J. Henderson (later Sir Charles Henderson, K.B.E.) was elected provisional Chairman and Lt. Colonel R.L.O. Beasley, D.S.O., Secretary.

At the first meeting of this committee the Treasurer, Mr. F.H. Lane, reported 905.90 frs shown as cash in hand, but which had actually been paid out by Mr. Barnes (the 1940 Treasurer), although the covering vouchers were not to be found. "Mr. Barnes was in the act of writing up his Cash Book when he was arrested by the Germans in 1940."

However, the Paris Branch of the British Legion, though dispossessed from 1940–1944, was not out of action. It set up in exile in London, and held meetings throughout the war. George Norbury remembered attending lunches and reunions of the Branch in London, at one of which, at least, Charles de Gaulle was guest of honour. There are no written records of this period available to us, sadly many were lost during the war or not passed to the Branch when a Committee person died.

It can be seen that the spirit of the Paris Branch, like that of the Free French, was not to be put down just because a certain Mr Hitler had occupied Paris!

The new committee, chaired by Sir Charles Henderson, and elected on 14th December, 1945, was soon at work, hampered by conditions of austerity and lack of funds at first. Nevertheless, the Chairman, in his address of 1946 said that they aspired 'not only to attain the position held prior to the war by the Paris Branch of the Legion, but to exceed it'. He reminded members of the aims of the Legion.

> "To promote comradeship; to remember the fallen; to care for the disabled, widows and orphans; to continue service in peace as in war".

He also mentioned in his speech the arrangements being made to cooperate with the British Charitable Fund to provide relief when required, an arrangement which still functions to this day.

In 1947 we find him suggesting that the 'young men' of the 1939-45 War be given a chance on the Committee, and on 20th February, 1948 at the A.G.M., Sir Charles stood down in favour of 'young' Brigadier E.R. Cawdron, OBE, who was 'eminently fitted to fill the position'.

Many of the subjects discussed in committee have a familiar ring – how to make the Club House a more attractive meeting place for members, arrangements for the rekindling of the Flame in August, the Annual Poppy Appeal and Notre Dame.

At the A.G.M., in February 1950, Brigadier Cawdron stepped down after a long illness and his place as Chairman was taken by Brigadier S. Swinton-Lee, DSO., who, according to George Norbury, was a very active, full-time chairman, and really made things hum.

Tragically, Swinton-Lee died in 1952, to be succeeded for two years by Lord Norwich, and then Colonel H.A. Wilsden, OBE., under whom the branch thrived for seven years until his death in August, 1961. During his chairmanship, membership of the Legion rose from about 650 to nearly a thousand, and on 4th May, 1962 the main room at the rue Boudreau was formally named after him by his widow.

He was actively helped over this period by a number of enthusiasts whose names have become legendary:

John Taleen, Bray Zeff, 'Robbie' Robinson, 'Mandy' Mandeville, Arthur Cooke, Bobby Gay, Barry Lynham, 'Nobby' Clarke, George Norbury, 'Rudolph' (Valentine) Burton.

For many of these of the 'Old Brigade' the rue Boudreau was their principal social centre in Paris, for a pint of beer, a game of cards, or 'chewing the fat'.

John Taleen was Parade Marshal, and in those days, with NATO troops and bands in support, the British Legion Standard and Union flag, together with flags of other service organisations used to be proudly paraded the length of the Champs Elysees on special occasions, such as the Rekindling of the Flame.

After the death of Colonel H.A. Wilsden in 1961, the Legion in Paris carried on with its good works under the chairmanship of Major L. Cunliffe David.

1964 was a landmark, the 50th anniversary of the outbreak of the 1914-1918 war, commemorated by many ceremonies in France, in which the Paris Branch took a leading part. 1964 was also the 20th anniversary of the Liberation of Paris, and there was one particularly poignant ceremony, the funeral of Wing Commander Forest Yeo-Thomas, "White Rabbit", at the Embassy Church, where the address was given by General Koenig, and among those present was the 97 year-old General Weygand.

Yeo-Thomas was the hero of the Second World War, and a comparatively young man, but those who had survived the holocaust of Flanders and Picardy in their twenties were now in their seventies, and during the '50s and '70s many of the 'Old Brigade' answered their last Roll Call. Not a few of them, knowing that their end was near, and the call of their maker, said, as 'Mandy' Mandeville did:

"Say 'goodbye' to all my good friends at the Legion".

But there were veterans of the Second World War to keep the standard flying and, when Major Cunliffe David had to resign in 1968 through ill health, his place was taken by Brigadier Barrie Wilson, DSO, who had served as Military Attaché in Paris. He was aided by such stalwarts as John Taleen, Major General R.B. Stockdale, Barry Lynham, Arthur Cooke, Reg Howarth, Robbie Robinson and George Norbury.

In 1971 the Legion worldwide was awarded the Royal Prefix. In 1972 members of the Legion were honoured by being presented to our Royal Patron, Her Majesty the Queen, on the occasion of her state visit to Paris and, in 1974, there were special ceremonies to mark the 50th anniversary of the unveiling of the Memorial Plaque in Notre Dame. On 11th November, the Remembrance Ceremony at Notre Dame was presided over by Admiral of the Fleet the Earl Mountbatten of Burma.

Another event in November 1974 was the 250th monthly luncheon in the series which was started in February 1951. Some of the guests of honour have included a succession of British Ambassadors who have always nobly supported the Legion cause and also Pierre Mendès-France, Madame La Maréchale Leclerc, General Koenig, Georges Carpentier, Maurice Chevalier, André Maurois, Georges Daninos, Forest Yeo-Thomas, Colonel 'Remy'; a chord striking names which is by no means exhaustive.

In 1976 Brigadier Wilson stepped down from the chairmanship, which was taken over by Lt. Col. Stanley Edwards, MC, TD., who had been for some years Vice-Chairman with special responsibility for administering the Relief Fund, and also Editor of the Newsletter.

In 1980 Stanley Edwards stood down as Chairman to be followed by Donald Kinloch, who in turn was followed by Geoffrey Cox, John Gardner, Gyles Longley, Richard Doggett, Roger Thorn, and now David Bean.

We still maintain a Poppy Appeal each year and the money we raise stays in the Paris region, with permission from RBL London and Poppy Appeal, to help ex-service persons who fall on hard times as in days gone by. We still work closely with the British Charitable Fund in Paris, who also help our 'clients' when the need arises.

In 1981 full membership was extended to serving members of H.M. Forces. Membership is now open to all who adhere to the aims of the Royal British Legion.

In September of 2009, the Paris Branch moved from rue Boudreau, having 'lived' there for nearly 81 years both as tenants and owners. The decision was taken to raise funds and buy rue Boudreau. In December 1953 we moved in. Our new premises are situated just a stone's throw from the Arc de Triomphe. We hope you will come and see us from time to time. We maintain the same spirit of our 'fore fathers' and still believe in the Legion motto 'Service Not Self'.

Our new address is:
28 rue des Acacias, 75017 Paris

In 2014/15 the Paris Branch was approached by a House Clearer in the UK who had found in amongst articles from the house of our first ever Chairman, Sir Edward Heaton-Ellis, mentioned in the early part of this history, a presentation conical desk ornament dedicated to him by the Paris Branch. The gentleman concerned had looked us up on the website and asked if we, the Paris Branch would like to buy it from him for our Branch Headquarters. After deliberation of the Committee and haggling over the price it was agreed to obtain the article. It now sits in the bookcase area. It is solid brass and very heavy, but we are glad it has found its way back home from whence it came. A photo of the item is included here.

'WE WILL REMEMBER THEM'

Presentation conical desk ornament dedicated to Sir Edward Heaton-Ellis.

Lift!

Chris O'Brien

Somewhat more anecdotal, this story comes from the period of the Gulf War era. It demonstrates some of the lighter side of military life amongst comrades in arms, from all walks of life.

Big Jim was a Royal Engineer of mammoth proportions — in the realms of the song Camouflage or Big Bad John by Jimmy Dean, a sapper with an Armoured Engineer Squadron and a driver of a Centurian tank. An old school squaddie, he worked hard, played hard, drank hard and fought even harder, but if there was work to be done he was first in the queue. I believe he was near the back of the queue though when the brains were dished out.

There was a clutch failure on his tank and it needed the gearbox lifted out to replace it. We (REME Vehicle mechanics) set to work and after 2-3 hours had the gearbox prepped and ready to lift out.

I told Jim that the lifting crane on our 434 was out of action (truth be told, it wasn't) and we had an issue lifting the gearbox out. There was going to be a manual lift required, I'd already told his two mates we were going to have some fun, courtesy of Jim. So, with one sapper (private) each side of the gearbox and Jim at the clutch end they were going to have to manhandle the gearbox out themselves; now, a Centurian gearbox must weigh nearly a ton!!

"Right Jim, on my count of 3-2-1 and lift, OK?"

"Yep" came the reply, I winked at his two mates who were by now smirking. They wrapped their arms around the relevant part in readiness.

"3-2-1 and lift".

Muscles bulged, eyes trained, legs shook and noises were made, up to a point where Jim had veins bulging in his neck and across his forehead as he went purple. They all stood up, took a deep breath and Jim said "heavy ain't it?"

"OK" I said, "you guy's really need to put all your effort in and once lifted we will slide it to one side to gain access and you can get your breath back, OK"?

"Yes" came the reply from all three.

"3-2-1 and lift".

Again, backs strained and muscles twitched and bulged, Jim had his eyes closed and was straining with every sinew in his body, no movement. The other two sappers were leaning in the right position but had no effort on their faces. The gearbox didn't move a millimetre, unsurprisingly.

Jim opened his eyes enough to see the other two not straining and stood up.

He looked, stared left then again stared right this time at the other two sappers. Before we could laugh, and explain we had wound him up, he shouted: "You're not fucking lifting" at the lad on his left and punched him square in the jaw with a right hook knocking him back off his feet. Without a thought and before he could duck, he threw a left hook at the other sapper on his right, and a mirror image shot had a mirror image effect on the other lad putting him straight on his backside.

We restrained Jim from killing the two sappers and explained we were just having some fun on his behalf and gave him a can of beer. He lifted the two sappers up, bruised and bleeding, dusted them down and laughing said "next time you might wanna lift".

How The Poppy Appeal Began

Janet Warby
Hon. Secretary, Royal British Legion, Paris Branch

We are often asked how the Poppy Appeal came to be our National Emblem of Remembrance. Once again as Remembrance tide looms, I have looked in two publications about The Royal British Legion and can inform young and old of the origins of the Poppy Appeal.

Poppy Day is essentially cosmopolitan in origin. The inspiration came from across the Atlantic: a Canadian medical officer serving in France had written a poem sitting on the step of the ambulance outside his dressing station on the banks of a canal during the Second Battle of Ypres in 1915. An American woman seized on the leading idea in that poem and applied it (in a sense) in the United States. A few years later a French woman made an unannounced visit to Legion Headquarters in London, from which the Poppy and Poppy Day was born.

The Canadian was Colonel John McCrae who had already served and survived the Boer War. He called his poem 'In Flanders Fields'. It begins:

> *In Flanders Fields the poppies blow*
> *between the crosses, row on row*

and concludes with the stirring lines :

> *If ye break faith with us who die*
> *We shall not sleep, though poppies grow*
> *In Flanders Fields.*

The poem was published anonymously in *Punch* magazine in December 1915. Among those affected by the verses was a young American woman, Miss Moina Michael. Receiving a gift of ten dollars, she used it to buy twenty-five artificial poppies from a store in New York. She persuaded some of her friends and colleagues to wear these poppies at a conference of YMCA overseas workers in November 1918.

In August 1921 a French woman, Madame Anne Guérin, marched into Legion Headquarters with some samples of artificial poppies which were made in France to support her charity, a joint French-American organization seeking to help restore the areas in France devastated by the war. She met with Colonel Crosfield, later Chairman of the Legion from 1927–1930, and the General Secretary. She showed them some of the small artificial poppies of the type made in France. Would not the Legion care to adopt the idea as a method of raising money for its own purposes? There were, she told them, two firms in France ready to supply the material. In return she wanted a certain percentage for her own organisation in France.

After much anxious deliberation, it was decided first to consult Sir Herbert Brown, Chairman of the Appeals Department of the Officers Association, and for a time of the Legion's Appeals Department, and then to despatch him to Paris to investigate, reporting on his return that at least the suppliers were genuine. He was then asked to return to Paris to place an order for one and a half million poppies. To this Colonel Heath, General Secretary, told Sir Herbert Brown, 'For goodness sake order three million, whatever else you do.' In the end, according to the Legion Journal of December 1921, nine million were supplied. The first suitable occasion for a poppy-linked appeal would be Armistice Day — 11th November 1921 — which was the chosen date.

The first Poppy Appeal was so successful that the NEC's thoughts turned to future Appeals. It then took steps to register the design of the poppy to prevent the sale of unauthorised sale of imitation poppies. Above all, arrangements were then made to manufacture poppies in the UK.

Major George Howson, after the war, launched the Disabled Society. He approached the Legion in due course with the suggestion that the Disabled Society should manufacture poppies for them. This was agreed. Having already gone into the artificial-flower trade to gain experience, Major Howson set up a factory, under the Legion umbrella, in a small workroom just off the Old Kent Road, in South-East London. The enterprise began with a staff of five badly disabled ex-Service men, three of whom were still employed in 1954. There were about 330 others working in more pleasant and spacious surroundings of Richmond Hill (Surrey). These men worked a five-day week and were expected to produce 1,000 poppies per day each. All the men had either single or double amputations and some travelled some distance to get to work, but they worked with a cheery disposition singing along to the gramophone as they made their poppies. It is thought that by 1924/25 the factory had moved to Richmond Hill from the Old Kent Road. A disused brewery donated by a well-wisher was converted into a factory and an adjoining estate purchased by the Legion, to erect flats for the workers and their families, together with a club. By this time the employees had risen to 190 with well over 300 on the waiting list.

By setting up their own arrangements for the manufacture of poppies the Legion had of course turned its back on Madame Guérin and the organization which had supplied not only the original idea but the means of putting it into effect. The same thing was to happen in Canada, which had also been visited by the enterprising French woman, but which turned to the local 'Vetcraft Industries' to make poppies from 1925 onwards. There is no evidence of any protest from the original manufacturer, but at the time no legislation existed to prevent the Legion appropriating the idea from another country. In any case, as has already been mentioned, the National Executive Council had by now patented the poppy buttonhole in the United Kingdom.

Who would have thought that from a poem written by a Canadian Colonel and two inspirational and dynamic women, we would still be wearing the poppy each Armistice Day on November 11th? Had the timing been different, we could have been wearing the poppy on 4th August, the day we entered the First World War.

If you would like to read more about the formation of The Royal British Legion, please let either the Chairman or myself know. We have in our possession two books written on the history of the RBL from which the information you have just read has come. The first book is called 'The Official History of The British Legion' by Graham Wootton, published in 1956, and the second is called 'Keeping Faith, The History of the Royal British Legion' by Brian Harding, published in 2001.

Remember...

by Alice

Remember as you see the crimson flower,
That small and frail blossom on your chest,
Drowned in the ocean of its scarlet sisters,
A strong reminder of the ones who rest.

Remember the fighter who went to war,
Commemorate him saving you;
For now he is but a monochrome image in our memories,
A picture that will stay with us forever.

So remember them with silence,
As words will never be enough.

About Janet Warby

Janet Warby, Honorary Secretary and Standard Bearer, Royal British Legion, Paris Branch

Janet Warby has worked tirelessly for the Royal British Legion over the last 30 years or so, both in Paris and Herne Bay, Kent branches. She has not only served the function of Honorary Secretary in both of these branches but also has been, and continues to be the Union Jack Standard bearer on various commemorative parades.

Janet Warby is married with two children, and lives in Paris.

About Grahame Warby

Grahame Warby lives and works in Islington, London. He is married with one child. Grahame read Law and History (BA Hons) and Public and Private International Law (LL.M) at University and has published three books to date along with various articles in International Relations and International Law. He is a member of the Royal British Legion, Paris Branch.

Index

W

Y

Z